Teaching Principles of Microeconomics

ELGAR GUIDES TO TEACHING

The Elgar Guides to Teaching series provides a variety of resources for instructors looking for new ways to engage students. Each volume provides a unique set of materials and insights that will help both new and seasoned teachers expand their toolbox in order to teach more effectively. Titles include selections of methods, exercises, games and teaching philosophies suitable for the particular subject featured. Each volume is authored or edited by a seasoned professor. Edited volumes comprise contributions from both established instructors and newer faculty who offer fresh takes on their fields of study.

Titles in the series include:

Teaching Research Methods in Political Science
Edited by Jeffrey L. Bernstein

Teaching International Relations
Edited by James M. Scott, Ralph G. Carter, Brandy Jolliff Scott and Jeffrey S. Lantis

Teaching Marketing
Edited by Ross Brennan and Lynn Vos

Teaching Tourism
Innovative, Values-based Learning Experiences for Transformative Practices
Edited by Johan Edelheim, Marion Joppe and Joan Flaherty

Teaching Sports Economics and Using Sports to Teach Economics
Edited by Victor A. Matheson and Aju J. Fenn

Creating Inclusive and Engaging Online Courses
A Teaching Guide
Edited by Monica Sanders

Teaching Undergraduate Political Methodology
Edited by Mitchell Brown, Shane Nordyke and Cameron G. Thies

Teaching Graduate Political Methodology
Edited by Mitchell Brown, Shane Nordyke and Cameron G. Thies

Teaching Political Theory
A Pluralistic Approach
Nicholas Tampio

Teaching Social Work
Neil Thompson

Teaching Principles of Microeconomics
Edited by Mark Maier and Phil Ruder

Teaching Principles of Microeconomics

Edited by

Mark Maier

Professor of Economics, Glendale Community College in Glendale, California, USA

Phil Ruder

Professor of Economics, Pacific University in Forest Grove, Oregon, USA

ELGAR GUIDES TO TEACHING

Edward Elgar
PUBLISHING

Cheltenham, UK • Northampton, MA, USA

Published by
Edward Elgar Publishing Limited
The Lypiatts
15 Lansdown Road
Cheltenham
Glos GL50 2JA
UK

Edward Elgar Publishing, Inc.
William Pratt House
9 Dewey Court
Northampton
Massachusetts 01060
USA

Paperback edition 2023

A catalogue record for this book
is available from the British Library

Library of Congress Control Number: 2022946167

This book is available electronically in the **Elgar**online
Economics subject collection
http://dx.doi.org/10.4337/9781800374638

ISBN 978 1 80037 462 1 (cased)
ISBN 978 1 80037 463 8 (eBook)
ISBN 978 1 0353 2370 8 (paperback)

Printed and bound by CPI Group (UK) Ltd, Croydon, CR0 4YY

Contents

Extended contents

PART III   INCLUSIVE TEACHING

PART IV   PEDAGOGY

Figures

Tables

Contributors

Abdullah Al-Bahrani is an Associate Professor of Economics and the Director of the Center of Economic Education at Northern Kentucky University in Highland Heights, Kentucky, USA.

Belinda Archibong is an Assistant Professor of Economics at Barnard College, Columbia University in New York, New York, USA.

Humberto Barreto is a Professor of Economics and Management at DePauw University in Greencastle, Indiana, USA.

Olivia Bobrownicki is a University Teaching Fellow at the National Education Equity Lab at Barnard College, Columbia University in New York, New York, USA.

George Cusack is a Senior Lecturer in English and the Director of Writing Across the Curriculum at Carleton College in Northfield, Minnesota, USA.

Tisha L.N. Emerson is the Ben H. Williams Professor of Economics at the Hankamer School of Business, Baylor University in Waco, Texas, USA.

Nathan D. Grawe is the Ada M. Harrison Distinguished Teaching Professor of the Social Sciences at Carleton College in Northfield, Minnesota, USA.

Steven Greenlaw is a Professor Emeritus of Economics at the University of Mary Washington in Fredericksburg, Virginia, USA.

Simon D. Halliday is an Associate Professor of Economics Education in the School of Economics, University of Bristol in Bristol, United Kingdom.

Gail M. Hoyt is a Professor of Economics and a Gatton Teaching Fellow at the Gatton College of Business and Economics, University of Kentucky in Lexington, Kentucky, USA.

Jennifer Imazeki is a Senate Distinguished Professor, a Professor of Economics, and the Associate Vice President for Faculty and Staff Diversity at San Diego State University in San Diego, California, USA.

Pratistha Joshi Rajkarnikar is the Associate Director of the Economics in Context Initiative at the Global Development Policy Center and a Lecturer at the Frederick S. Pardee School of Global Studies, Boston University in Boston, Massachusetts, USA.

Mary J. Lopez is a Professor of Economics at Occidental College in Los Angeles, California, USA.

Fernando Lozano is a Professor of Economics at Pomona College in Claremont, California, USA.

Mark Maier is a Professor of Economics at Glendale Community College in Glendale, California, USA.

Emily C. Marshall is an Associate Professor of Economics and Data Analytics at Dickinson College in Carlisle, Pennsylvania, USA.

Martha Olney is a Teaching Professor of Economics at the University of California, Berkeley, in Berkeley, California, USA.

Darshak Patel is a Senior Lecturer of Economics and the Director of Undergraduate Studies at the Gatton College of Business and Economics, University of Kentucky in Lexington, Kentucky, USA.

Jack Reardon is a Senior Lecturer at the University of Wisconsin-Eau Claire in Eau Claire, Wisconsin, USA, and is founding editor of the *International Journal of Pluralism and Economics Education.*

Phil Ruder is a Professor of Economics at Pacific University in Forest Grove, Oregon, USA.

Geoffrey E. Schneider is a Professor of Economics and the Economics Department Co-Chair at Bucknell University in Lewisburg, Pennsylvania, USA.

Rajiv Sethi is a Professor of Economics at Barnard College, Columbia University in New York, New York, and an External Professor at the Santa Fe Institute in Santa Fe, New Mexico, USA.

Brandon Sheridan is an Associate Professor of Economics at Elon University in Elon, North Carolina, USA.

Scott P. Simkins is an Associate Professor of Economics and Economics Department Chair at the Willie A. Deese College of Business and Economics, North Carolina Agricultural and Technical State University in Greensboro, North Carolina, USA.

Wendy A. Stock is a Professor of Economics at Montana State University and Co-Director of the MSU Initiative for Regulation and Applied Economic Analysis in Bozeman, Montana, USA.

Erin A. Yetter is a Lecturer in Economics at the Eller College of Management, University of Arizona in Tucson, Arizona, USA.

Homa Zarghamee is an Associate Professor of Economics at Barnard College, Columbia University in New York, New York, USA.

1. Improving the Principles of Microeconomics course

Phil Ruder and Mark Maier

More than 40 percent of United States (US) college students take an introductory economics course, most beginning with Principles of Microeconomics (Bowles and Carlin 2020; Prante 2016). And for the vast majority of those students, the introductory courses are the last economics they will ever study.

The Principles of Microeconomics course offers the chance to introduce students to the study of how markets have made possible the specialization, trade, and innovation that create the vast wealth of the rich countries of the world. At the same time, the basic tools of microeconomics yield important insights for addressing the pressing challenges of modern society, including predatory monopolies, pollution and climate change, the unequal distribution of resources among and within nations, and ongoing discrimination on the basis of gender and race; topics that our students are eager to explore.

In this book (and in the online supplement at https://www.e-elgar.com/textbooks/maier) we have assembled the wisdom of eminent scholars of economic education on how best to introduce students to our discipline and to inspire a passion for microeconomics. The practical suggestions for teaching Principles of Microeconomics will improve the courses of new teachers and those who have taught economics for many years.

We, the editors of this book, together have 70 years of teaching experience and have taught more than 200 sections of Introductory Microeconomics in that time. We have learned a great deal from our contributors and are eager to share these great ideas with our fellow economics instructors.

Beyond the primary goal of improving the learning of students in our courses, the chapters in this book offer measures for addressing many of the vexing challenges that face the discipline of economics, and have their roots in how we teach Principles of Microeconomics and Macroeconomics.

One problem with the way we teach the introductory sequence stems from the limited learning in the courses. Students who take the introductory courses typically recall only a few of the core concepts by the time they are seniors (Walstad and Allgood 1999). Thus, economists are missing our chance to elevate the economic literacy of the citizenry. Improved pedagogy in the courses holds the promise of improving student learning.

Another problem with the Principles of Economics courses is that students become more selfish after taking them (Spiegelman 2021). The typical narrow focus of the introductory course on *Homo economicus* gives students a false sense of economists' understanding of altruistic behavior, and does lasting harm to the students' social behavior.

Yet another problem with the introductory courses arises from the poor job they do at attracting students to major in economics. Overall, the number of students majoring in economics has stagnated between 2001 and 2014 (Stock 2017). Women and underrepresented African-Americans and Hispanics seem especially discouraged from studying economics. Our discipline lags significantly behind nearly every other, including math and the natural sciences, in the share of women and minorities majoring, going on to pursue PhDs, and securing academic appointments in economics (Bayer and Rouse 2016).

Economic educators have identified several reasons for the shortfalls of the Principles course. Most frequently cited is the common overload of concepts, each presented in a shallow manner without sufficient examples of application (Hansen et al. 2002). Learning science shows us that to ensure the retention of new concepts, introductory courses must repeatedly apply a few core models and emphasize the transfer of conceptual understanding to unfamiliar situations (Schwartz et al. 2005). Economic educators often dispute which concepts are key and worthy of deep study, but agree that fewer concepts are needed in introductory courses.

A related problem with the Principles of Microeconomics course is its typically abstract, mathematical approach to key concepts, unmotivated by big questions that are of inherent interest to students (Bowles and Carlin 2020, pp. 178, 191–192). Ironically, in recent years economic researchers are giving more attention to questions such as inequality, climate change, family relationships, race, and gender; 60 of the 110 articles in the current issue of *AEA Papers and Proceedings* (2021) focus on these topics. There is every reason to expect that the Principles of Microeconomics course can show students that economics is relevant, even as we convey the core concepts of the subject.

Finally, pedagogy in the Principles course has failed to engage students. Despite well-documented insights from the learning sciences and evidence-based research on the benefits of active learning elements in each class, economics instructors continue to use primarily a lecture approach (Asarta et al. 2021), and assessments that emphasize computational exercises rather than economic reasoning.

This book is organized (roughly—most chapters fit into multiple categories) according to which of the challenges facing the Principles of Microeconomics course the chapter addresses. The first set of chapters (Chapters 2 through 6) focus on concerns about how the whole course should be taught and what materials are available to support different approaches. The next two chapters (Chapters 7 and 8) identify content that lies in the mainstream of the economics discipline but that is often underemphasized or omitted entirely from the course. Next, five authors (Chapters 9 through 12) offer suggestions on how to make the course more inclusive of all students, particularly women and people from underrepresented groups. The book concludes with an eclectic set of proven pedagogical strategies (Chapters 13 through 18) to improve the Principles of Microeconomics courses.

To begin our re-thinking of how best to teach Principles of Microeconomics, Gail Hoyt (Chapter 2) considers the crucial decisions that instructors must make as they develop their plan to teach each concept, and identifies a short list of essential content. Erin Yetter (Chapter 3) follows with a careful examination of the instructor's decision to use one of 28 textbooks, and additional resources that exist to support the course.

Belinda Archibong, Olivia Bobrownicki, Rajiv Sethi, and Homa Zarghamee (Chapter 4) introduce readers to the Curriculum Open-Access Resources in Economics (CORE) Project that has re-imagined the Principles of Microeconomics course, adopting a novel rhetorical strategy, and creating materials that add consideration of the institutional underpinnings, historical and social context, and current research to the study of markets. The authors also describe the Equity Lab and Outlier projects that increase access to high-quality college economics courses for members of underserved communities.

Wendy Stock (Chapter 5) recommends that the Introductory Microeconomics course focus first on economic issues to stimulate student interest and establish the relevance of the material under study. Only then should we present the analytical framework used by economists to gain insight into the issue. The result is a compelling course that gives the "one-and-done" students economic tools to apply to their personal, professional, and public lives, while preparing future majors for the Intermediate courses just as well as do the traditional Principles courses.

Geoffrey Schneider (Chapter 6) argues that a critical analysis of the assumptions of the neoclassical model and a consideration of alternative perspectives should be part of Principles of Microeconomics. Dr Schneider also recommends that the course should include consideration of important social issues such as inequality and climate change. Such an approach develops the critical thinking skills that feature prominently in student learning objectives for the course.

Simon Halliday and Emily Marshall (Chapter 7) describe how insights from behavioral economics can extend the neoclassical model to consider other-regarding preferences, biases, and faulty "rules of thumb." Adding the behavioral perspective to the course improves students' ability to explain observed human behavior. Students also develop a better sense of how maximizing behavior by individuals can lead to inferior outcomes for society.

Jack Reardon (Chapter 8) offers suggestions for weaving sustainability concepts throughout the course, to increase understanding of what markets can do well and of how incomplete markets can lead to excessive harm to the ability of the planet to sustain human life.

Economists must do everything possible to increase the diversity of people and ideas in our discipline. When problems are examined from multiple highly diverse perspectives, the solutions we arrive at are more likely to work. The task of attracting women and other underrepresented people to economics must begin in the Principles of Microeconomics classroom; or even before students arrive there. Jennifer Imazeki (Chapter 9) establishes the importance of creating an inclusive classroom environment, and offers practical suggestions for doing so.

Mary Lopez and Fernando Lozano (Chapter 10) describe three elements of anti-racist pedagogy: setting clear and equitable rules; implementing strategies to reduce differences in student achievement; and adjusting course content to align with students' interests, backgrounds, and personal histories. They offer specific, feasible suggestions for including anti-racist content and student assignments in the course that will lead all students to a better understanding of the economy.

Pratistha Joshi Rajkarnikar (Chapter 11) explains how adopting a gender-aware and inclusive approach in the Introductory Microeconomics course enables us to see important things that we otherwise miss. For example, the non-market economy, in which women do most of the work, provides great social value and supports the market economy but receives little attention in most courses. Dr Joshi Rajkarnikar recommends measures for adding a feminist perspective to the course, which leads to a more robust view of the economy.

Martha Olney (Chapter 12) identifies ways to teach the Introductory Microeconomics course in order to encourage women to continue in the study of economics. Further, Dr Olney argues that economics instructors can make efforts outside of the classroom to reach students who would not otherwise be likely to take the course. Without such interventions, the extreme gender imbalance in our profession probably will persist.

The consideration of other pedagogical strategies to improve the Introductory Microeconomics course begins with an exhortation from Nathan Grawe and George Cusack (Chapter 13) to include writing even in large courses. The authors explain the great importance of writing for learning, provide a number of possible short assignments, and offer tips for giving useful feedback and grades without spending inordinate amounts of time on those tasks.

Scott Simkins, Mark Maier, and Phil Ruder (Chapter 14) summarize the benefits of including highly structured cooperative learning activities in the Principles of Microeconomics course. The pedagogy enables frequent practice and immediate feedback for every student, without Herculean instructor effort. The authors offer examples that range from simple applications for student work in pairs, to more complex tasks that are suitable for six-student groups in team-based learning pedagogy.

Tisha Emerson (Chapter 15) shares her success in using experiments to give students first-hand knowledge of the core concepts in the course. Experiment pedagogy has led to gains in learning and engagement for all students. What is more, because women experience greater learning gains from experiment pedagogy than do men, the strategy promises to contribute to closing the gender gap in the discipline. Dr Emerson gives detailed guidance to instructors interested in adding experiments to their Introductory Microeconomics courses.

Abdullah Al-Bahrani, Darshak Patel, and Brandon Sheridan (Chapter 16) elucidate the gains in student outcomes that occur when instructors include social media references and assignments in their courses. The authors help instructors to select appropriate social media platforms and tasks, providing advice that will be useful even when the options change in the years to come. The many example assignments in the chapter provide a clear path to adding one or several engaging elements to the Principles of Microeconomics course.

Even before the recent coronavirus pandemic, online education was growing rapidly in its share of the college economics courses being taught. During the pandemic, we all learned that simply trying to do what one does in a face-to-face class does not result in a good online course. Steven Greenlaw (Chapter 17) carefully articulates the challenges of developing a high-quality online course, and goes on to offer design principles and examples that lead to great online courses.

As Humberto Barreto (Chapter 18) explains, including MS Excel examples in class and student assignments gives students the concrete illustrations that they need to become competent at using the abstract concepts in the Principles of Microeconomics course. The easy access to data that the Federal Reserve Bank of St Louis (FRED) database provides makes it possible to develop data-rich cases on a wide variety of microeconomic topics. Along with developing quantitative reasoning skills by means of Excel-based assignments, students become adept at manipulating spreadsheets, which they recognize as important for future job performance.

The possibility of continued improvement throughout a long career comprises one of the joys of teaching. The ideas in this book highlight many feasible improvements to the Principles of Microeconomics course. Every chapter in the book makes a compelling argument to implement the strategy being described. We recommend that instructors take the long view and gradually improve each iteration of their course. Implement a few changes each time, prioritizing the aspects of the course that you judge to be most urgently in need of adjustment.

We close by thanking our all-star roster of contributors. When we set out to assemble this guide to teaching the Principles of Microeconomics course, we made a list of the ideal colleagues in the field of economic education to write each chapter. To our delight—and surely that of our readers—our choice for every chapter agreed to contribute to the book. We are deeply grateful for the careful thought each author put into writing their chapter, and we are honored to be a part of bringing the chapters in this book to teachers of the Principles of Microeconomics course.

REFERENCES

Asarta, C.J., Chambers, R.G., and Harter, C. (2021). Teaching methods in undergraduate introductory economics courses: Results from a sixth national quinquennial survey. *American Economist 66* (1), 18–28.

Bayer, A., and Rouse, C.E. (2016). Diversity in the economics profession: A new attack on an old problem. *Journal of Economic Perspectives 30* (4), 221–242. DOI: 10.1257/jep.30.4.221.

Bowles, S., and Carlin, W. (2020). What students learn in Economics 101: Time for a change. *Journal of Economic Literature 58* (1), 176–214.

Hansen, W.L., Salemi, M.K., and Siegfried, J.J. (2002). Use it or lose it: Teaching literacy in the Economics Principles course. *American Economic Review 92* (2), 463–472.

Prante, G. (2016). A comparison of Principles of Economics curriculum across US colleges and universities. *E-Journal of Business Education and Scholarship of Teaching 10* (1), 73–84.

Schwartz, D.L., Bransford, J.D., and Sears, D.L. (2005). Efficiency and innovation in transfer. In J. Mestre (ed.), *Transfer of learning from a modern multidisciplinary perspective* (pp. 1–51). Information Age.

Spiegelman, E. (2021). Embracing the dark side? Testing the socialization of a maximizing mindset. *Economic Inquiry 59* (2), 740–761.

Stock, W. (2017). Trends in economics and other undergraduate majors. *American Economic Review* 107(5), 644–649.

Walstad, W.B., and Allgood, S. (1999). What do college seniors know about economics? *American Economic Review 89* (2), 350–354.

PART I

Traditional and alternative approaches

2. The deep work of teaching essential Microeconomic Principles

Gail M. Hoyt

Developing and delivering a high-quality Principles of Microeconomics course can be a daunting task for new and seasoned instructors alike. There are several moving parts in the teaching enterprise, and even identifying the pieces, let alone harnessing their potential in a unified and effective way, might seem overwhelming. Our content choice is often determined by a pre-existing syllabus shared by a colleague, or is selected for us by a textbook author as we rigidly adhere to a table of contents. And as this handbook attests, accomplished economic educators have developed a vast array of approaches and contexts for teaching Microeconomic Principles. Each approach garners its own unique appeal. Which one do we choose? Additionally, with teaching economists' websites, publications on economic pedagogy, and textbook publisher-produced materials, teaching resources abound. While this abundance is a boon to the profession, to economic educators in the throes of developing a course, it can be a source of anxiety as we contemplate the time-cost required to sort through our options and the uncertain outcomes of our choices.

Some aspects of developing and teaching a Microeconomics Principles course are straightforward, while others are more complex and complicated. Cal Newport, in his book *Deep Work*, makes the distinction between what we might consider the "shallow" busy-work of a job and the more complicated "deep" work that requires our undivided attention (Newport 2016). The concentrated mental focus for deep work requires a sufficient block of uninterrupted work time to achieve focus and productivity, but finding a peaceful, protected block of time in a distraction-filled world is no easy feat. We can make this same distinction between shallow and deep work in considering the tasks we face in our work as economic educators, keeping in mind that classifying work as "shallow" is not a statement about importance. The shallower work might involve the production of tangible items or the completion of concrete tasks, such as preparing an assignment, grading an assignment, writing an exam, or finishing a lecture or the deck of power point slides for the next class session. The more complicated, yet equally vital, deep work involves concentrated thought as we figure out ways to convey relevance, provide context, determine goals, match our goals to our teaching actions, and assemble the results of our shallow work into a cohesive teaching package with purpose and effect. The shallower work is the low-hanging fruit of teaching, the type of work to which we naturally gravitate. The second type of work requires deeper thought and mental focus and is often less likely to happen, as one can still deliver content without it, albeit less effectively.

Not only is it time- and thought-consuming, but the deep work of teaching is also the hard work of teaching. In his 2000 lecture to the Southern Economic Association, renowned economic educator Kenneth Elzinga said, "Most good teaching does not come as much from inspiration as from perspiration, or what is sometimes called sweat equity" (Elzinga 2001, p. 257). Elzinga is not describing the perspiration of energetic teaching in the classroom, but rather the mental sweat induced by preparatory thinking. The best economic educators exert significant time and energy toward doing the difficult thought exercises required for high-quality teaching. And it is not a "do it once and you are done" scenario. Both new and seasoned instructors alike must engage in deep work. This necessitates that economic educators at all stages of their careers embrace the same growth mindset in their teaching endeavors that we ask our students to embrace in their learning processes.

While I cannot clear blocks of distraction-free time in your schedule for deep work, and nor can I simplify the difficult labor that deep work entails, I can offer a series of guiding questions to help you identify the aspects of deep teaching work that you must address, on a topic-by-topic basis, when developing an effective course. This chapter is in three main sections. The first provides this series of questions to guide the deep work process for economic educators. The second section identifies ten essential concepts for the microeconomics principles course. And the third demonstrates the application of these guiding questions to one of those essential concepts. The final section concludes.

THE DEEP WORK QUESTIONS FOR TEACHING MICROECONOMIC PRINCIPLES

Relevance: Why Am I Teaching This Concept?

This is the most important question, and the best place to start because this question should ultimately drive our course content choices. Further, this is the question we must consider as we try to convey the relevance of any individual economic concept to our students. To understand the depth and complexity of this question, consider the series of queries that might inform our answer to the overarching query of "why": Why is this topic integral to the discipline? Why is it essential for my students to know this concept and related skills?

Is there something about this topic that can make the world a better place? Is there something about this topic that can improve the day-to-day lives and the future lives of my students? Is this topic essential for learning other economic concepts? If, after asking yourself these questions, you still end up teaching the topics as they have been laid out by a textbook author, at least you have made a deliberate choice rather than taking the default list of topics as a given. This exercise empowers you as an instructor.

There are a variety of philosophies that might drive your answer to the question of "why." For instance, one targeted philosophy might involve content selection with the end goal of helping students to achieve economic literacy (see "The issues approach to teaching Principles of Microeconomics," Chapter 5 in this book); or consider Avi Cohen's (2015) literacy-targeted (LT) approach in his textbook, *Microeconomics for Life: Smart Choices for You*. Additionally, topic selection might be intended to promote accessibility and emphasize application to pressing issues; the CORE project (Chapter 4 in this book) takes this approach.

Sometimes our answer to the "why" question for content is interwoven with a broader educational objective, of which content choice is the vehicle. In this handbook you will see how content choice in Microeconomic Principles might be driven by the desire to design a course with contextual emphasis such as offering a heterodox perspective (Chapter 6), taking a feminist approach (Chapter 11), focusing on behavioral economics (Chapter 7), or focusing on environmental issues (Chapter 8). For approaches to teaching microeconomics with targeted emphasis, there is often a natural endogeneity between area of emphasis and specific topic choice. You might choose one of these broader philosophical or contextual approaches to teaching Microeconomic Principles and apply its tenets to the selection of your full content list, or you might apply a variety of approaches, using your preferred criteria on a topic-by-topic basis. But either way, it is crucial to choose each concept which you teach with deliberate purpose.

It is worth considering the unique merits of individual topics as well as their relevance to the broader context of the course. Truly conveying the significance of a particular economic concept to students is a challenging task even for seasoned instructors. If you have not wrestled with the "why" regarding a concept and nurtured your own understanding of a topic's relevance, it is very difficult to convey that relevance to your students. Each semester, you should ask yourself why students need to know the economic concepts and skills on the syllabus; and before walking into a class on any given day, you should ask yourself why students need to know the topic you are covering in class that day. An instructor's well-defined perception of a concept's relevance will lead to a well-informed selection of strategies for conveying that relevance. Often, when instructors leave a class session feeling that things fell flat, the inability to convey relevance is the culprit.

Endgame: What is My Endgame for This Concept?

Travelers rarely begin a journey without a destination, and instructors should therefore not begin teaching a concept without an end goal in mind. If we consider what students should know and be able to do after studying a concept, we can more effectively devise our plan for sharing the concept and assessing student learning down the road. In fact, when our learning goals align with the subsequent content delivery mechanisms and our assessment strategies, this intentionality and consistency engenders student learning.

Many economic educators look to W. Lee Hansen's (2001) proficiencies for a thoughtful discussion of what students should be able to do with the economic concepts they learn. More recently, and specific to economic principles, many economic educators adopt the broader set of course learning objectives that Allgood and Bayer (2017) propose for the Microeconomic Principles course. They derive their five learning objectives from what they call "five essential competencies in economics." These competencies reflect the things that students of economics should be able to do in any economics course, such as applying the scientific process to economic phenomena, analyzing outcomes using economic concepts and models, using quantitative approaches, thinking critically about economic methodology and application, and communicating economic ideas (Allgood and Bayer 2017, pp. 661–662).

Take, for instance, a relatively straightforward concept such as weighing costs and benefits when making a decision. We would hope to teach this topic in a way in which students become capable of applying the process to a variety of situations. We might also intend for students to comprehend and appreciate the potential shortcomings of such a process, and we might hope that they could articulate their decision-making processes and outcomes to others. When we teach a concept by first identifying these anticipated end goals for students, we design a far more focused and effective plan for content delivery and assessment that can profoundly impact the student learning experience.

Context: How Can I Provide Context for This Concept?

If we think of building a wall of content as we teach a course, we might think of each piece of content as a brick in that wall. Most instructors have an idea of how to deliver concepts and stack the bricks in front of students, but often struggle with providing the mortar to make the bricks adhere to each other in a sturdy way. The mortar that holds the bricks together is comprised of the ways we convey relevance along with the things that we do to contextualize a topic. If the "why" of a topic leads an instructor to consider its relevance and significance, context is a key tool that allows us to convey that relevance to students.

It is crucial to pay attention to context on a topic-by-topic basis, taking into account key considerations that facilitate the formation of context. Why is this concept essential, and how does it fit in with the other concepts in the course? How does this current topic connect to a previous topic, or how will it connect to subsequent topics? From whose perspective do we consider this concept? We also provide context in the ways that we introduce a concept at the start and re-emphasize key points at the end. To avoid a dry-stacked wall of bricks that will not stand the test of time, connective discussion/context is key. When intentionally providing this context, as you transition from one concept to the next, you might even walk to a different part of the room to a more intimate position, as if you are having a different type of conversation with your students. Stepping away from delivering content to provide context signals the significance of what you are about to say, and serves as a format change that punctuates the lecture and productively changes the flow.[1]

One foolproof way to provide context that connects to the student information set and adds a sense of immediacy and relevance is to have students consider a concept from the point of view of some specific role. There are many roles that we might ask students to adopt regarding a concept, including the viewpoint of policy-maker, business owner, manager, social planner, and consumer, just to name a few. Role play provides context for students that accommodates alternative perspectives, and empowers students with a sense of agency as they call upon course content to make decisions in varied roles. One type of contextual role that especially resonates with students is to imagine themselves in a job interview, answering some content-specific question that might make sense in such a setting.[2] For instance, when discussing a potential increase to the federally mandated minimum wage, you might ask students to answer questions regarding the possible impacts and responses to them from the point of view of a business owner, and then from the perspective of an employee who engages in job markets where the minimum wage is a consideration. You might also ask them to assume that they live in a state that has a minimum wage exactly at the federal level, and then assume that they are from a state with a state-level wage that is already higher than the federal minimum. Students could answer these questions in many formats, such as electronic polling or in discussion with small groups. As students consider the topic from an array of relevant perspectives, they gain a much more nuanced understanding of the various dimensions of a topic and any related issues.

Hurdles: What Are the Biggest Student Hurdles to Understanding This Concept?

Many of the concepts and skills that we teach in Microeconomic Principles have aspects that act as hurdles or hindrances to student learning. Instructors must carefully evaluate the concepts and skills which they include in their course to identify these potential learning obstacles for students. If we can anticipate the cognitive hurdles inherent in a topic, we can figure out ways to help students navigate around the obstacles or work through them.[3]

Hurdle identification can be especially difficult for instructors, as expert-level understanding makes it difficult to remember what was confusing about the topic at our own first exposure. New instructors are often flummoxed at the points in the semester when students seem to hit bottlenecks of confusion, and learning starts to wane. However, a little deep work might help us to anticipate and weaken the effects of the specific learning obstacles associated with any given concept.

Chew and Cerbin (2020) identify and explain specific cognitive challenges related to student mental mindset, student fear and mistrust, metacognition and self-regulation, prior knowledge, misconceptions, ineffective learning strategies, transfer of learning, constraints of selective attention, and the constraints of mental effort and working memory or "cognitive load." They also offer general strategies for dealing with these cognitive challenges that can easily be tailored to the economics classroom and the specific economic topic.

As economic educators focus more attention toward promoting diversity and inclusion in the economics classroom, the presence of certain cognitive challenges and hurdles to learning are especially disconcerting if they are systematically related to factors such as poor academic preparation due to family socio-economic status or perhaps weak training in a poorly financed school system. Conscience requires our time and attention in addressing these challenges, and I refer the reader to Chapter 9 in this book for advice in this regard.

Mathematical ability and graphical understanding are the biggest hurdles for many students in a microeconomics class. For instance, students might understand a definition of consumer surplus, they might be able to calculate the amount of consumer surplus for individuals, and they might be able to calculate the amount of consumer surplus as the area of a triangle on a graph. However, for many students there is a cognitive jump in understanding the definition of consumer surplus and how it translates into the area of a triangle on a graph. How do we address the learning obstacle that this cognitive leap creates? Sometimes, just acknowledging to students the presence of a hurdle helps. This alerts students that they might need to work a little harder to make the connection, and it is calming to know that other students might also find this connection confusing. Additional review might be required if the roadblock involves a necessary skill, such as how to calculate the area of a right-angled triangle. We might also offer multiple examples and alternative contexts that specifically target the learning hurdle, such as constructing demand, consumer surplus for individual consumers, and total consumer surplus, using data from students about their willingness to pay for something. Identifying and addressing the cognitive obstacles of an economic concept are two of the most difficult aspects of our deep teaching work, but the payoff is big.

Engaging and Accessible Points of Entry: What Is the Best Engagement Trigger and Accessible Point of Entry to Intellectually Engage Students as I Initiate Discussion of This Concept?

It makes logical sense to launch discussion of a concept by providing a key definition or graph, and this is what many instructors do. Sadly, in taking this approach, the instructor forfeits an important opportunity to fully engage students. When we initiate discussion of a topic by using an engagement trigger or learning hook, we tap into the natural curiosity of our students and increase the likelihood that they will learn the subsequent concept. Engagement triggers can take many forms, and are often most effective if couched contextually in the student information set, current events, and issues of import. By starting with something straightforward and relatable, this method creates an "accessible point of entry" for students to approach a more complex concept. For instance, before showing a market shortage in the context of a supply and demand graph, you might first show a photo depicting a shortage of something in a local store. The photo captures student attention and allows for a more accessible and relatable understanding before considering the same shortage graphically.

Devising effective engagement triggers that serve as accessible points of entry to concepts is the fun and creative deep work of teaching Microeconomic Principles. The only limit to the possibilities is your own imagination, as learning hooks can take myriad forms. Some instructors like to begin by telling a relevant story, sharing an analogy, applying a related case study, or highlighting a current event. Many instructors lean toward the visual, with evocative, relevant photographs or physical objects. For instance, one might auction an item in class on the first day to demonstrate multiple concepts. Holding a physical object up to the class, as we initiate discussion, captures attention and excites students about the learning to come. Many instructors like to mix media and cross-curricular divides by sharing relevant video clips, cartoons, literature, music, and even art. In this handbook, Al-Bahrani et al. provide a helpful discussion of the use of pop culture and social media (Chapter 16).

One way to engage students is to use "just in time telling" (Schwartz et al. 2016, pp. 114–126). This requires an engagement trigger that comes in the form of a problem which students might face, or a situation of cognitive dissonance they might encounter, before their first exposure to the relevant course content. The content needed to understand and solve the problem is more readily and effectively learned as the situation has generated curiosity and interest in content-based solutions. For instance, before discussing the tragedy of the commons and the role of property rights, I use electronic polling to ask students whether elephant herds in African countries fare better in A countries where elephant herds roam freely, hunting is illegal, and to hunt is to poach; or in B countries where hunting is legal, and local tribes have property rights to elephant herds and can profit from allowing hunting. With no prior exposure to the content and no opportunities to discuss their answer with classmates, typically about 70 percent of students select answer A and about 30 percent select answer B. I then give them a chance to discuss their answer with a neighbor and I ask the question again, and the answer distribution changes to about 50 percent A and 50 percent B. I still have not said anything about right and wrong answers, but the students are very curious now and want to understand the situation better. We then go on to discuss the issue and other applications of the tragedy of the commons and the role of property rights. Students get one more attempt to answer the question, and by this point they understand and have a greater appreciation of the topic than if I had just started with definitions and examples, rather giving them an opportunity to wrestle with the issues.

Engagement triggers, in addition to capturing student attention and serving as an accessible point of entry, serve the dual function of anchoring student recognition of content and serving as memory triggers when taking exams. Years after taking a class, students often indicate the things that they most remember and appreciate about the class as being the content tied to especially effective engagement triggers. Also, if we close our discussion of a concept with a reiteration of the engagement trigger that we used to introduce the concept, we form a cognitive frame around the content that boosts learning.

Delivery: What Is the Most Engaging and Effective Pedagogic Technique or Combination of Techniques for Teaching This Concept?

"Active learning," a term describing the use of pedagogic technique to actively engage students in the learning process, has been in common use in the academy for over 30 years. There is no doubt that a key consideration in delivering an economic concept or skill is that we actively engage students, giving them agency and ownership of content. Incorporating a reliable and effective pedagogical vehicle for conveying a concept is deep work indeed, calling upon the instructors to avail themselves of the resources needed to learn about techniques, set goals, plan, and prepare. And as is the case with any deep work, it can be taxing, but comes with a significant learning payoff if done well.

Engaging pedagogical techniques take a variety of forms, and this handbook serves as a manual, providing valuable, easy-to-follow guidance from experts on specific methods. Chapter 14 describes the use of collaborative learning techniques, Chapter 15 advises on the use of experiments, Chapter 13 explains how to incorporate writing, and Chapter 18 explains how to use Excel for engaged learning. Another engaging, active approach when sharing a concept with students is the interactive discussion technique, which includes activities such as questioning students, open-ended discussion, debate, brainstorming, and role play.

When selecting the delivery strategy for a specific concept, there are a couple of ways to go. An instructor might adopt one technique with regularity, allowing students to become familiar with a consistent approach and develop a productive rhythm. Another strategy is to mix things up and select different techniques or combinations of techniques for different topics. The latter approach offers variety, and by coming at the same topic from a variety of angles can offer a richer and more complete picture of the concept. In fact, one recently constructed educational paradigm, called universal design for learning (UDL), articulates the connection between variety in the classroom and enhanced learning equality.[4] UDL includes a set of guidelines for implementation that offer concrete suggestions for how educators can ensure that all learners can access and participate in learning opportunities. Based on cognitive science research, the guidelines center around three key tenets; the inclusive learning experience must incorporate: (1) multiple means of engagement; (2) multiple means of representation; and (3) multiple means of action and expression.

Whether you choose uniformity in your delivery method or a mix, for new instructors it is also a good idea to start with easier "gateway" pedagogies and work your way up to more elaborate and complex strategies. Some of the easiest starter techniques are quick activities such as discussion and collaboration in a think–pair–share setting, or a one-minute paper to get students thinking. It is not uncommon for economic educators to have a lecture-based class session which is frequently punctuated with short learning activities.

Assessment: How Will I Assess Student Competency Regarding This Concept?

When doing the deep work of contemplating the assessment of a concept, it is important to bear in mind the distinction between "formative" and "summative" assessment techniques. While formative assessment allows us to monitor student understanding and provide feedback to students to facilitate immediate learning, summative assessment is intended to evaluate student learning compared to some benchmark, and appraise performance. Both are important elements of a Microeconomic Principles course, but instructors lean toward summative assessment as a default, since graded quizzes, assignments, papers, and exams are typically integral to course design and necessary for assigning grades. However, in considering what is useful for teaching a specific topic, formative assessment techniques can be valuable pedagogic devices. Gibbs and Simpson (2005, pp. 6–7) find that carefully tailored assignments and formative assessments can lead to higher-quality learning and longer-lasting learning. Concepts that are more complex and rigorous typically warrant more frequent use of formative assessment.

What makes this work especially deep is that our assessments must align with our learning goals if we hope to let our students and ourselves know whether we are hitting the mark, or whether we need to alter course in some way. Suppose you assign a one-minute paper in which you ask a question about a concept, the answers to which reveal whether a learning goal has been achieved; but upon reflection, you realize it has not. Do you forge ahead to the next concept, or do you backtrack and present the topic in a new context and then reassess? Effective economic educators are attuned to the signals which formative assessment provides, and flexible enough to make the necessary adaptations to ensure that students master a concept.

Learning Environment: Have I Created a Learning Environment Conducive to Learning This Concept?

The learning environment permeates the student experience and profoundly influences how well a concept is received by students and how much students learn. The learning environment encompasses many things, including the general mood, attitude, and tone of a class, and these factors ultimately influence a student's sense of comfort and belonging in a course as well as the instructor's interpersonal rapport with the class. These in turn affect student responsiveness to learning and willingness to participate. Some aspects of the learning environment are set in place for the course as a whole and impact all learning, and some aspects are specific to individual topics. Although we must address issues of classroom atmosphere from the start, I list this question last because it is best reconsidered when we can look back at how we have answered the other deep work questions for a particular concept and see how they contribute to atmosphere in a holistic way.

In this handbook, Chapters 9, 10, 11, and 12, while coming at the issues from varied angles, all offer outstanding expert advice on promoting inclusion at the overall class level and in teaching specific topics. I leave the offering of detailed instructional advice to them. While I work to the best of my ability to make all of my students feel included, I claim no expertise, and realize that I learn new things and grow in this regard each semester. That said, I suggest two ways to think about inclusion when teaching a specific concept. The first is to "do no harm" and the second is to "deliberately do right." When teaching a concept, look long and hard at the context, examples, and activities which you select to determine whether there is anything offensive, insensitive, or inappropriate. If you are unsure, you can ask someone; but typically, if you feel the need to check, that is a signal that something is off. And from the positive side, have you explicitly taken steps in your design to add broad, universal appeal and promote inclusivity in the learning environment when teaching a topic? Ultimately, accessibility and inclusivity are intertwined, so incorporating the aforementioned accessible points of entry when introducing a topic can fortify the inclusivity of your approach. Attention to inclusivity on a topic-by-topic basis is vital for learning in the economics classroom and for ultimately promoting diversity in the economics major and profession.

TEN ESSENTIAL CONCEPTS IN MICROECONOMIC PRINCIPLES

I would like to share ten concepts that I view as essential to a Microeconomic Principles course, and apply my deep work questions to one of these concepts to demonstrate the approach.[5] To provide context for the reader regarding my top ten list, in the spring semester of 2021, I polled 50 students in an honors section of Microeconomic Principles, asking them which three concepts they found to be most useful or important, and why. Granting that there might be endogeneity between my delivery of a concept and their perceptions of a concept's value, student views still add interesting insights that I incorporate when sharing my top ten list.

Students frequently mention opportunity cost and the fact that we weigh costs and benefits when making decisions as two of the most important concepts that we cover in Microeconomic Principles. They indicate that these two concepts have had the biggest impact on their day-to-day lives, influencing and improving their decision-making processes. In learning these concepts, students say that understanding sunk costs, and the idea that we make decisions at the margin, considering marginal benefit and marginal cost, has altered their decision-making processes in especially useful ways.

The next most frequently mentioned topic is supply and demand analysis, for which students see value in their daily lives as consumers, and potential value in their work lives. While many students indicate that the mechanics of the graphical supply and demand analysis present an obstacle to learning, the frequent applications that we consider, and the wide variety of contexts, eventually make them comfortable with supply and demand analysis.

Students also list elasticity and cost curves as important, saying that they see value in what they might do in the workplace or as policy-makers. I might also mention that students unanimously identify these two concepts as the most difficult content in the course. Given performance on summative assessments and the number of office hour visits to discuss these concepts, I would agree. The biggest hurdles to mastering these concepts relate to interpreting graphs, and general mathematical understanding. With elasticity, just when students feel that they understand price elasticity of demand, we then introduce other elasticities, and when considering all seven cost curves at one time, some students say they feel a cognitive overload. For this reason, frequent formative assessment combined with multiple examples that present the concepts from varied perspectives and contexts are especially useful. Additionally, when the whole seems overwhelming to students, we must break the concept down into smaller, more digestible pieces to facilitate learning.

Students also place high value on understanding the difference in how government planners and market economies answer questions of allocation, indicating that it gives them a clearer understanding of political differences as they relate to government intervention in economic activity. Basic ideas of trade and specialization make the top ten cut, as students say that they help them to understand why we choose our areas of specialization, and it helps them to understand the interaction of countries, adding a global dimension to their awareness. They value the concepts of efficiency and welfare analysis that we use to analyze the impacts of policies and market failures, and they find the application of government intervention in markets through price controls to be especially interesting. And finally, students say that they like thinking about market failure, especially in the case of the fan favorite: externalities.

A DEEP WORK APPLICATION

I will apply the deep work approach to the distinction between non-market allocation and market allocation processes, with non-market generally referring to government allocation. I think the value of deliberately covering this distinction is underestimated by many economic educators and often given short shrift by the newest instructors. Please keep in mind that my answers to the deep work questions reflect my perceptions and preferences, and your answers may be very different.

Relevance

Almost all Microeconomic Principles textbooks include discussion of the economic allocation questions of what to produce, how to produce, and who gets the output of the economy. Most textbook authors explain the difference between the answers to these questions in centrally planned economies and in decentralized, market-based economies. Although many countries in the world have changed drastically in this regard over the last few decades, and most departments no longer offer courses in comparative systems or economic transition, understanding the distinction between markets and other allocation mechanisms, as it applies to economic allocation, should remain an integral element of the Microeconomic Principles course, with coverage that is deliberate rather than incidental. Students have a much clearer understanding of how a market works when considered in juxtaposition to government approaches to allocation. A student's view on the role of government in market activity is foundational to many of the student's political views. A clearer understanding turns the student into a more politically aware citizen who can develop informed opinions and take responsible actions. This understanding also serves as the basis for more sophisticated policy discussion in class.

Context and Endgame

When providing context for this concept, I articulate my endgame to students: I want them to understand the mechanics of government allocation and market allocation, and to be able to compare the two and form their own impressions of the pros and cons of these two approaches to answering the economic questions. I want them to begin to form opinions on economic issues; and while I emphasize that their views may vary, all views should be informed. I hope that students can look at a current event and understand what role the government plays and what role the market plays. In addition to transparency regarding my learning goals for this topic, the reader will see the additional ways in which I provide context with my choice of engagement trigger and learning activity.

Engagement Triggers, Accessible Points of Entry, and Hurdles

I open discussion of this topic with an anonymous polling question: "Do you feel that you have a well-developed set of political views? Yes or no." Obviously, the distribution of answers to such a question is likely to vary by institution. In my classes, the 40 percent or so who say "yes" are on the edge of their seats, thinking they are going to be asked to share their views, and the other 60 percent who say "no" are squirming with discomfort, fearing what is to come. But my next step is to ask why it is that over half of the students in the class do not feel they have well-developed political views. This aspect of the engagement trigger captures students' attention and provides the class and I with a full list of the hurdles regarding this topic. Additionally, this discussion creates an accessible point of entry to the topic, as there are no right or wrong answers. It is a moment of self-reflection for students that is designed to provide safety and comfort with the process. Some students say that they listen to over-the-top political discussion in a variety of settings and it turns them off, and they do not want to be a part of it. Some say that they feel they must take extreme, polarized positions, and there is no middle ground. Others say that the topics of discussion are all so complicated that they cannot get their minds around such complex issues and know how to intelligently participate in the conversation. Others say that they just do not care.

It is important to help students understand that their views on the role of government in economic activity, and their opinions about the best ways to answer the economic questions of allocation, are integral to forming many of their political views on economic matters. For students who have not yet developed their views on various issues, college provides an opportunity to begin the process and, for students who do have opinions, to make sure their views are grounded and that they have arrived at their beliefs through their own reasoning. For the students who feel overwhelmed with the complexity of issues, we offer reassurance that in our role as instructors we introduce them to the issues one by one, help them to understand what economics has to say about the issues, and then they can form their opinions on a topic-by-topic basis. They do not have to decide everything at once, and they do not have to know everything to know something. College is a time for students to learn to engage in the world and form their own opinions.

There are two compelling visual engagement triggers that I have seen other economic educators present and that I now include as well. One involves a comparison of two photos, the Shanghai cityscape in 1990 and the same cityscape in 2010. The other is a satellite image of North Korea and South Korea at night. In addition to the engagement that the visual aspect engenders, the images also serve demonstrative purposes.

Delivery and Assessment

The initial classroom presentation of the concept is discussion-oriented, and involves asking students about different ways that we answer the three big allocation questions with market forces and with government decision-making. My next step is to use a learning activity developed by Keenan and Maier (2004) called the "Dreaded Disease." This activity provides a scenario with an island economy that is struck with a disease that is deadly for children. There are 1000 children on the island and the island has produced 1000 doses of a vaccine. A series of accompanying questions asks students to explain how allocation takes place if the island has a market economy, and how the medicine would be allocated if the island has a more command-oriented economy.

I make this learning activity collaborative, and ask students to work in groups as they complete a worksheet to answer these questions. The activity and the worksheet provide formative assessment to help students, and I, see whether they are learning the concept; and if submitted, also provide summative assessment to ensure that students are staying on-task during the group work. To add a contextual element of role play, I have modified the activity, and ask each student group to take the role of government planner who must decide, if they only had 200 doses, the best way to allocate it among the 1000 children, assuming that their goal is to do what is best for their society. Groups come up with solutions, and a spokesperson from each group shares their policy solution with the class. Students are stunned to find the variation in policy recommendations, and it helps them to understand how even with the best intentions, policies can be vastly different. This exercise demonstrates some of the difficult aspects of centrally planned allocation, and requires students to call upon higher-order thinking skills to evaluate the situation, synthesize ideas, and formulate a policy.

Learning Environment

Obviously, as students consider the role of government and markets in answering crucial questions of allocation, and we apply this thinking to specific, real-world policy and events, attention to the elements of the learning environment is crucial. With varying opinions, there is the potential for emotionally charged discussion. To prepare for this eventuality, many instructors allow the students to form a community agreement early in the semester that outlines rules for civil discourse. This is a good point in the semester to remind the students of the terms of their self-designed agreement. This is vital to create an atmosphere of inclusivity that is comfortable for students of varying viewpoints.

For students who are apprehensive regarding the complexity of applying this aspect of economics to real-world issues, and beginning or continuing the process of developing their views, you might reiterate that they can move beyond where they are in their understanding, and they can tackle the issues one topic at a time. This is consistent with the notion of helping students to develop a growth mindset. We might also remind students that even if they have difficulty in grasping all of the complexities of an issue, their thoughts and opinions still have value. You might emphasize to students the importance of the process of mentally wrestling with different ideas, and the value of understanding the logic of competing positions.

Additionally, I have students complete a pre-course survey in Qualtrics, and one question gathers information about current issues that most concern students. I identify some of those issues while covering this topic in the course, and explain how understanding ways to allocate helps us to think about these issues and evaluate policy. The intent is to connect course content to real issues, especially the ones that students identify as of concern to them, providing students with a sense of ownership of the content. And finally, the cooperative nature of the learning exercise is intended to promote inclusivity by fostering peer instruction, helping students to connect with other students, and providing an alternative way for students to contribute to the discourse that is consistent with the aforementioned tenets of universal design for learning.

CONCLUSION

It is a privilege to introduce students to all that economics has to offer. Teaching Microeconomic Principles can be an incredibly rewarding experience for the instructor, and a valuable learning experience for the student. The application of the deep work approach to economic concepts only serves to enhance the experience, and this handbook is an excellent resource to call upon when tackling the deep work aspects of teaching Microeconomic Principles. Each of you will answer the deep work questions in your own way, looking for the unique combination of teaching elements that works for you and your teaching style. Much of the joy and excitement of teaching emanates from the lifelong adventure of striving for that perfect combination.

NOTES

1. If instructors choose a broad, overarching context for teaching a course, such as an emphasis on behavioral economics, then by design they provide context for the individual concepts in the course. Textbook authors sometimes adopt a broad approach that puts content into context as well, such as Karlan and Morduch's (2021) text, Micro*economics: Improve Your World*. In this handbook, Chapter 3 provides a more detailed discussion of the varied approaches that textbook authors take.
2. In their textbook, Stevenson and Wolfers (2020) frequently use role play as context when explaining concepts.
3. Volume 52, issue 1 of the *Journal of Economic Education* in 2021 has a useful series of papers on the cognitive challenges of teaching economics.
4. CAST (2018). Universal Design for Learning Guidelines version 2.2. Retrieved from http://udlguidelines.cast.org.
5. I teach more than ten concepts in my principles course, but am only sharing the top ten here for brevity's sake.

REFERENCES

Allgood, S., and Bayer, A. (2017). Learning outcomes for economists. *American Economic Review: Papers and Proceedings 107*(5), 660–664.
CAST (2018). Universal Design for Learning Guidelines Version 2.2. Retrieved from http://udlguidelines.cast.org.
Chew, S.L., and Cerbin, W.J. (2020). The cognitive challenges of effective teaching. *Journal of Economic Education 52*(1), 17–40.

Cohen, A. (2015). *Microeconomics for Life: Smart Choices for You* (2nd edition). Pearson Education Canada.

Elzinga, K. (2001). Fifteen theses on classroom teaching. *Southern Economic Journal 68*(2), 249–257.

Gibbs, G., and Simpson, C. (2005). Conditions under which assessment supports students' learning. *Learning and Teaching in Higher Education 1*, 3–31.

Hansen, W.L. (2001). Expected proficiencies for undergraduate economics majors. *Journal of Economic Education 32*(3), 231–242.

Karlan, D., and Morduch, J. (2021). *Microeconomics: Improve Your World* (3rd edition). McGraw Hill Education.

Keenan, D., and Maier, M. (2004). *Economics Live! Learning Economics the Collaborative Way* (4th edition). McGraw Hill.

Newport, C. (2016). *Deep Work: Rules for Focused Success in a Distracted World.* Grand Central Publishing.

Schwartz, D.L., Tsang, J.M., and Blair, K.P. (2016). *The ABCs of How We Learn.* W.W. Norton & Company.

Stevenson, B., and Wolfers, J. (2020). *Principles of Microeconomics.* Worth Publishers and Macmillan Learning.

3. Considerations for the textbook selection process in Principles of Microeconomics

Erin A. Yetter

INTRODUCTION

This chapter provides information on the 28 best-selling Principles of Microeconomics textbooks in the United States. To help make the textbook evaluation process easier, it provides 13 areas, or dimensions, that you can consider when selecting a textbook for adoption. Those dimensions are approach, authors' background, contemporary issues, content and organization, course length, diversity, online platform (courseware) and instructional aids, price, product differentiation, publisher, readability, rigor, and style. Each dimension poses relevant questions for an instructor to consider, well as advice on those considerations. Additionally, the chapter provides information on changes to the textbook market, some critiques, the future of the textbook market, and common content differences across textbooks.

You should know that some research shows that textbooks do not affect student learning, which is attributed to their heterogeneity (Allgood et al. 2015). However, an alternative explanation could be that students are not utilizing them as a learning tool. Fitzpatrick and McConnell (2009) found that only 17 percent of their students completed the course readings in a Principles of Macroeconomics course. Thus, if we want our students to gain knowledge from the textbook, they actually have to read it. Jaan Mikk, who conducts extensive research on textbook construction evaluation, concludes that "a textbook is efficient if students are motivated to read it. The motivational effect of the textbook depends on its content and the way of presenting the material" (Mikk 2000, p. 335).

Further, if you are established instructor, I encourage you to read the free response section of your student evaluations. Or, if you are a new instructor, speak with your advisor or new colleagues about their experience. You will find plenty of comments on the textbook, the publisher's website, and materials. Thus, while textbook selection may not directly affect how much your students learn, it can affect their perception of the course and your teaching evaluations (Lee and Cho 2014). When there is an issue with the textbook, courseware, or instructional supplements, students will not blame the publisher or author; they will blame you for selecting that textbook for the course. Furthermore, when properly selected according to your students, their abilities, and your preferences, textbooks make the job of teaching easier. Students have another resource from which to learn the content. Instructors have another method to differentiate their instruction. Taking time now to invest in a book that best fits the dimensions important to you will benefit you in the long term. It can save you time during the semester in the form of less preparation, fewer emails from students, and a smoother-running course overall.

Finally, if you find that a book is not the best fit after trying it out, do not be afraid to switch. Most publishers update their books every two to three years, so there is an ever-present cycle of new material, technology, and resources. Staying tuned into the state of the textbook market can help to ensure that your course is the best possible experience for you and your students.

Table 3.1 provides a list of the books that are part of this chapter. I list the books alphabetically, by author last name, to avoid any illusion of preference. If a separate Principles of Microeconomics textbook was available, it is used. If only a Principles of Economics book is available (that is, Asarta and Butters) it is used. Additionally, through the lens of helping you to evaluate and select a textbook for your course, I provide information on changes to the textbook market, some critiques, and the future of the textbook market. I also provide some of the common content differences across the books. This is important if you are switching textbooks and/or teach students who took an economics course in high school.

If you have no idea where to start, I have a few suggestions. Ask around among colleagues within and outside of your institution to find out what they are using. Try to ask people with economic viewpoints and teaching styles similar to your own. At conferences you attend, make it a point to visit exhibitors. There are always textbook booths at all of the major economics conferences (for example, Allied Social Sciences Association Conference). Read periodicals relating to economics education such as the *Journal of Economics Teaching* and *Journal of Economics Education*. As recommended by Wooten et al. (2020), connect with other economics professors across the country and the world using the #TeachEcon or #EconTwitter hashtags on Twitter. Join groups such as Econ Professors UNITE! on Facebook. Join the National Association of Economics Educators (NAEE) (for more information: www.naee.net). Finally, Doug McKee dedicates a blog post (McKee 2014) and podcast (McKee 2017) to the topic.

Table 3.1   *Most popular Principles of Microeconomics textbooks in the United States*

Title	Author(s)	Publisher	Edition	Year published	Number of pages
Microeconomics	Acemoglu, Laibson and List	Pearson	2	2018	512
Microeconomics	Arnold	Cengage	13	2019	624
Connect Master Principles of Economics	Asarta and Butters	McGraw-Hill	3	2022	639
Foundations of Microeconomics	Bade and Parkin	Pearson	9	2021	600
Microeconomics: Principles and Policy	Baumol, Blinder, and Solow	Cengage	14	2020	528
CORE: The Economy	Bowles, Carlin, and Stevens (CORE Team)	Oxford University Press	1	2017	1000
Principles of Microeconomics	Case, Fair, and Oster	Pearson	13	2020	528
Microeconomics: Principles for a Changing World	Chiang	Macmillan	5	2020	512
Microeconomics	Colander	McGraw-Hill	11	2020	501
Modern Principles: Microeconomics	Cowen and Tabarrok	Macmillan	4	2018	608
Principles of Microeconomics	Frank, Bernake, Anotonovics, and Heffetz	McGraw-Hill	7	2019	480
Principles of Microeconomics	Greenlaw and Shapiro	OpenStax	2	2017	570
Microeconomics: Private and Public Choice	Gwartney, Stroup, Sobel, and Macpherson	Cengage	16	2018	504
Microeconomics	Hubbard and O'Brien	Pearson	7	2019	720
Microeconomics	Karlan and Murdoch	McGraw-Hill	3	2021	744
Microeconomics	Krugman and Wells	Macmillan	6	2021	688

Title	Author(s)	Publisher	Edition	Year published	Number of pages
Principles of Microeconomics	Mankiw	Cengage	9	2021	528
Principles of Microeconomics	Mateer and Coppock	W.W. Norton	3	2020	704
Microeconomics	McConnell, Brue, and Flynn	McGraw-Hill	22	2021	573
ECON MICRO	McEachern	Cengage	6	2019	390
Economics Today: The Micro View	Miller	Pearson	19	2018	544
Microeconomics: Principles, Applications, and Tools	O'Sullivan, Sheffrin, and Perez	Pearson	10	2020	448
Microeconomics	Parkin	Pearson	13	2019	576
The Micro Economy Today	Schiller and Gebhardt	McGraw-Hill	15	2019	528
Exploring Microeconomics	Sexton	SAGE	8	2019	616
Microeconomics	Slavin	McGraw-Hill	12	2020	592
Principles of Microeconomics	Stevenson and Wolfers	Macmillan	1	2020	592
Microeconomics for Today	Tucker	Cengage	10	2019	640

Notes: For all Macmillan books, they are published under the Worth imprint, which is a division of Macmillan, so I use the latter. CORE stands for Curriculum Open-Access Resources in Economics. The CORE text authorship is credited to the CORE Team, which consist of Samuel Bowles, Wendy Carlin, and Margaret Stevens. To be consistent with the other texts, I use their last names here.

CONSIDERATIONS FOR EVALUATING A BOOK

Below are a variety of dimensions for an educator considering adopting a Principles of Microeconomics text. The dimensions range from the authors' approach to the number of teaching resources that are available from the publishers.

These dimensions are offered as general guidance in determining which aspects of a textbook are most important to you as the instructor. Some dimensions may be more important than others depending on teaching style and student characteristics, thus I list them alphabetically so as to not impart value judgments. The dimensions are heavily based on the work of Leamer (1972, 1974), but have been updated to account for technological changes and updated expectations. Each dimension poses relevant questions for an instructor to consider well as advice on those considerations.

Dimension 1: Approach

What is my approach to teaching economics and does it align with the textbook?

To determine the approach of the authors (or author), read the preface. Here, the authors explicitly tell you their approach to teaching economics. Some common approaches are:

- Balanced: covers both theory of application, does not favor one economic point of view over another.
- Free market: favors the conservative or neoclassical approach to studying economics.
- Policy: recent economic events and policy developments.
- Pedagogy: focused on how instructors best teach and students best learn economics.
- Traditional: focuses mostly on theory, does not favor one economic point of view over another.
- Data: uses data to explain economic concepts. Focuses on data literacy.
- Modern: presents concepts in a novel way, often through the use of technology and/or media.
- Business: examines economics through the lens of business.

Dimension 2: Authors' Background

Where, and when, did they get their degrees? Do they appear innovative or are they more established? Is their research agenda based in pedagogy? Do they have unique experiences (that is, Nobel prizewinner, president of the American Economic Association (AEA), regularly published in the New York Times, *etc.)? Is one more likely to connect better with your students?*

Most textbooks offer author biographies online or in the introductory material of the book. Many authors also have websites, blogs, or other social media presences that you can review. This may help to understand their approach to economics.

Dimension 3: Contemporary Issues

Does the book address contemporary economic problems and issues? Should the book reference Covid-19? Does the book include economic issues that are important to you? Are the issues woven into the text or presented separately?

Students learn more easily when they are able to make real-world connections to the material, but the types of issues presented in textbooks differ. While all the books make real-world connections, their approach to doing so varies widely. Some books, such as Baumol et al., present policies and ask the students to think through them with an economic lens. Others present news articles, case studies, references to popular culture. Some books present special issues as their own chapter (for example, Mateer and Coppock provides a 'Healthcare' chapter; Gwartney et al. provides 12 special-topic chapters). These chapters could be an excellent extension opportunity if you have time in your course to cover them. Finally, in the newer editions many books are dedicating chapters, or sections within, to the impact of the pandemic.

Dimension 4: Content and Organization

What content is covered and what is missing? How many chapters does the text-book include? Do you want a book that briefly hits all the main points, or one that covers fewer concepts, but more in depth, or one that covers everything? In what order is content covered? Do you want a text in which each chapter is self-contained, and thus you are able to freely change the order? Or do you want a text where each part explicitly builds on prior chapters?

There are no content standards by which to measure what should be taught in a particular post-secondary class. The Council for Economic Education has published the nationally normed assessment known as the Test of Understanding of College Economics (TUCE) in an effort to establish what students should know after completing introductory microeconomics and macroeconomics courses (Walstad and Rebeck 2008). The content covered on the microeconomic portion of the TUCE exam can be compared to the content in the textbooks. The six categories, and the subcategories, covered by the TUCE are: the basic economic problem (scarcity, opportunity cost, choice); markets and price determination (determinants of supply and demand, utility, elasticity, price ceilings and floors); theories of the firm (revenues, costs, marginal analysis, market structures); factor markets (wages, rents, interest, profits, income distribution); the (microeconomic) role of government in a market economy (public goods, maintaining competition, externalities, taxation, income redistribution, public choice); and international economics (comparative advantage, trade barriers, exchange rates) (National Council on Economic Education 2007).

The sampled books presented in Table 3.1 differ in their topic coverage, with the greatest variation occurring in the sections related to factor markets, the role of the government, and international economics. Most books do not include a section on maintaining competition, income redistribution, public choice, and exchange rates. If a topic is not present in the textbook that has been adopted, supplementary readings may be necessary.

A book's length includes the physical length of the volume, but also depth of coverage. The average page length in this sample is 589 pages, but ranges from 390 (McEachern) to 1000 (Bowles et al.). Pictures, tables, and graphs take up a lot of space, so a pure page count is not necessarily representative of the amount of content covered. Some books follow the motto that less is more (Frank et al.), and specifically state that they focus on depth, not breadth. On the other hand, some books try to cover it all.

Sequencing matters if you are someone who likes to teach topics in a particular order. Knowing whether your book builds later content on earlier content will be imperative to your students' understanding. If you choose to deviate from the textbook's sequencing, you have to cover any missing material briefly so that students have the background knowledge to comprehend the reading. Most books are cumulative. Sexton and Chiang has self-contained chapters.

Dimension 5: Course Length

Do students need a standalone microeconomics book or will they need a book that covers both microeconomics and macroeconomics? Can book selection be coordinated across instructors to select a book that can be used in multiple courses? How well does this book prepare students for the material taught in intermediate microeconomics?

If students are required to complete both Principles of Microeconomics and Macroeconomics, it may benefit instructors to work with colleagues on adopting a single book that students can use across semesters. Most of the books in this sample have a "Principles of Economics" option that covers both microeconomics and macroeconomics.

Dimension 6: Diversity

Does this book include women and people of color in its illustrations? When the authors show illustrations or use names associated with unrepresented people, what are they doing? Does the book feature a variety of economists, business leaders, policy-makers, entrepreneurs, and celebrities?

Authors should make an effort to diversify their illustrations, examples, and featured people, but should not display bias in what these people are doing. It takes very little to switch an example name from "Tyler" to "Monique." Stevenson and Zlotnik (2018) found that women are less likely to be a fictionalized character (that is, "Larissa bought an apple") and when women are mentioned, they are more likely to be consuming (instead of producing) food, fashion, or household tasks. Textbooks should also feature women in leadership positions, as policy-makers, and/or prominent economists. Further, Bayer et al. (2020) found that low-cost steps to increase diversity boost the sense of belonging and persistence in economics of women and underrepresented minorities.

Dimension 7: Online Platform (Courseware) and Instructional Aids

Does the publisher offer an online platform, and does it integrate well with your learning management system (LMS)? How does the publisher handle technical support, and is it available on demand when students need help? What is the typical response time? Is the support team in-house or outsourced? How do publishers support instructors who are new to using the system? For you, as the instructor, how easy is it to change due dates (that is, give time extensions) for students who require extended time on assessments? What instructional aids does this text offer to make your job easier? Are any publisher-provided videos closed-captioned? Are resources available in other languages? Are students who need disability accommodations able to fully engage with the materials?

Six of the eight publishers across the 28 major books have online platforms, which they call "courseware." Through each online platform, students have access to the e-book, homework (regular and adaptive), and other resources. It is easiest to think of the online platform as the LMS for the publisher. Each publisher believes their courseware is superior, but most are very similar. Here is the courseware for each of the publishers:

- Cengage: MindTap.
- McGraw-Hill: Connect.
- Pearson: MyLab.
- Worth/Macmillan: Achieve.
- W.W. Norton: Online Learning Tools (that is, no formal name, but this is how it refers to its online offerings).

- SAGE: no platform, LMS plug-in in only. Plug in works on Blackboard, Canvas, Brightspace by Desire2Learn (D2L), and Moodle. It will have courseware (called Vantage) for the next edition of Sexton.
- OpenStax: no platform, LMS plug-in only. Plug-in only works on Canvas and BlackBoard.[1]
- Oxford University Press: no courseware but plenty of instructional aids through the CORE website.

From personal experience, some platforms experience fewer technical errors and pair better with specific LMSs than others. Colleagues in your department or college may have different experiences, so it is important to ask around. Each textbook representative should be able to demonstrate how their courseware works. Inquire about special features of the platform, frequent student/ faculty complaints that they hear, and whether trial accounts can be set up for instructors.

In addition to the courseware, all of the titles include figures, tables, end-of-chapter questions, and appendices to help explain information to students. They all also include test banks and PowerPoints to help instructors. While these elements may seem quite similar, there can be great variability in the quality of these tools, such as end-of-chapter questions. When considering textbooks, keep in mind the type of questions you want your students to be able to answer. For example, consider whether you need well-differentiated (that is, covering a broad spectrum of cognitive demand), only low-level (for example, remembering, understanding), or only high-level (that is, synthesizing, evaluating) questions, based on your students.

Where the online platforms differ most is in the extra material offered. Most include instructor manuals, but these vary in robustness. The manual for Mateer and Coppock is the most robust on the market, but Arnold is a close second, providing tips for teaching, worksheets, additional readings, and so on. Each provides solutions to the end-of-chapter problems, with explanations. Many manuals provide only the answer, with no explanation of how to derive it. Other supplements that are offered by the publishers may include student study guides, suggested additional readings or podcasts by topic, discussion guides, lecture outlines, newsletters, worksheets, and media clips. Finally, textbook representatives should be able to demonstrate the tools for students that may help to meet different learning needs. For example, some e-books have a read-aloud option.[2]

Dimension 8: Price

What is the final cost to students? Can earlier editions be adopted to reduce cost? Is inclusive access available from the publisher and supported by the university?

Keep in mind that the campus bookstore will likely add a mark-up to the price quoted by publishers. This final price may be such that some of your students are priced out of your class and will not be able to fully participate in the course. OpenStax specifically mentions focusing on diversity and inclusion as part of its mission, and part of the reason for offering its text at low or no cost.

The vast majority of the textbooks in Table 3.1 can be purchased as an electronic book (e-book) bundled with their courseware. If the online courseware will not be a component of the course, some publishers offer a standalone e-book as an option.

A more recent development is the concept of inclusive access (IA), which is digital access to required course materials through the LMS at a reduced price. Access to the required textbook begins on the first day of classes, but is complementary through the drop/add date. Depending on the university, students may be able to opt out of IA if they believe they can obtain the material at a lower cost or do not wish to purchase the material. The goal of IA is to ensure that students have immediate access to course material from the start of the term, since the material is billed through their bursar's account. Not all institutions have an IA program, but the textbook representative and/or campus bookstore will likely have information specific to your university.

Prices for the e-book version of those listed in Table 3.1 range from $0 (OpenStax and Oxford University Press) to $130 (various Cengage titles) and from $19.00 (Macmillan) to $95 (SAGE) for a physical copy to accompany your e-book.[3] These prices may differ by region and institution. Depending on the bargaining power of the university, some institutions may be able to negotiate a lower price for students, or publishers may offer discounts for larger adoptions. Coordinating with other instructors may also result in considerable cost savings for students.

Dimension 9: Product Differentiation

How does the product stand out? What does this book or publisher offer that others do not?

Each product has its own unique aspects, which is why are there many dimensions to consider when selecting a book. In addition to those mentioned elsewhere, here are a few additional standout features that help to differentiate the products:

- Adaptive learning software. Adaptive learning provides a personalized learning path based upon individual knowledge, confidence level, and retention ability. If students struggle with a concept, the software provides more questions on that topic, and/or prompts them to read that passage in the book. If students have mastered a concept, the program progresses to more challenging content. Most publishers include adaptive learning exercises through their courseware.[4]
- Cengage Unlimited. Cengage offers the students the option to have unlimited access to all of its titles for a specific time period. Students can access all Cengage e-books for four months at a price of $69.99, or e-books and courseware for $199.99. If a student uses a Cengage title in at least one other course during the semester, they will likely benefit from Cengage Unlimited. Students would need to determine this on their own by checking their other course syllabi.
- OpenStax Allies. OpenStax has collaborated with various educational entities, including publishers such as McGraw-Hill, to offer over 70 course supplements to accompany their titles. Many are fee-based (for example, Perusall). See the full list at https://openstax.org/partners:
- MobLab. Moblab was created specifically for teaching economics with the use of online games and experiments. There are currently more than 60 simulations available that can be assigned to students.
  - Moblab can be bundled with Macmillan and McGraw-Hill offerings for an additional fee, but the resources are not integrated through their courseware. Students will have to go to MobLab's site to access content.
  - Moblab is included at no additional cost for Cengage MindTap users and is integrated directly through MindTap. Students do not have to go to another website.
- Video-based textbook. Asarta and Butters is a digital-first product and is based on over 260 short videos. Each chapter consists of between four and 17 videos, offered in English and Spanish. Videos can be assigned with questions that are native to the video and can hold students accountable for viewing.
- CORE. The most non-traditional of all of the offerings, the CORE text provides a full outline of the differences, a mapping to traditional textbooks, suggestions for how to implement in different courses, and more here: https://www.core-econ.org/the-economy/book/text/0-5-note-to-instructors .html#a-note-to-instructors.

- W.W. Norton's *The Ultimate Guide to Teaching Economics*. The guide includes over 1000 teaching tips from classroom instructors. A physical copy comes with adoption of Mateer and Coppock, but an online version is available as well.

Dimension 10: Publisher

Does the publisher provide a variety of economics textbooks or specialize in just one? How often does the publisher update editions? What level of support does the publisher provide and how frequently is support available? Will the publisher help set up the course and integrate reading and courseware to the LMS?

Textbook representatives and colleagues are good resources for learning about the quality of customer service that a publisher provides new adopters. The consolidation of product lines over the past few years has meant that representatives are now generalists instead of specialists, which means that your representative may have little to no background in economics.

In respect of how many books each has, Pearson and McGraw-Hill each have seven titles; Cengage has six; Macmillan has four; W.W. Norton, SAGE, OpenStax, and Oxford University Press each have one. The best-sellers (or only offering) at each publisher are as follows:

- McGraw-Hill: McConnell et al.
- Cengage: Mankiw.
- Pearson: Hubbard and O'Brien.
- Worth/Macmillan: Stevenson and Wolfers.
- SAGE: Sexton.
- OpenStax: Greenlaw and Shapiro.
- Oxford University Press: Bowles et al./CORE Team.
- W.W. Norton: Mateer and Coppock.

In this sample, the publisher with the most experience publishing economics textbooks is McGraw-Hill, which first published the 2nd edition of Lynn in 1970. The least experienced publisher is SAGE, which took over the publishing of Sexton's *Exploring Economics* in 2019.

Dimension 11: Readability

Is the reading level of the textbook appropriate for my students?

Readability should be an important consideration when selecting a textbook. Prior research has shown that textbooks are often too difficult for students (Mikk 2000). In addition, the average college student does not read at the college level. On the 2019 National Assessment of Educational Progress in reading, only 37 percent of twelfth-grade students tested scored at or above the proficient level (NCES 2020).

For each book listed in Table 3.1, I score the first chapter using the Flesch Reading Ease Formula[5] (Flesch 1948). I choose to only score the first chapter for several reasons. First, just like the introductory section of an article sets the tone for the entire paper, so too does the first chapter of the book. It should be the best-written chapter in the entire text. Second, because economic content builds in complexity, later chapters will likely be more complex in terms of readability. Third, and last, if a student reads the first assigned chapter and finds that to be over their head, then the chances that they complete subsequent readings declines. This reasoning is similar to Tinkler and Woods (2013).

Results are presented in Table 3.2 in the online supplement to this chapter (https://www.e-elgar.com/textbooks/maier). The Flesch Reading Ease score ranges from 0 to 100; the higher the score, the easier the reading. All of the books fall into one of three categories based on interpretation scales provided by Flesch (1948): Difficult (30–49), Fairly Difficult (50–59), and Standard/ Average (that is, Plain English) (60–69). The book with the most difficult first chapter is Miller, which scored a 42. It would take the average person about 13 years of formal schooling (or one year post-secondary) in order to comprehend this chapter. The book with the most readable first chapter is Bade and Parkin, which scored a 68. It could be understood by an average student in eighth grade.

Dimension 12: Rigor

Is math included in the main text as part of the explanation, as a math supplement, or in an appendix? Do the authors provide example problems with worked solutions? How many economic models are expressed graphically?

Being aware of your students' general math ability is of the utmost importance. There does not seem to be a consensus on what determines economic rigor; however, Leamer (1972) defined rigor as, "the complexity of theoretic constructs ... and the amount of algebra and geometry used."

For each publisher, here are the most and least rigorous and/or math-intensive titles according to their marketing materials and/or conversations with their marketing teams. Publishers with only one title are included as "Others."

Most:

- McGraw-Hill: Frank et al.
- Cengage: Baumol et al.
- Pearson: Case et al.
- Worth/Macmillan: Krugman and Wells, or Cowen and Tabarrok.
- Others: None.

Least:

- McGraw-Hill: Slavin, or Asarta and Butters:
  - If you are just looking for the book with the least amount of math from McGraw-Hill, it is Slavin. It includes step-by-step solved problems (with simplification steps, not present in other texts).
  - Asarta and Butters has more math comparatively, but also includes more step-by-step solved problems called "worked examples" throughout.
- Cengage: Tucker.
- Pearson: Miller.
- Worth/Macmillan: Stevenson and Wolfers.
- Others: Mateer and Coppock.

Dimension 13: Style

What is the overall look and feel of the book? Would students find it aesthetically pleasing? Is it easy to navigate?

The organization of information on a page also affects student learning (Committee on Undergraduate Science Education 1997). Further, the stylistic choices of a book can affect students' overall impressions of its usefulness. For example, the presentation of definitions, which varies, can signal the level of accessibility of a text. Some texts bold them and define them within the body of the text; some bullet them within the body of the text; others bold them within the text and define them in the margin; others just define in the margin.

The majority of the texts in this sample are written as large bodies of text, with each section touching on multiple concepts. Sexton, however, is highly segmented. It is written with many headers and only one paragraph under each. Another stylistic choice is the number of columns used. Most textbooks are written traditionally as one column. McEachern and O'Sullivan et al. are written in two columns per page, giving those texts the feel of a periodical.

Another stylistic choice is the number of illustrations included. One of the most effective types of illustration, especially for students with low verbal aptitude, is a simple multicolor line drawing (Mikk 2000). Although more visually appealing, and more prevalent in the current textbook market, realistic drawings or photographs are less effective at enhancing student learning. The books in this sample also vary widely in the number of illustrations included. Mateer and Coppock includes 264 photographs, while Slavin only includes 16. Acemoglu et al. includes 26 diagrams, while Schiller and Gebhardt does not include any.

CONSIDERATIONS FOR SWITCHING TEXTBOOKS

More than 20 states require an economics course as part of high school graduation requirements, so there is a very good chance that many of your students will have studied economics in high school (Council for Economic Education 2020). It is extremely important for instructors to recognize that different books cover things differently, even when they share the same publisher. The material presented in a previous course could affect students' ability to succeed in your course. Across publishers, textbooks differ in terminology, calculations, and even what factors shifts the supply and demand curves.

The following are the most common differences that I noticed across the texts listed in Table 3.1:

- Calculating opportunity cost. All books use some variation of the "next best alternative" definition. Some books, however, only include implicit costs, while others include both implicit and explicit costs (e.g., Mateer and Coppock).
- Price elasticity of demand. There is no consensus on whether or not to keep the negative sign in the interpretation of the value. Some books (e.g., Mankiw), for ease of interpretation and because the answer will always be negative, drop the negative sign and use only absolute values in the interpretation. Others (e.g., Mateer and Coppock) keep the negative sign as part of the interpretation. Depending on the text, elastic values will be presented as greater than one, but in others, the elastic values will be considered less than negative one. While mathematically identical, differences in terminology can confuse students.
- Shifters of supply and demand. Some books include shifters that others do not, and all books vary in their terminology for the shifters.[6] Across books, the same supply shift could be referred to as the costs of inputs (Mateer and Coppock), prices of inputs used to produce the product (Miller), resources costs (Asarta and Butters), changes in the seller's input prices (Sexton), or input prices (Mankiw; Stevenson and Wolfers; Greenlaw and Shapiro). In addition, there is no consensus on which factors shift each curve. Many include input prices, technology, expectations about price, and the number of sellers, but "unique" shifters include taxes and subsidies (Mateer and Coppock; Miller; Asarta and Butters; Greenlaw and Shapiro), changes in

the prices of related goods and services (Sexton), prices of related outputs (Stevenson and Wolfers), and conditions affecting factors of production (Greenlaw and Shapiro). A similar lack of consensus occurs with demand shifters. Most include income, the price of related goods, tastes and preferences, the expectation about price, and the number of buyers, but "unique" shifters of demand include taxes and subsidies (Mateer and Coppock), congestion and network effects (Stevenson and Wolfers), buyer composition (Stevenson and Wolfers; Greenlaw and Shapiro), and other factors (Greenlaw and Shapiro).

- Competitive markets. There are at least four different ways in which authors refer to the same market structure: competitive (Mateer and Coppock), pure competition (McConnell et al.), perfectly competitive (Sexton), and perfect competition (Bade and Parkin). The most common are the last two.
- Value of marginal product. There are at least four different ways to refer to the value of resources: factor demand (MRP) curve (Arnold), marginal revenue product of labor (Hubbard and O'Brien), marginal revenue product (McConnell et al.), and value of the marginal revenue product (Acemoglu et al.).
- Factors of production. Across almost all of the books in the sample, there is disagreement about the number of factors of production based on how entrepreneurship (entrepreneurial skill or ability) and human capital are treated. The books that do not include entrepreneurial ability as a separate factor treat that resource as being a form of capital, specifically human capital. The books that do include entrepreneurial ability deem the special talents or skills to coordinate factors or production to bring goods and services to the market to merit identification separately from other types of human capital. As an outlier, O'Sullivan et al. presents five factors of production, with capital split into physical capital, human capital, and entrepreneurship.

CONCLUDING THOUGHTS

Textbooks are an important tool for learning. They provide an alternative way for students to learn the course material. They also provide a means for instructors to differentiate their instruction. If chosen properly, they make our job as instructors easier. As the instructor of record, you have the important task of knowing what alternatives are available and how those materials fit with your students, their abilities, and your instructional style. This task can seem overwhelming, but I encourage you to give the task careful attention. By reading this chapter (and book) you are already on the path toward improving your course.

NOTES

1. It is piloting a courseware called OpenStax Tutor, but this is not yet available for its economics textbooks.
2. If the native courseware does not allow this, VitalSource (www.vitalsource.com) has this ability.
3. Leamer (1972) found that textbook prices ranged from $3.95 to $12.95 during the sample period, which after adjusting for inflation would be between $25.44 and $83.40.
4. Specific brands are as follows. W.W. Norton: InQuizitive; McGraw-Hill: LearnSmart; Pearson: Dynamic Study Modules; Macmillan: LearningCurve. No adaptive learning: Cengage and SAGE do not offer adaptive learning products. OpenStax offers access to its Allies feature.
5. The specific mathematical formula is: $RE = 206.835 - (1.015 \times ASL) - (84.6 \times ASW)$.
   Where: RE = readability ease; ASL = average sentence length (that is, the number of words divided by the number of sentences); and ASW = average number of syllables per word (that is, the number of syllables divided by the number of words). The output, RE, is a number ranging from 0 to 100.
6. For brevity, I compared one book per publisher: Mankiw (Cengage), Mateer and Coppock (W.W. Norton), Miller (Pearson), Asarta and Butters (McGraw-Hill), Sexton (SAGE), Stevenson and Wolfers (Macmillan), and Greenlaw and Shaprio (OpenStax). The Bowles et al. text (Oxford University Press) treats the supply and demand model very differently and was not part of this comparison.

REFERENCES

Allgood, S., Walstad, W.B., and Siegfried, J.J. (2015). Research on teaching economics to undergraduates. *Journal of Economic Literature 53*(2), 285–325.

Bayer, A., Bhanot, S.P., Bronchetti, E.T., and O'Connell, S.A. (2020). Diagnosing the learning environment for diverse students in Introductory Economics: An analysis of relevance, belonging, and growth mindsets. *AEA Papers and Proceedings 110*, 294–298.

Carbaugh, B. (2020). The decline of college textbook publishing: Cengage Learning and McGraw-Hill. *American Economist 65*(2), 284–299.

Committee on Undergraduate Science Education (1997). *Science Teaching Reconsidered: A Handbook*, Washington, DC: National Academy Press.

Council for Economic Education (2020). Survey of the States 2020: The state of economic, financial and entrepreneurship education in our nation's schools. Council for Economic Education.

Fitzpatrick, L., and McConnell, C. (2009). Student reading strategies and textbook use: An inquiry into economics and accounting courses. *Research in Higher Education Journal 3*, 1–10. https://citeseerx.ist.psu.edu/viewdoc/download?doi=10.1.1.561.7242&rep=rep1&type=pdf.

Flesch, R. (1948). A new readability yardstick. *Journal of Applied Psychology 32*(3), 221–233.

Leamer, L.E. (1972). A guide to the selection of college Introductory Economics textbooks. Economic Growth Institute, State University of New York.

Leamer, L.E. (1974). A guide to college Introductory Economics textbooks. *Journal of Economic Education 6*(1), 47–56.

Lee, J., and Cho, J. (2014). Who teaches economics course better? Using student–professor matched data for the Principle of Economics course. *Applied Economic Letters 21*(13–15), 934–937.

Lynn, R.A. (1970). *Basic Economic Principles* (2nd edition), McGraw-Hill Book Co.

McKee, D. (2014). Choosing the right textbook for a class. *Teach Better Blog*, May. https://teachbetter.co/blog/2014/05/30/choosing-textbooks/.

McKee, D. (2017). Podcast #58: Digital textbooks. *Teach Better Podcast*, July 10. https://teachbetter.co/blog/2017/07/10/tbp-episode-58/.

Mikk, J. (2000). *Textbook: Research and Writing*, Frankfurt am Main and New York: Peter Lang.

National Center for Education Statistics (NCES) (2020). NAEP report card: Reading. https://www.nationsreportcard.gov/reading/?grade=12.

National Council on Economic Education (2007). *Test of Understanding of College Economics (Fourth Edition) Examiner's Manual*, William B. Walstad, Michael Watts, and Ken Rebeck. https://www.econedlink.org/wp-content/uploads/2018/09/TUCE-4th.pdf.

Stevenson, B., and Zlotnik, H. (2018). Representations of men and women in Introductory Economics textbooks. *AEA Papers and Proceeding 108*(May), 180–185.

Tinkler, S., and Woods, J. (2013). The readability of Principles of Macroeconomics textbooks. *Journal of Economic Education 44*(2), 178–191.

Walstad, W.B., and Rebeck, K. (2008). The Test of Understanding of College Economics. *American Economic Review 98*(2), 547–551.

Wooten, J., Al-Bahrani, A., Holder, K., and Patel, D. (2020). The role of relevance in economics education: A survey. *Journal for Economic Educators 21*(1), 11–34.

Textbooks

Acemoglu, Daron, David Laibson, and John List (2018), *Microeconomics*, New York: Pearson Education, 2nd edition.

Arnold, Roger (2019), *Microeconomics*, Boston, MA: Cengage Learning, 13th edition.

Asarta, Carlos and Roger Butters (2022), *Connect Master Principles of Economics*, New York: McGraw-Hill Education, 3rd edition.

Bade, Robin, and Michael Parkin (2021), *Foundations of Microeconomics*, New York: Pearson Education, 9th edition.

Baumol, William J., Alan S. Blinder, and John L. Solow (2020), *Microeconomics: Principles and Policy*, Boston, MA: Cengage Learning, 14th edition.

Bowles, Samuel, Wendy Carlin, and Margaret Stevens (CORE Team) (2017), *The Economy: Economics for a Changing World*, New York: Oxford University Press, 1st edition.

Case, Karl E., Ray C. Fair, and Sharon E. Oster (2020), *Principles of Microeconomics*, New York: Pearson Education, 13th edition.

Chiang, Eric (2020), *Microeconomics: Principles for a Changing World*, New York: Worth Publishers, 5th edition.

Colander, David (2020), *Microeconomics*, New York: McGraw-Hill Education, 11th edition.

Cowen, Tyler, and Alex Tabarrok (2018), *Modern Principles: Microeconomics*, New York: Worth Publishers, 4th edition.

Frank, Robert, Ben Bernake, Kate Anotonovics, and Ori Heffetz (2019), *Principles of Microeconomics*, New York: McGraw-Hill Education, 7th edition.

Greenlaw, Steven, and David Shapiro (2017), *Principles of Microeconomics*, Houston, TX: OpenStax, 2nd edition.

Gwartney, James, Richard Stroup, Russell Sobel, and David Macpherson (2018), *Microeconomics: Private and Public Choice*, Boston, MA: Cengage Learning, 16th edition.

Hubbard, Glenn, and Anthony O'Brien (2019), *Microeconomics*, New York: Pearson Education, 7th edition.

Karlan, Dean, and Jonathan Murdoch (2021), *Microeconomics*, New York: McGraw-Hill Education, 3rd edition.

Krugman, Paul, and Robin Wells (2021), *Microeconomics*, New York: Worth Publishers, 6th edition.

Mankiw, N. Gregory (2021), *Principles of Microeconomics*, Boston, MA: Cengage Learning, 9th edition.

Mateer, G. Dirk, and Lee Coppock (2020), *Principles of Microeconomics*, New York: W.W. Norton & Company, 3rd edition.

McConnell, Campbell, Stanley Brue, and Sean Flynn (2021), *Microeconomics*, New York: McGraw-Hill Education, 22nd edition.

McEachern, William (2019), *ECON MICRO*, Boston, MA: Cengage Learning, 6th edition.

Miller, Roger (2018), *Economics Today: The Micro View*, New York: Pearson Education, 19th edition.

O'Sullivan, Arthur, Steven Sheffrin, and Stephen Perez (2020), *Microeconomics: Principles, Applications, and Tools*, New York: Pearson Education, 10th edition.

Parkin, Michael (2019), *Microeconomics*, New York: Pearson Education, 13th edition.

Schiller, Bradley, and Karen Gebardt (2019), *The Micro Economy Today*, New York: McGraw-Hill Education, 15th edition.

Sexton, Robert (2019), *Exploring Microeconomics*, Corwin, CO: SAGE Publications, 8th edition.

Slavin, Stephen (2020), *Microeconomics*, New York: McGraw-Hill Education, 12th edition.

Stevenson, Betsey, and Justin Wolfers (2020), *Principles of Microeconomics*, New York: Worth Publishers, 1st edition.

Tucker, Irvin (2019), *Microeconomics for Today*, Boston, MA: Cengage Learning, 10th edition.

4. Asynchronicity, access, and content: teaching economics in a shifting landscape

Belinda Archibong, Olivia Bobrownicki, Rajiv Sethi, and Homa Zarghamee

INTRODUCTION

The novel coronavirus that began to ravage societies worldwide starting in early 2020 left no part of the global economy untouched. The resulting effects can usefully be partitioned into those affecting the composition of production, and those affecting its scale. The scale effects included a dramatic rise in layoffs and furloughs, and a collapse in aggregate demand. The composition effects involved a rise in demand for some sectors even as others were contracting. Demand for online communication technologies and home delivery rose, for example, even as that for travel and lodging fell catastrophically.

The scale effects in the United States were addressed by a number of policy initiatives, including the $2 trillion commitments in the Coronavirus Aid, Relief, and Economic Security Act (the CARES Act), as well as actions by the Federal Reserve to sustain borrowing by businesses and municipalities. These effects have largely been contained. But some of the composition effects may well be irreversible, and certain sectors will experience long-term structural transformation. We believe that the delivery and content of higher education will belong to this group. Indeed, incipient trends in the content and delivery of instruction—including asynchronous or livestreamed course components—were accelerated under the force of the pandemic, and new approaches to pedagogy are starting to crystallize.

In this chapter, we focus on instruction in microeconomics and describe three recent innovations—the Curriculum Open-Access Resources in Economics (CORE) Project, the National Education Equity Lab, and Outlier—that provide a glimpse into the pedagogy of the future. The first two are non-profits, while the third is a commercial venture that, like Equity Lab, depends on partnerships with existing educational institutions for course accreditation.[1]

We focus on these particular innovations because we—along with other colleagues at Barnard College, Columbia University in New York—have been closely engaged with them. We have used CORE materials as the basis for instruction for several years. More recently, we have assisted Outlier in syllabus construction and recorded lectures for its courses. And we have developed and taught a course for Equity Lab. We do not discuss other innovative resources with which we have less experience. Most conspicuously absent from our discussion is OpenStax, a non-profit initiative housed at Rice University in Texas that offers high-quality textbooks, assessment tools, and learning management software integration without charge online. Much of what we say about the manner in which CORE, Equity Lab, and Outlier are transforming content and delivery in the teaching of economics is also applicable to OpenStax.

THE CORE PROJECT

Historical Background

In January 2013, with many economies still reeling from the global financial crisis, Wendy Carlin of University College London convened a meeting of concerned economists in Cambridge, Massachusetts. The goal was to "consider how we could better teach economics to undergraduates," by building "a curriculum that places before students the best of the current state of economic knowledge addressed to the pressing problems of concern."

This initiative led to the development of a project called Curriculum Open-Access Resources for Economics or CORE, dedicated to the production of high-quality open-access resources for teaching economics. In August 2017, CORE released *The Economy*, an introductory textbook that is available free of charge worldwide in digital form.[2] The provision of digital resources that could effectively replace much costlier alternatives increased access and equity at a stroke.

These materials are now in use at almost 400 colleges and universities worldwide. From January to October 2021, over 1 million visits to the CORE website were logged, culminating in more than 6 million page views. Over 11 000 teachers have registered to access CORE's teaching resources. Several additional projects are underway, with two additional texts—*Doing Economics* and *Economy, Society, and Public Policy*—already posted online, and a print version of the latter available at modest cost (CORE Team 2019). A second edition of *The Economy* is in preparation.

Building Content

The handful of individuals who attended the initial 2013 meeting grew to encompass *The Economy*'s 23 contributors, each with varying levels of participation in content creation. A small team led by Carlin developed a skeletal outline of the book, identifying key topics and potential authors. Approximately 20 units were originally conceived, and 22 eventually written. The task of drafting early versions of each unit was then delegated to selected authors. While this method allowed for individual units to be written by specialists in their respective fields, it raised a problem of coherence. Not surprisingly, these early drafts were largely stand-alone pieces, bearing little relation to each other. Even naturally connected topics were treated independently across different units.

The task of building connectedness and coherence was undertaken using a combination of centralized and decentralized processes. Wendy Carlin, Sam Bowles, and Margaret Stevens solicited revisions from unit authors and then stitched together the material into a seamless whole. These three were the primary authors for many units and played a role in writing several more. Twelve authors contributed to just a single unit, and another four to just two units. This allowed for a division of labor in which expertise in diverse fields could be harnessed.

The Economy contains several content innovations, which we discuss below. But in the long run, the process innovation may turn out to have the broadest impact, since it provides a proof of concept for the development of teaching materials in a manner that is both openly collaborative and carefully coordinated. This has implications not just for the economics discipline, but indeed for any discipline in which standard writing practices have thwarted content innovation.

Instead of using an existing textbook (or set of texts) as a template and improving content at the margins, the CORE team started from scratch and tried to produce something without precedent. Traditional processes for content development often begin by identifying the models to be taught, and then building the content by selecting examples that fit these models. In comparison, CORE's distinctive approach to pedagogy begins with a question or problem, and then introduces students to new concepts and models so that they may investigate the issue from multiple angles. CORE has set a new benchmark for economics instruction by integrating nuanced topic perspectives that are often reserved for higher-level courses (Bowles and Carlin 2017, 2020). In particular, the team sought to incorporate substantive historical content, data, experimental results, and recent developments in theory; including models of social preferences, strategic interaction, incomplete information, incomplete contracts, and disequilibrium dynamics. We next describe these content innovations in some detail.

Expanded and Refitted Foundational Tools

Compared with standard textbooks, CORE builds introductory economics on an expanded and refitted set of basic tools. While supply and demand analysis is introduced and invoked in a variety of applications, it is not the primary mode of analysis.

One of the main shortcomings of the reduced-form model of supply and demand on which standard introductory texts so heavily rely is that it glosses over the process of price discovery and trading. Markets are viewed as abstractions rather than as concrete institutions with established rules and norms. To rectify this, considerable attention is paid in *The Economy* to describing the rules that govern trading in particular environments.

For instance, trading in many modern financial markets is typically governed by the rules of the continuous double auction, with anonymous participants electronically submitting bids to buy or offers to sell. Orders either trade on arrival—if they are compatible with an earlier order that has yet to trade—or enter a limit order book where they become available for future trades. The prices at which trades occur, and the priority with which orders are executed, are all subject to the rules of the exchange. Students learn about price–time priority, and the determination of price when two compatible orders are associated with different prices (as when a buyer is willing to pay more than a seller is willing to accept).

Along similar lines, students are introduced to the Dutch auction that is used in the Ancona fish market, and the process of pairwise bargaining that occurs in the Marseille fish market. These are contrasted with the posted-price markets with which they are already familiar. This approach gives students a feel for how different markets operate, and how prices and quantities are actually determined in various environments. Rather than simply manipulating demand and supply curves to reach mechanical solutions, they can clearly visualize the underlying process at work, based on a deeper understanding of how markets operate.

More broadly, instead of demand and supply curves, the recurrent microeconomic foundation in CORE is constrained optimization, and is illustrated with feasible sets and some standard tools such as isocost, isoprofit, and indifference curves. The same indifference curve and feasible set analysis applied to individual choice over two goods in Unit 2 is used in Unit 4 to model individual choice over own–other payoff combinations under different social preferences, and again in Unit 5 to illustrate the expansion of the feasible set in intertemporal choice under different finance regimes.

This approach decouples efficiency and equilibrium from the start; or rather, avoids presenting them as a benchmark tradeoff that would then require decoupling. The emphasis on constrained optimization allows for a more flexible and comprehensive "pluralistic integration" of recent research into fundamental economic models.

For example, consider the model of the labor market. Standard economic textbooks treat labor as any other variable input used by the firm, with a price (namely the wage) that emerges from the same competitive supply and demand conditions used to determine the price of bread. Unemployment occurs as a result of distortionary government policies such as minimum wages and unemployment benefits in this orthodox conception.

In CORE, labor contracts are introduced as inherently incomplete, with the employer able to contract authority over the employee's time, not productive ownership over the worker themself. The interaction is modeled as the employer setting wages to produce optimal effort from the employee, while constrained by the feasible set of effort–wage combinations the employee is willing to accept over unemployment or job search. As such, labor markets, because of their institutional foundation, inherently give rise to unemployment. Students are then exposed to discussions of alternative labor arrangements such as cooperatives and the role of labor unions.

Historical and Social Contextualization

CORE presents economic models within historical and social contexts. The opening unit provides a bird's-eye view of the dramatic changes in production, technology, inequality, and environment attendant on the Industrial Revolution and its accompanying institutions. Students see a series of "hockey-stick" graphs that show the breaks in trend relative to the previous millennium, not just in income per capita, but also in the speed at which information travels, the price of luminosity, carbon concentration in the atmosphere, and other measures of economic, social, and environmental transformation. The raw data underlying the figures are available at the click of a mouse, including high-resolution data such as income by decile within a large set of countries for each year over several decades.

The second unit then grapples with the kink in the hockey-stick, addressing the question of why exponential growth began where and when it did. Students learn how colonial expansion, wage pressures, and the price of coal combined to incentivize the capital innovations in eighteenth-century Britain that fueled the Industrial Revolution and ensuing escape from the Malthusian trap. Research from economic historians is featured throughout, as is the history of economic thought.

The third unit considers the manner in which the choice of work hours in different countries has varied historically, under the conflicting influences of income and substitution effects. The interplay of cultural preferences and economic pressures can result in different outcomes under similar economic circumstances, as with the relatively long vacation times in Northern Europe compared with South Korea's lengthy work hours. These historical narratives and data visualizations are interwoven with the development of the benchmark microeconomic model of constrained optimization.

Through this historical lens, students interact with introductory principles at a deeper level. The result is a more tangible, less abstract understanding of the ideas and their application. Moreover, the connections between economics and other social and historical sciences is made apparent. This allows for a balanced and self-contained introduction to the field, which is especially valuable for the many students for whom this will be the only formal exposure to economics.

The standard tools—including supply and demand curves, constrained optimization, intertemporal choice, equilibrium, externalities, and efficiency—are all covered in subsequent units, but within this historical and institutional context throughout.

Understanding the Economy as a Whole

CORE's second pedagogical innovation is its sustained emphasis on the economy as a whole. Though it can be tailored for separate courses in micro- and macroeconomics, *The Economy* is not yet divided along these lines. Even the most fundamental microeconomic material is embedded in a macroeconomic framework, and vice versa. As such, students are encouraged to think carefully about the role of models in economic reasoning and their ability to serve as good representations of the real world.

In Unit 3, the section on scarcity, work, and choice, students learn to use models of feasible frontiers and indifference curves to solve constrained optimization problems and understand the role of income and substitution effects in decision-making pertaining to work and consumption. They then use these models to explain the reduction in work hours that has occurred in many economies since the Industrial Revolution, and analyze current data showing a positive cross-country relationship between per capita gross domestic product and average annual work hours. In Unit 4, students are introduced to "social interactions" using game theory and models of social dilemmas. Experimental research on altruism and coordination is featured, as is the crucial role of social norms and institutions in attaining desirable economic outcomes, and addressing collective action problems both local and global.

Units 5 through 9 cover material on inequality as well as the role of bargaining power in firm–worker and firm–customer relations. The microeconomic labor model depicting the power- and norm-dependent interactions of employees and employers culminates in the measurement of the effectiveness of policies and institutions combatting economy-wide income inequality and unemployment, such as labor unions in the Organisation for Economic Co-operation and Development (OECD) and Operation Barga in West Bengal. In Units 10 through 15, a microeconomic model of intertemporal consumption leads to a discussion of the business of banking, balance sheets, asset valuation, bubbles and crashes, and the role of the central bank.

The textbook ends with "capstone" chapters that provide a thorough theoretical and historical background on important topics, incorporating methods and concepts learned throughout the text. These topics include the Great Depression and financial crises, globalization, economic inequality, the economics of the environment, and politics and public policy.

The forthcoming edition of *The Economy* will be composed of two separate volumes, making it easier for instructors to adapt the text to specialized courses in microeconomics and macroeconomics. Until then, the introduction to the current version provides a "note to instructors" that explains how the text can be organized into distinct courses along these lines. For instance, an introductory microeconomics course can be constructed based on the units on scarcity, work, choice, social interactions, property and power, firms, supply and demand, the labor market, banks, money, the credit market, rent-seeking, price-seeking, and market efficiency and public policy, coupled with one or more capstone units.

Incorporation of Frontier Research

The Economy (and the CORE vision more generally) connects students with cutting-edge research and the economists who are conducting it. References are not just relegated to end-of-chapter lists, but are directly linked throughout the text, providing the curious student with direct access to further readings and datasets.

Interspersed throughout the online text are 30 "Economists in Action" videos, in each of which a leading economist concisely presents their research, methodology, and analyses. These videos feature, among others: Joseph Stiglitz discussing the financial crisis as a market failure; Thomas Piketty discussing the long-run dynamics of wealth inequality; Esther Duflo discussing women's empowerment in India; and Kathryn Graddy discussing competition in fish markets.

In addition, *The Economy* features a recurrent "Great Economists" section, presenting intellectual biographies of pioneering economists. These include household names such as Smith, Marx, Keynes, and Hayek, as well as highly original but less often featured interdisciplinary thinkers such as Herbert Simon, Albert Hirschman, and Elinor Ostrom.

Through these resources, students are exposed to ideas and economists that they would not normally encounter in an introductory textbook. Information about each economist is embedded in the unit that relates to their work; their descriptions complement the base material and enable students to better understand the origins and applications of concepts. For example, in her video, Kathryn Graddy describes her research on price discrimination at the Fulton Fish Market in New York City. In her analysis, she applies principles such as competition and barriers to entry, while also assessing their limitations.

Similarly, as students delve into the work of Elinor Ostrom, they are introduced to social preferences, reciprocity, and trust. They learn that norms sustained by decentralized punishment can avert a tragedy of the commons, even in the absence of private or state property. Ostrom's challenge to conventional economic thinking on common property exposes students to an original thinker and an alternative perspective that departs from standard textbook material. Furthermore, exposure to the economists behind the various concepts in the textbook has the potential to diversify the field, as students may update their beliefs about who economists are.

CORE Insights

Given its origins in a team of collaborators spanning multiple countries, CORE is not adapted to particular local conditions. In order to facilitate such adaptation, introduce new material, and cover existing topics in greater depth, the organization has started to publish a series of stand-alone units, collected together as CORE Insights. These units can be used to augment the main texts for introductory courses, or can be used to supplement other sources in a variety of more advanced elective courses.

CORE Insights make the project's content dynamic. As new topics of economic importance are identified, they can be easily added to the digital repertoire of open-access content.[3] In this way, the CORE texts function like a hub-and-spoke system, with texts such as *The Economy* operating as a hub, and instructors and students selecting specific spokes to complement the material based on individual needs and local conditions. This innovation allows for significant flexibility and regional adaptability in curriculum construction.

The ease of adopting CORE Insights as supplements to existing classroom content makes them a viable option for instructors who may be unwilling or unable to change their primary text to *The Economy*. This is an important consideration, since CORE's content innovations have run up against deeply entrenched pedagogical practices. For example, in the United States, most introductory courses are offered as micro-specific or macro-specific units. These courses are often taught by different instructors. Students take them in different sequences, and may take one but not the other. Some instructors are also required to teach courses that are aligned with state-mandated or department-prescribed learning objectives. *The Economy*, therefore, can be difficult to adopt even when there are instructors in a department who favor it. CORE Insights are a response to such challenges because they may be added to any economics course, regardless of its primary focus. Instructors who can only make incremental changes to their curricula can use them to supplement other texts.

Three CORE Insights have been published to date, with others in development. A unit on *Financing American Government* addresses the manner in which a sudden and significant expansion of federal spending can be attained even as tax revenues are collapsing, as with the $2 trillion dollar CARES Act of 2020 (Jasova and Sethi 2020). More generally, the unit considers the role of the United States Treasury and Federal Reserve in stabilizing the economy in ordinary conditions and in times of crisis. Students learn about the underlying microeconomic principles in the Treasury's issuing of securities, including the structure of Treasury auctions.

A unit called *Too Big to Fail: Lessons from a Decade of Financial Sector Reforms* examines the processes that can cause the collapse of a systemically important bank to threaten the stability of the global financial system (Buch et al. 2021). It reveals how governments have adapted their monetary policies following the 2008 financial crisis to decrease the likelihood of such collapses, and the risks associated with them.

Finally, *A World of Differences: An Introduction to Inequality* considers the causes, consequences, and ethical evaluation of economic inequality (Naidu et al. 2021). It enables students to quantify and compare inequality across time and space using tools such as the Lorenz curve and the Gini coefficient. The text provides students with the vocabulary to understand economic inequality and possible policy solutions. It explains concepts such as disposable income, market income, and income shares, that are a critical basis for interpreting measures of inequality and drawing comparisons. This unit offers instructors an organized, robust discussion of inequality that is often missing from or scattered throughout introductory texts. These CORE Insights, and others under development, can be easily incorporated into a range of courses, including higher-level electives focused on specific topics.

Delivery

The digital version of *The Economy* and a camera-ready version for print were both produced from the same source content by Fire & Lion, a publishing firm based in Cape Town, South Africa. The effort was led by Arthur Atwell, using open source tools and pioneering methods for multi-format publishing. As Atwell (2017) describes, bridging the gap between print and digital publishing required considerable innovation. Not only are the CORE materials published under a creative commons license, but the publishing process itself involved the use of open source tools, without compromising production values. In fact, the digital version contains many features that go beyond what is available in online versions of standard texts. Aside from embedded video, there are figures generated from data that can be accessed directly, quizzes with solutions that are displayed on demand, and slide decks that build individual figures step-by-step as one is reading.

But publishing is simply the first stage of delivery; subsequent stages involve the design and execution of courses by instructors. The material can certainly be used in conventional courses taught in standard face-to-face classroom settings, replacing traditional textbooks for this purpose. But the CORE resource ecosystem is especially well suited for asynchronous or remote instruction, which can broaden access and reach. CORE provides a number of resources for online instruction, including video tutorials, self-assessment exercises throughout the text, interactive simulations, and guidance and infrastructure for running online economics experiments and relating them to the text. The pandemic forced a shift to such modes of instruction, and these changes will not be entirely reversed.

We next describe two significant partnerships that involve new modes of content delivery by instructors: Equity Lab and Outlier. The former is a non-profit working with underserved high schools. The latter is a commercial venture targeting adult learners and college students who stand outside the existing system of elite education. Both are reliant on partnerships with academic institutions for course accreditation in the United States. The for-profit nature of Outlier raises issues related to mission alignment with partner institutions, which we discuss below.

EQUITY LAB

Equity Lab is a non-profit that provides high school students in underserved communities access to free, credit-bearing college courses. The organization is founded on the belief that "while talent is evenly distributed, opportunity is not." It seeks to create new opportunities for high school students by bringing together Title 1 high schools, universities, and non-profit organizations. Working with instructors, Equity Lab adapts college curricula for a high school setting, awards scholarships to teachers and students to enable their participation, and cultivates a support network of affiliated schools. In the process, it creates a new pipeline of applicants for colleges and universities, and potentially allays subsequent costs for students by providing them with college credit.[4]

While the courses are taught at a high level of rigor, students are offered extensive support in mastering content by classroom co-teachers from their high schools, and teaching fellows from the college or university at which their course originates. Faculty at several institutions—including Arizona State, Barnard, Cornell, Howard, the University of Connecticut, and Yale—have already developed and offered courses through this program.

At each high school, a cohort of students completes their Equity Lab class together under the guidance of a high school teacher, who is known as the classroom co-teacher. Cohorts watch asynchronous lectures recorded by the college faculty member responsible for the course, and then attend synchronous class sessions with their classroom co-teacher to review and discuss the material, receive feedback on assignment drafts, and develop time management strategies. Beyond class, Equity Lab students are required to complete homework assignments to test and deepen their understanding of a subject. To assist, teaching fellows meet with the students in small groups weekly to answer homework questions, clarify concepts, share grades and feedback, and talk about their experience at college. A student success manager works as a liaison among the students, course professor, classroom co-teachers, and teaching fellows. They track each student's progress to identify whether additional support is needed, communicate this need to the instructors, and then plan and implement solutions to academic barriers that may arise. Overall, Equity Lab prepares students for the demands of a rigorous college curriculum, while allowing them to demonstrate their potential and secure transferable credits.

Equity Lab's programs are funded by its partnerships with various philanthropies—such as the Gates Foundation and the Carnegie Corporation—and enhanced by its partnerships with organizations such as the Common Application (Common-App). For example, Common-App provides participating students with college mentors through programs such as Strive for College, while Michelle Obama's Reach Higher program supports them as they traverse the financial aid and college application process (Davis 2020). Partnerships also increase Equity Lab's ability to expand its program, as new collaborators such as Amazon Web Services (AWS) are willing to facilitate courses that train students for high-demand work positions. AWS is currently working with Equity Lab to bring 10000 students into cloud computing courses by 2025 (Ascione 2021). As employers recognize the importance of expanding educational access, Equity Lab provides them with a viable avenue for reaching underserved students.

Over 2019–2020, Equity Lab's courses reached 3000 students in over 75 Title 1 high schools across 22 cities. In all, 86 percent of enrolled students passed their courses, earning a cumulative 2248 transferable, free college credits. Each passing student demonstrates their capability to complete college-level work, develops the skills necessary to apply for and succeed in college, gains confidence through their experience, and faces a reduced cost of college attendance due to the early completion of credits. By 2022, Equity Lab expects to reach 10 000 students by expanding its program to 18 additional cities, furthering this positive impact, and further expanding access to a college-level education.

Equity Lab piloted its first microeconomics course in the fall of 2021 at four high schools: three in New York City and one in Orlando. The course is taught by Homa Zarghamee of Barnard College, and utilizes content from her asynchronous recorded lectures, the open-access CORE resources, and supplemental readings. This course demonstrates the synergies between the CORE ecosystem of modular open-access resources for economics, and the structured delivery mechanisms maintained by Equity Lab. In principle, very similar approaches could be used to reach new audiences such as adult learners, students from non-traditional backgrounds, and those who cannot gain admission to the nation's elite academic institutions. For example, colleges can enhance the support they provide to students by replicating Equity Lab's extensive network of support systems.

Equity Lab exposes students to each topic three times: by providing recorded lectures; requiring high schools to review the material in smaller, teacher-guided groups; and organizing weekly recitations led by teaching fellows. This degree of interaction with the content and access to different teaching styles increases students' ability to master the material. Following this blueprint, college instructors can structure their economics courses to provide threefold exposure to key concepts. Although this level of support may not be feasible for a large college course due to the many resources it requires, it can be targeted toward students who are struggling to better ensure the success of the entire class. This general approach to instruction is similar to that offered by Outlier, as we discuss next.

OUTLIER

Outlier is a for-profit company that partners with the University of Pittsburgh to award its students transferable college credits. Its business model is based on the development of a set of introductory courses in high demand among college students and adult learners. The focus is on quality, accessibility, and affordability: the courses are online, feature faculty from elite institutions, and are offered at a substantially lower price than their more conventional counterparts.[5]

As is the case with Equity Lab, Outlier courses are based on asynchronous recordings by college faculty, augmented by a team of assistants who handle interactions with students and grading. One significant difference lies in curriculum construction, which is delegated to a team of content experts. A single course may involve recordings by several faculty spread across multiple institutions, with each professor handling a small number of units.

Although lectures are recorded and delivered asynchronously, the program strives to replicate an in-person classroom experience in other respects. Courses include access to live assistance during office hours, facilitate the submission of inquiries during practice exercises and lectures, and share a discussion community consisting of all of a course's students, tutors, and success advisors. Numerous problems and exercises are provided to increase student engagement.

Outlier's Introduction to Microeconomics course features several faculty members who have taught with and helped develop CORE materials: Simon Halliday, Suresh Naidu, Rajiv Sethi, and Homa Zarghamee. Moreover, Introduction to Macroeconomics features Peter Mathews, Rena Rosenberg, and Elham Saeidinezhad, all of whom have also been associated with CORE. Several of the innovations in the CORE curriculum are accordingly represented, though embedded in a course with more conventional coverage and a more traditional structure.

Equity Lab has a mission that aligns well with those of its partner academic institutions. Outlier's position as a commercial venture, by contrast, raises some thorny issues of mission alignment. For example, a number of Outlier's courses, including those in introductory economics, are accredited by the University of Pittsburgh. Meanwhile, curriculum development and the recording of lectures have been largely delegated to faculty at other institutions. If faculty at accrediting institutions are to be more involved in the design, production, and delivery of content, several issues would need to be addressed, including ownership of intellectual property, and the conditions under which the university's own students could take courses. Such concerns do not preclude ongoing collaboration with Outlier, but do demand careful attention to maintaining a harmony of goals.

CONCLUSION

Simon Wren-Lewis (2017) has argued that the radical departure from the standard curriculum that CORE embodies would not have been possible under the conventional model of textbook publishing. In a sense, the content innovation was made possible by the process and publishing innovations. A transformation of economic instruction that could not have been made one step at a time was accomplished by taking multiple steps simultaneously.

Having established a new free online curriculum in economics, CORE has been able to expand its reach as a result of initiatives such as Equity Lab and Outlier that leverage the scalability of asynchronous instruction. Recorded lectures allow students to learn from instructors who may be thousands of miles away, while they simultaneously study under the daily guidance of an in-person high school teacher or the weekly instruction of a synchronous, online teaching assistant. This structure facilitates collaboration among physically distant entities, while maintaining an extensive support network for students. Scalability, along with the targeting of underserved students, has furthered progress toward the fulfillment of a key CORE mission, to "help change who studies economics to include more women and other underrepresented groups by changing content, pedagogy and access to knowledge."[6]

Although each of these initiatives began before the Covid-19 pandemic, the world's shift away from live instruction revealed the practical advantages and greater accessibility that can accompany digital delivery of higher education, if designed with sufficient care. Changes that were forced upon institutions by public health concerns may well point the way to lasting structural transformation, and greater access to the best content that higher education can offer.

ACKNOWLEDGMENTS

The initiatives described in this chapter have been made possible thanks to generous financial support and guidance provided by the Teagle Foundation, the Hewlett Foundation, and the Omidyar Network. We are especially grateful to Loni Bordoloi Pazich, Jennifer Harris, and Tracy Williams. We also thank Sam Bowles, Wendy Carlin, Mark Maier, Phil Ruder, and Sarah Thomas for comments and suggestions.

NOTES

1. Our discussion of CORE draws on material in Archibong et al. (2018), presented at the Eighth Annual AEA Conference on Teaching and Research in Economic Education (CTREE), San Antonio, 2018. We shall refer to the National Education Equity Lab simply as Equity Lab.
2. See https://www.core-econ.org/ for this text and all other resources published online by CORE. A print version was published by Oxford University Press shortly after the digital release of *The Economy*, and sold at a fraction of the price charged for standard introductory-level textbooks (CORE Team 2017).
3. The Covid-19 collection published by CORE exemplifies this dynamism. This is a series of classroom lectures, videos, interactive learning simulations, prepared assignments, and instructor resources to facilitate the adoption and integration of Covid-19 economics content into existing classes. The collection may be found at https://www.core-econ.org/selection/covid-19-collection/.

4. See https://edequitylab.org/ for further details. Some of the information in this section is drawn from a presentation at Barnard College by Shaquille Dunbar of Equity Lab.
5. Outlier's courses cost $400 each, and students who complete all requirements but do not pass can get a full refund. In comparison, the average two-year institution in the United States cost $4230 in tuition and required fees during the 2019–2020 school year, and the average four-year institution was $19081 (National Center for Education Statistics 2022).
6. See https://www.core-econ.org/about/ for CORE's mission statement.

REFERENCES

Archibong, B., Sethi, R, Thomas, S., and Zarghamee, H. (2018). Four innovations in economics education: The CORE Project. Available at SSRN: https://ssrn.com/abstract=3305726.
Ascione, L. (2021). New initiative targets 10,000 underserved students for in-demand cloud computing careers. *eSchool News*, July.
Atwell, A. (2017). Producing *The Economy* with the electric book workflow: A case study in multi-format book production. *Electric Book Works*, August 29.
Bowles, S., and Carlin, W. (2017). A new paradigm for the introductory course in economics. *VoxEU*, September 7.
Bowles, S., and Carlin, W. (2020). What students learn in Economics 101: Time for a change. *Journal of Economic Literature* 58(1), 176–214.
Buch, C.M., Dominguez-Cardoza, A., and Ward, J. (2021). Too big to fail: Lessons from a decade of financial sector reform. *CORE Insights*.
CORE Team (2017). *The Economy: Economics for a Changing World*. Oxford University Press.
CORE Team (2019). *Economy, Society, and Public Policy*. Oxford University Press.
Davis, J. (2020). The National Education Equity Lab announces first-ever national pilot a success in Title 1 underserved high schools in 11 cities from Flint, Michigan, to Baton Rouge, Louisiana, and NYC. *Common App*, February 5.
Jasova, M., and Sethi, R. (2020). Financing American government. *CORE Insights*.
Naidu, S., Sethi, R., and Thomas, S. (2021). A world of differences: An introduction to inequality. *CORE Insights*.
National Center for Education Statistics (2022). Digest of Education Statistics: Table 330.40, 2021. Retrieved February 10, 2022 from https://nces.ed.gov/programs/digest/d20/tables/dt20_330.40.asp.
Wren-Lewis, S. (2017). Undergraduate economics teaching moves into 21st century. *Mainly Macro*, September 19.

5. The issues approach to teaching Principles of Microeconomics

Wendy A. Stock

The Principles course fails to improve economic literacy of not only those who take it, but also those frightened away by its reputation as a technical course. The course fails because it does not teach students how to apply economics to their personal, professional, and public lives.

(Hansen et al. 2002, p. 464)

INTRODUCTION

An internet search for "why study economics" returns a long list of websites from universities, businesses, and others describing how taking economics promotes critical thinking and problem-solving, helps one better understand how the world works, makes one a more informed voter or policy-maker, and improves one's job and graduate school prospects. These answers make a lot of sense. Unfortunately, the typical Principles of Microeconomics course taught in universities today falls far short of its potential to improve students' economic literacy and increase their interest in economics more generally.[1]

Approximately 2 million students in the United States take Principles of Economics each year, but just 2 percent of them major in economics (Bowles and Carlin 2020; Stock 2017). For the vast majority of students, Principles will be their only formal exposure to economics. Unfortunately, Principles courses are not geared toward these "one-and-done" students, but instead tend to be more focused on preparing students to take upper-level field and intermediate theory courses. The result is that much of the focus in Principles courses is on topics and theory that only a select few students are likely to use in the future, while leaving most students with relatively little that they can apply in their personal, professional, and public lives. In addition, the traditional Principles course structure likely turns off students on the margin who might otherwise enroll in the course and perhaps continue in economics if it had more obvious application and relevance to the issues that they face in their lives. This may be especially true among women and other underrepresented demographic groups, with the result that the traditional Principles course exacerbates the lack of diversity in economics.

In 2002, Allgood et al. (2004) surveyed students in the United States who took economics courses in 1976, 1986, and 1996 to ask which topics regularly covered in economics courses they remembered studying, and which topics they viewed as being important (and unimportant) since leaving school. The general agreement among respondents was that studying markets/supply and demand, imperfect competition, and scarcity and opportunity cost were at the top of the list of things they remembered studying. Unfortunately, when asked about the importance of the topics or concepts in their lives since leaving school, microeconomics topics such as perfect and imperfect competition ranked near the bottom of the list. Because perfect and imperfect competition comprise about three weeks of a typical 12-week Principles course, one could argue that Microeconomics Principles instructors spend 25 percent of the time teaching concepts that are not particularly important to students' lives. At the same time, topics such as race, inequality, unemployment, and poverty— problems that students say they want to learn more about in economics courses—are given scant (if any) attention.

In this chapter, I assert that using an issues-oriented approach to teaching Principles of Microeconomics can increase student interest and help students to see the applicability of economics to addressing current social issues.[2] The approach can also help instructors to implement teaching methods that researchers in cognitive science have found to increase learning, and can enhance the impact of the Principles course for "one-and-done" students while at the same time not short-changing continuing economics students.

WHAT IS THE ISSUES APPROACH TO TEACHING ECONOMICS?

There is no formal definition of the "issues approach" to teaching economics, but an example can illustrate the method.[3] In a traditional Principles course, the course's textbook chapters provide the framework and structure as students progress through the course. A quick review of the tables of contents of top-selling Microeconomics Principles books shows that most have an introductory chapter describing the scope of economics using key principles or foundational ideas, followed by chapters on supply and demand or comparative advantage, and then proceeding through consumer and producer theory, competitive and monopoly markets, and finishing up with other market structures and market failures. When covering a topic such as comparative advantage, for example, a typical Principles instructor would present the concept of opportunity cost, build the production possibilities model, and show how comparative advantage provides the foundation for mutually advantageous trade. Social issues are incorporated after economic concepts are presented, and are typically used as examples or applications of a given concept or theory.

As described by Randall (1975), the issues approach reverses this process. The social issues come first, to provide the motivation and framing, and economic concepts are introduced to illustrate how economists approach the issue, use models to explain and predict behavior around the issue, and use data to evaluate policies related to the issue. While the traditional Principles syllabus would set the class schedule based on the sequence of economic concepts or topics to be covered, an issues-oriented Principles syllabus would set the schedule based on the issues covered in the course, and would then link those issues to specific economic concepts and topics.

Table 5.1 provides an example of the issues approach by comparing a simplified version of the schedule for Harvard's fall 2019 EC 10a Principles of Microeconomics course to that of a potential issues-oriented Microeconomics Principles course. Column 1 presents the typical Principles course schedule, column 2 presents a schedule for an issues-oriented course, and column 3 lists relevant economics topics and concepts that can be linked to each issue in the issues-oriented course. In the typical Microeconomics Principles course, the schedule proceeds from the introduction of basic economic concepts, to supply and demand, consumer and producer theory, perfect competition, and various types of market failures. In an issues-oriented course, the schedule starts with an introduction to highlight how economics can shed light on a wide array of issues that students face in their lives, and then proceeds through a set of issues or questions used to motivate the underlying economics (I discuss ways to select the issues to cover later in this chapter).

As illustrated in column 3, most of the key topics covered in the traditional Principles course are also covered in the issues-oriented course, but not necessarily in the same order or with the same emphasis. For example, when teaching comparative advantage, an instructor in a typical Principles course would start by explaining what comparative advantage is, illustrating how to compute opportunity costs, and then showing students how comparative advantage can be applied. In an issues-oriented course, the instructor does the reverse. An issues approach to teaching comparative advantage would start with a discussion of a news article on, say, Chinese import restrictions on United States (US) agricultural goods, and would then proceed to challenge students to identify and explain key components of the issue (perhaps with prompts from the instructor to move the discussion toward the question of why the US and China trade at all). The instructor would then deliver a mini-lecture showing how international trade (and indeed all voluntary trade) is linked to the economic concept of comparative advantage. The primary difference is perspective and framing. In the issues-oriented course, the issue comes first and the economics behind it comes second, consistent with research in cognitive science which

Table 5.1   Traditional and issues-oriented Principles course schedules

	1	2	3
Week	Traditional Principles of Microeconomics	Issues-Oriented Microeconomics	Issues Course Linked Topics
1	Introduction to Economics, Principles of Economics and Economic Methods, Demand, Supply and Equilibrium	What Can Economics Teach Us About Addressing Social Issues?	marginal analysis, maximization, models, scientific method, correlation/causation
2	Consumers and Incentives, Psychology and Economics	US–China Relations	comparative advantage and trade, comparative economic systems
3	Perfect Competition and the Invisible Hand, Equity and Efficiency	Affordable Housing	demand and supply, taxes, elasticity, discrimination
4	Externalities and Public Goods, Climate Change	The Minimum Wage	welfare economics, price and output controls, policy analysis, inequality
5	Government in the Economy: Taxation and Transfer Programs	The Student Loan Crisis	consumer theory, labor–leisure tradeoff, present value, expected value, externalities, inequality
6	Inequality and Economics of Labor Markets	Why Do MLB Players Earn $ Millions while Teachers Earn $ Thousands?	producer theory, factors of production, short/long run, discrimination, inequality
7	Sellers and Incentives	The Microbrew Revolution	producer theory, costs, shutdown rule, entry, competition
8	Monopoly, Game Theory, and Strategic Play	Why Are EpiPens So Expensive?	competition and monopoly, output, price, profit, monopoly regulation, inequality
9	Oligopoly and Monopolistic Competition	Big Tech	oligopoly, monopolistic competition, game theory, collusion

	1	2	3
Week	Traditional Principles of Microeconomics	Issues-Oriented Microeconomics	Issues Course Linked Topics
10	Tradeoffs Involving Time and Risk	Climate Change	externalities and public goods, government intervention, market solutions, game theory
11	Economics of Information: Adverse Selection, Moral Hazard, and Healthcare	Healthcare	externalities, asymmetric information, adverse selection, moral hazard, government intervention, inequality, discrimination
12	Social Economics	Poverty and Inequality	measurement, government intervention, discrimination

Note: The schedule for the traditional Principles of Microeconomics course is based on the syllabus used by Jason Furman and David Liabson (2019), for EC 10a Principles of Economics (Microeconomics) at Harvard University in fall 2019.

finds that telling students about procedures and concepts before engaging them in problem-solving undermines student learning (Schwartz et al. 2011, 2016). Apart from organizational differences, issues-oriented courses also tend to cover fewer topics than traditional Principles courses. This is by design. In addition to mitigating instructors' curse of knowledge (we underestimate how long it will take another person to learn something we have already mastered), covering fewer topics allows for repeated exposure to key ideas, which in turn promotes a deeper understanding and a working knowledge of fundamental concepts and helps students to apply their understanding to new situations (Wieman 2007; Brown et al. 2014).

A BRIEF HISTORY OF THE ISSUES APPROACH

The issues approach to teaching economics is not new. In reviewing the history of what he terms the "economics made fun" movement, Fleury (2012) notes that the first issues-oriented Principles textbooks emerged in response to criticism that economics and its teaching were lacking relevance to real-world issues facing students in the mid-1960s. Although students at the time wanted economics and other disciplines to focus more on subjects such as war, poverty, racial discrimination, civil rights, drugs, and other social phenomena, these subjects were generally considered outside the traditional boundaries of economics and were not typically taught in Principles courses. George Stigler argued in the *American Economic Review* at the time that:

> The watered-down encyclopedia which constitutes the present course in beginning college economics does not teach the student how to think on economic questions. The brief exposure to each of a vast array of techniques and problems leaves [the student with] no basic economic logic with which to analyze the economic questions [they] will face as a citizen. The student will memorize a few facts, diagrams, and policy recommendations, and ten years later will be as untutored in economics as the day [they] entered the class. (Stigler 1963, p. 657)

He goes on to ask, "Would intense concentration on the basic logic of price theory, applied to two score of real problems, give a vastly better and more lasting training than the current encyclopedic texts? Surely, the answer is yes" (Stigler 1963, p. 659).

Building on the notion that students learn more when the subject is interesting and relevant, and when students are repeatedly exposed to key topics, Leftwich and Sharp (1974) developed and introduced the first issues-oriented economics textbook. They presented concepts and topics in mostly non-technical language, and kept the focus on key features of the economic way of thinking, including scarcity, opportunity costs, supply and demand, marginal analysis, market clearing, elasticity, and efficiency. The goal for their issues-oriented course was to increase students' economic and financial literacy and to create more interest in economics than would be generated by the traditional approach.

Several others have followed Leftwich and Sharp's lead and developed their own textbooks, and now there are several issues-oriented textbooks on the market. In addition, Fleury (2012) argues that many of the popular "economics made fun" books such as Landsburg's (1993) *The Armchair Economist*, Wheelan's (2002) *Naked Economics*, and Dubner and Levitt's (2005) *Freakonomics*, are built on the foundations of the issues-oriented approach.

COSTS AND BENEFITS OF THE ISSUES APPROACH

As with any teaching technique, using the issues approach involves tradeoffs. For the instructor, the largest up-front cost comes from the time and energy it takes to redesign syllabi and lectures. Some instructors may also adjust course readings and assignments, although this is not a necessary condition for using the issues approach. Once the structure is in place, ongoing costs of using the issues approach are relatively low, and depend on how often an instructor decides to update the issues addressed in the course. Because of its flexibility, instructors can also spread the up-front costs over time by adopting the issues approach incrementally in subsections of a course.

Another cost of implementing the issues approach may involve over-coming resistance from colleagues who perceive issues-oriented courses as "Principles-lite." While an issues approach may be more valuable for non-majors, they argue, it may disadvantage students who go on to complete intermediate economic theory courses because they do not have an adequate foundation on which to build. As noted below, research shows that these con-cerns are unfounded.

The beneficial impact of the issues approach for students has been studied in several contexts. The earliest assessment is from Sharp et al. (1975), who compared pre-course and post-course scores on the Test of Understanding of College Economics (TUCE) for students who took their newly developed issues course, and students who instead took a traditional Principles course. They found no difference in the relative gain in post-course TUCE scores for those who took the issues course relative to those who took a traditional course.

Grimes and Nelson (1995) also compared pre-course and post-course TUCE scores for students in their issues-oriented course to those of their peers at the same university who enrolled in traditional Principles of Macroeconomics and/or Principles of Microeconomics courses in the same semester. They found that students in the issues-oriented course were more likely to complete the course than students in the traditional Principles courses, consistent with notion that issues-oriented courses are better at sparking students' interest. They also found that students in the issues-oriented course performed better than their peers in Principles of Macroeconomics on the post-course TUCE exam. However, the students in the issues course scored lower on the post-course TUCE exam than their counterparts in Principles of Microeconomics. Grimes and Nelson (1995) attribute at least some of this to the difference between the content of the issues course and the content of the TUCE exam, since the TUCE was designed to evaluate the traditional Principles course and is thus biased to include concepts (for example, indifference curves, cost curves) that were not covered in the issues-oriented course.

Gilleskie and Salemi (2012) examined whether students who completed a literacy-targeted Principles course performed differently in intermediate theory courses than their peers who completed a traditional Principles course. They found that students who completed the literacy-targeted course earned slightly higher grades in Intermediate Microeconomics and Intermediate Macroeconomics than students who completed the traditional Principles course. They also found that the students in the literacy-targeted course were more likely to continue in economics and enroll in Intermediate Macroeconomics and Intermediate Microeconomics than the students in traditional Principles courses. Benjamin et al. (2020) also compared performance in intermediate courses among students who took a literacy-targeted Principles course and those who took a traditional Principles course. Like Gilleskie and Salemi (2012), they found no difference in students' grades in Intermediate Microeconomics, Intermediate Macroeconomics, or Statistics. They also found that women who took the literacy-targeted course performed significantly better in later statistics courses, suggesting that issues-oriented courses may provide an avenue to reduce the male–female gap in economics. Similarly, Owen and Hagstrom (2021) found that a curricular reform aimed at showing students the broad range of social issues that economists study resulted in more majors from both under- and overrepresented groups at their college.

Finally, Bowles and Carlin (2020) compared students' grades in Intermediate Microeconomics, Intermediate Macroeconomics, and Econometrics courses for the first cohort of students introduced to the Curriculum Open-Access Resources in Economics (CORE, a problem-centered approach to introductory economics that is described in Chapter 4 in this book), and the last cohort of students taught using traditional Principles course structure and methods. They found that students taught using CORE earned higher grades in Intermediate Microeconomics and Intermediate Macroeconomics than students in the traditional Principles courses.

In sum, the research findings consistently indicate that issues-oriented courses do not sacrifice student learning. The issues approach also generates better course completion rates, and increased likelihood of students taking additional courses in economics. As Benjamin et al. (2020) argue, given that a literacy-targeted approach is more accessible and interesting to a broader spectrum of students, and makes the "one-and-done" students (who represent the vast majority of Principles students) better off while not making continuing economics students worse off, it is Pareto-improving for students.

IMPLEMENTING THE ISSUES APPROACH

The issues-oriented approach to teaching can be implemented in an infinite number of ways, ranging from whole-cloth adoption of the method, to applying the method at the margin when covering a particular concept or topic. Leftwich and Sharp (1974) describe the four key steps used in developing and implementing their issues course. First, the nature of the issue is presented in a general and easily accessible way. Then, second, the instructor introduces the economic aspects of the problem and how economists conceptualize the issue. Third, relevant economic concepts and principles are developed; and fourth and finally, the concepts and tools are applied to the issue, and policy changes suggested by the economic analysis are discussed.

Regardless of whether one is thinking of using the issues approach for teaching a single concept or an entire course, it is beneficial to apply the same fundamentals of backward course design used more generally. In particular, rather than formulating a course around a set of content to be covered, we instead focus on essential competencies that we want students to develop, and then generate learning outcomes by intersecting those competencies with key economic concepts. Beginning with competencies such as "applying the scientific method to economic phenomena," and linking them to course content (for example, by using applications of supply and demand), provides a framework to guide course design, helps instructors to decide what and how to teach, and aids in assessing students' learning. Sharing the desired competencies with students can also reduce their cognitive load and better motivate their study of economics (Allgood and Bayer 2016).

There have been robust debates about the essential competencies that economics students should be able to demonstrate, and the appropriate content to include in economics courses (see, e.g., Stigler 1963; Hansen 1986; Krueger et al. 1991; Allgood and Bayer 2016; Bowles and Carlin 2020). The concepts, competencies, and learning outcomes presented by Allgood and Bayer (2016), and summarized in Table 5.2, build on past efforts and represent the general consensus among experts in economics education. The competencies reflect skills that we want students to acquire, and that they can apply in a myriad of situations in the future. The concepts reflect the cornerstones of economic analysis (individual decision-making, interactions between economic agents, the aggregation of individual decisions, and the role of institutions in affecting social welfare) that students study while developing essential competencies. Finally, instructors can develop learning outcomes (statements describing the knowledge or skills students should acquire by the end of the course, and why that knowledge or skill will be useful) by linking concepts with competencies.

For example, to develop competency in applying the scientific method to economic phenomena using the concept of individual decision-making, one learning outcome could: have students develop a hypothesis to explain how an increase in their wages would affect how many hours they work per week; identify which model (for example, supply and demand, indifference curves, and so on) is appropriate to use to assess the hypothesis and why; find data or research on wages and hours worked; assess whether the data support their hypothesis; and describe whether the data are appropriate for determining causality. To develop competency in using quantitative approaches using the concept of markets and other interactions, a learning outcome would have students solve a set of demand and supply equations to find an equilibrium.

Table 5.2   Economic concepts, competencies, and learning outcomes

Panel A: Essential Economic Concepts	Description
1 Individual Decision Making	agents make decisions about how to use the resources they control, which affects their well-being and the welfare of others
2 Markets and Other Interactions	agents interact through markets, which help determine the production, consumption, and distribution of goods and services
3 The Aggregate Economy	individual decisions and interactions combine to form aggregate outcomes for an economy, which are described, predicted, and assessed in macroeconomic analyses
4 Role of Government and Other Institutions	governments and other institutions can regulate or influence economic activity in ways that affect the distribution of resources, individual well-being, and social welfare
Panel B: Economic Competencies	**Description**
1 The Ability to Apply the Scientific Process to Economic Phenomena	be able to ask good questions about economic phenomena, know how to gather and organize information to answer them
2 The Ability to Analyze and Evaluate Behavior and Outcomes using Economic Concepts and Models	use economics to explain, predict, and evaluate choices
3 The Ability to Use Quantitative Approaches in Economics	use mathematical reasoning, understand when it is appropriate to employ a given method and how to interpret results
4 The Ability to Think Critically about Economic Methods and Their Application	choose appropriate models and methods, connect to real events, identify assumptions
5 The Ability to Communicate Economic Ideas in Diverse Collaborations	understand terminology, mathematical representations, communicate through writing, listening, and speech

Source: Allgood and Bayer (2016).

Strategies from Cognitive Science

The issues approach is particularly amenable to implementing best practices for learning based on cognitive science (for a summary, see Brown et al. 2014). First, as noted above, issues-oriented courses generally cover fewer concepts than traditional Principles courses in order to allow time for more intense concentration on, and repeated exposure to, key concepts throughout the course. Repeated exposure that is spaced across time promotes a deeper understanding and working knowledge of fundamental concepts. Unlike blocked practice (that is, thoroughly practicing one skill at a time before moving to the next), spaced repetition and retrieval helps to mitigate the law of diminishing marginal returns when studying a particular concept or idea. Incorporating frequent low-stakes quizzes, and encouraging students to engage in self-testing (for example, by providing old exams) rather than simply re-reading the material, encourages reflection and metacognition and helps students to avoid illusions of knowing (Nowell and Alston 2007; Carpenter et al. 2012).

Second, presenting and discussing the issue before the economics around the issue is taught allows students the opportunity to generate their own ideas and potential solutions. Allowing students to struggle with a problem or issue, attempt solutions, fail, and try again, presents a "desirable difficulty" that engages students with the questions, fixes ideas into long-term memory, and promotes learning better than introducing a concept by showing students the "right way" to achieve an answer (Schwartz et al. 2011, 2016).

Third, focusing on issues that students find important encourages students to connect new knowledge and concepts to their own personal examples. Having students elaborate on ideas by expressing concepts in their own words, connecting issues to their own lives, adding layers of meaning, and putting concepts into a larger context, is highly effective for embedding new material in the brain (Weinstein et al. 2018).

Fourth, framing the course around issues and then linking them to economic concepts and competencies allows for interleaved practice. Learning two or more concepts or skills together while focused on a particular issue, and then returning to those concepts throughout the course when focused on other issues, better develops students' problem-solving and organizational skills. Using interleaving also leads to better long-term retention and transfer of knowledge to new situations than using blocked practice (Dunlosky et al. 2013).

Choosing the Issues

Instructors have wide latitude in choosing which issues to focus on in their courses, including whether to focus on a mix of issues or to focus on one particular issue as a theme throughout the course. Because the issues that instructors find important may differ from what students find important, it is worth consulting polls that assess young adults' interests and concerns.[4] For example, Bowles and Carlin (2020) report results from a 2016–2018 poll of roughly 4500 introductory economics students in universities throughout the world that asked, "What is the most pressing problem economists should be addressing?" "Inequality" was the most dominant response, followed by "unemployment," "poverty," and "the environment." Instructors can also poll students directly on the first day of class regarding which issues to cover, and then either integrate the 2–3 most-raised issues into the existing course schedule, or leave time to cover them in the last few weeks of the course. This is also an opportunity to make the course more inclusive by choosing issues relevant for students from diverse backgrounds, and by covering topics such as discrimination or inequality, which many students might not even know fall under the umbrella of economics.

Choosing a Text

A wide range of textbooks can be used when teaching using the issues approach. First, it is entirely possible to teach an issues-oriented course using a standard Principles textbook. Nearly all of the bestselling microeconomics Principles textbooks include chapters on scarcity and choice, comparative advantage, supply and demand, consumer theory, producer theory, competition, monopoly, imperfect competition, and externalities. One tradeoff of using a traditional textbook is the time it takes for the instructor to decide which chapters (or sections of chapters) to utilize, and how to link the chapters to particular issues. In addition, applications and issues incorporated into traditional texts often read as though they are merely appended to the material as an afterthought, or they are relegated to special call-out sections at the end of chapters and sections. This makes it easier for instructors to bypass the very material that is most applicable to students.

Second, there are several issues-oriented textbooks on the market, with Guell's (2010) *Issues in Economics Today*, and Register and Grimes's (2016) *Economics of Social Issues*, being the most utilized. Issues-oriented books generally have a set of introductory "toolkit" chapters that focus on specific tools (for example, marginal analysis, maximization, supply and demand) that can be applied to a wide range of issues. These toolkit chapters are followed by short chapters focused on particular issues that illustrate how the economics toolkit can be applied. Issues-oriented textbooks tend to have a large number of relatively short chapters, so instructors have flexibility in choosing which issues they want to cover.

Third, an array of online resources can be used as textbooks for issues-oriented courses. The open access platform and free online textbook, *The Economy*, developed by the CORE Project (core-econ.org) is becoming widely adopted (*The Economist* 2021). The book is adaptable to a variety of course structures, and includes color-coded themes (for example, inequality, environment, innovation) that appear throughout the chapters, as well as stand-alone "capstone" chapters on each of the themes. The website for the book also includes interactive test questions, classroom experiments, data, and other exercises linked to the themes. More broadly, curating a set of online resources gives instructors another opportunity to provide students with examples of economists from underrepresented identities by sharing work by diverse authors.

Finally, issues-oriented courses are also particularly amenable to incorporation of outside readings or other material related to the issue being covered. For example, when covering the issue of affordable housing as a way to teach supply and demand, taxes, price controls, and welfare analysis, one could assign students episode 373 of the Freakonomics podcast, "Why Rent Control Doesn't Work," beforehand. When teaching consumer theory using the issue of the student loan crisis, one could assign students the video "The Student Debt Crisis: Explained" from the *Economics Explained* YouTube channel. It is also relatively easy to find newspaper articles and other media coverage of various issues and assign them as pre-lecture readings. One could even assign students to find outside readings, which would also provide an opportunity to discuss credible sources, verifying information, and social media bubbles.

Issues-oriented courses are also ideal for having students complete a writing or oral presentation assignment based on Robert Frank's "The economic naturalist writing assignment." The assignment is for students to write a short essay or give a short presentation where they pose an interesting question or observation about something that occurs in their day-to-day life, and use basic economic principles to answer it (Frank 2006).

CONCLUSION

In the conclusion to his 2020 John R. Commons Award lecture, Gregory Mankiw writes:

> When students leave our classes, they should read the news, follow political debate, and evaluate alternative perspectives with greater understanding and more finely tuned critical skills. They should take with them not a set of conclusions or even a set of techniques but rather the beginnings of a worldview, a way to make sense of what occurs around them. (Mankiw 2020, p. 17)

Because of its primary focus on news, events, and policy choices that students face in their daily lives, rather than on a set of techniques and tools, an issues-oriented Principles of Microeconomics course represents a superior way to teach students the economic way of thinking and its associated worldview.

NOTES

1. I use the course titles "Principles of Microeconomics," "Microeconomic Principles," and "Principles" interchangeably in this chapter.
2. Although I describe the issues approach in Principles of Microeconomics, the approach is highly flexible and can be used for any type of course.

3. The issues approach is similar to the "literacy-targeted" (LT) approach in that the focus is on higher-level mastery of a shorter list of concepts that students can apply throughout their lives, although the LT approach need not center around a set of issues.
4. The Pew Research Center, for example, conducts a variety of surveys of teens and young adults (pewresearch.org).

REFERENCES

Allgood, S., and Bayer, A. (2016). Measuring college learning in economics. In R. Arum, J. Roksa, and A. Cook (eds), *Improving Quality in American Higher Education: Learning Outcomes and Assessments for the 21st Century* (pp. 87–134). Jossey-Bass.

Allgood, S., Bosshardt, W., van der Klaauw, W., and Watts, M. (2004). What students remember and say about college economics years later. *American Economic Review: Papers and Proceedings 94*(2), 259–265.

Benjamin, D., Cohen, A., and Hamilton, G. (2020). A Pareto improving way to teach principles of economics: evidence from the University of Toronto. *American Economic Review Papers and Proceedings 110*(2), 299–303.

Bowles, S., and Carlin, W. (2020). What students learn in Economics 101: time for a change. *Journal of Economic Literature 58*(1), 176–214.

Brown, P., Roediger, H., and McDaniel, M. (2014). *Make It Stick: The Science of Successful Learning.* Harvard University Press.

Carpenter, S., Cepeda, N., Rohrer, D., Kang, S., and Pashler, H. (2012). Using spacing to enhance diverse forms of learning: review of recent research and implications for instruction. *Educational Psychology Review 24*(3), 369–378.

Dubner, S., and Levitt, S. (2005). *Freakonomics: A Rogue Economist Explores the Hidden Side of Everything.* Penguin Books.

Dunlosky, J., Rawson, K., Marsh, E., Nathan, M., and Willingham, D. (2013). Improving students' learning with effective learning techniques: promising directions from cognitive and educational psychology. *Psychological Science in the Public Interest 14*(1), 4–58.

The Economist (2021). Efforts to modernize economics teaching are gathering steam. *The Economist*, March 20. https://www.economist.com/finance-and-economics/2021/03/20/efforts-to-modernise-economics-teaching-are-gathering-steam.

Fleury, J. (2012). The evolving notion of relevance: an historical perspective to the "economics made fun" movement. *Journal of Economic Methodology 19*(3), 303–316. DOI: 10.1080/1350178X.2012.714145.

Frank, R. (2006). The economic naturalist writing assignment. *Journal of Economic Education 37*(1), 58–67.

Furman, J., and Liabson, D. (2019). EC 10a – Principles of Economics (Microeconomics) (course syllabus). Harvard University. https://drive.google.com/file/d/1mMzYZUTw_KJbdmXvR_8fVbTCORq_ib7s/view.

Gilleskie, D., and Salemi, M. (2012). The cost of economic literacy: how well does a literacy-targeted Principles of Economics course prepare students for intermediate theory courses? *Journal of Economic Education 43*(2), 111–132.

Grimes, P., and Nelson, P. (1995). The social issues pedagogy vs. the traditional principles of economics: an empirical investigation. *American Economist 42*(1), 56–64.

Guell, R. (2010). *Issues in Economics Today.* McGraw-Hill Education.

Hansen, W.L. (1986). Expected proficiencies for undergraduate economics majors. *Journal of Economic Education 32*(3), 231–242.

Hansen, W.L., Salemi, M.K., and Siegfried J.J. (2002). Use it or lose it: teaching literacy in the Economics Principles course. *American Economic Review Papers and Proceedings 92*(2), 463–472.

Krueger, A., Arrow, K., Blanchard, O., Blinder, A., Goldin, C., et al. (1991). Report of the Commission on Graduate Education in Economics. *Journal of Economic Literature 29*(3), 1035–1053.

Landsburg, S. (1993). *The Armchair Economist*. Free Press.

Leftwich, R., and Sharp, A. (1974). *Economics of Social Issues*. Business Publications Incorporated.

Mankiw, N.G. (2020). The past and future of Econ 101: the John R. Commons Award lecture. NBER Working Paper 26702. DOI 10.3386/w26702.

Nowell, C., and Alston, R. (2007). I thought I got an A! Overconfidence across the economics curriculum. *Journal of Economic Education 38*(2), 131–142.

Owen, A., and Hagstrom, P. (2021) Broadening perceptions of economics in a new introductory economics sequence. *Journal of Economic Education, 52*(3), 175–191.

Randall, A. (1975). Economics and public policy for the undergraduate: a review article. *Journal of Economic Issues 9*(1), 81–86.

Register, C., and Grimes, P. (2016). *Economics of Social Issues*. McGraw-Hill Education.

Schwartz, D., Chase, C., Oppezzo, M., and Chin, D. (2011). Practicing versus inventing with contrasting cases: the effects of telling first on learning and transfer. *Journal of Educational Psychology 103*(4), 759–775.

Schwartz, D., Tsang, J., and Blair, K. (2016). *The ABCs of How We Learn: 26 Scientifically Proven Approaches, How They Work, and When to Use Them*. W.W. Norton.

Sharp, A., Leftwich, R., and Bumpass, D. (1975). An examination of trade-offs in teaching Economics Principles. *Journal of Economic Education 7*(1), 56–58.

Stigler, G. (1963). Elementary economic education. *American Economic Review Papers and Proceedings 53*(2), 653–659.

Stock, W. (2017). Trends in economics and other undergraduate majors. *American Economic Review Papers and Proceedings 107*(5), 644–649.

Weinstein, Y., Madan, C., and Sumeracki, M. (2018). Teaching the science of learning. *Cognitive Research: Principles and Implications 3*(2), 1–17.

Wheelan, C. (2002). *Naked Economics*. Norton & Co.

Wieman, C. (2007). The "curse of knowledge" or why intuition about teaching often fails. *American Physical Society News 16*(10). https://www.aps.org/publications/apsnews/200711/backpage.cfm.

6. Revising the traditional Microeconomics course: engaging students via problem-based, positive, paradigmatic pluralism

Geoffrey E. Schneider

INTRODUCTION

The traditional Principles of Microeconomics course can be a dreary affair in which students learn to apply the tools of neoclassical analysis to analyze economic man's participation in widget markets. There is typically little or no critical analysis of the standard models and their assumptions, nor is there consideration of alternate perspectives. Even more problematic, there tends to be little effort to address the major economic problems and policy debates confronting modern society, such as climate change and inequality.

Fortunately, there is an alternative that offers greater opportunities for critical thinking. In this chapter I argue for a broader, more engaging approach to teaching Principles of Microeconomics that focuses on important issues and policy debates and that is pluralistic in nature. This approach is embodied in my new series of pluralistic principles textbooks (Schneider 2018, 2019, 2022, forthcoming) but also can be used to reshape the content and approach of the traditional Principles of Microeconomics course. It is based on a philosophy that evolved from teaching in a pluralist department at Bucknell University. Being surrounded by economists from a variety of perspectives, including mainstream, feminist, institutionalist, Marxist, social, and post-Keynesian economists, caused me to examine aspects of economics with which I was only somewhat familiar. Furthermore, it prompted me to consider the appropriate way to teach courses within a contested discipline in a manner that was fair to all perspectives and engaging for students. For additional alternative approaches see the CORE project (Chapter 4), the issues approach (Chapter 5) and de Muijnck and Tieleman (2022).

The philosophical approach developed here for Principles of Microeconomics is based on the following core tenets. First, as instructors we have an ethical obligation to teach pluralistically, with all of the major strains of economics covered in our courses, including those we disagree with. Second, we should strive to teach each perspective in a positive light, stressing its major contributions to the discipline. Where perspectives come into conflict, we should present the best arguments on both sides to help students understand the logic behind each perspective and to foster critical thinking (Thoma 1993; Perry 1970; Allgood and Bayer 2016). Third, given that we cannot cover all perspectives on every topic, we should strive to include each perspective where its contributions to the discipline are most distinctive and well-supported. Fourth, we should strive for an approach in which students are taught to think like real, modern economists, including recent advances in the field such as behavioral economics, game theory, agent-based modeling, new institutional economics, and heterodox economics, rather than adhering to the Samuelsonian orthodoxy that dominates mainstream textbooks and courses. Fifth, the balance of the material should lean toward the mainstream, while offering at least one alternative perspective on each major topic, and usually two alternate perspectives in cases of policy debates. This will more accurately convey the contested nature of the discipline while acquainting students with the full breadth of perspectives. Sixth, the course should focus on the major "big think" issues and problems confronting modern society (Colander and McGoldrick 2009, p. 33), along with the policy debates and perspectives embodied in those issues.

I label this approach to teaching the principles of economics problem-based, positive, paradigmatic pluralism (PPPP), reflecting the principles outlined above. If implemented successfully, students report finding this approach engaging and empowering, enabling them to develop their critical thinking about the various approaches to the major economic problems facing modern society. The PPPP approach works best if it is established at the very beginning of the semester, and applied consistently to policy debates throughout the course.

In what follows below, the chapter lays out the arguments for the PPPP approach to teaching Principles of Microeconomics. The chapter illustrates how the PPPP approach can be used to make microeconomics engaging and more reflective of the rich, contested terrain that is modern economics.

A MODERN, PARADIGMATIC APPROACH

Mainstream principles courses and texts have remained largely unchanged even as the discipline has evolved. While mainstream economics has taken some small steps toward pluralism and a broader scope, especially in the realm of behavioral economics, game theory and new institutional economics, this "certainly does not apply to the largely standardized (if not petrified) and orthodox higher mass teaching and textbook writing" (Decker et al. 2018,

p. 2). The model originally established by Samuelson's (1948) *Economics* text remains the norm (Allgood and Bayer, 2016, p. 100). Most importantly, mainstream and heterodox approaches to various topics are rarely compared and contrasted, and heterodox ideas are almost never covered systematically, even in the areas where heterodox economists have made the most significant advances. Given these limitations of the traditional, textbook-based Principles of Microeconomics course, some significant rethinking is warranted.

The first key to engaging students in a Principles of Microeconomics course is to make the subject relevant to their lives. The most compelling way to do this is to engage students in issues that are of deep concern to them, or to make them aware of economic problems that they should care about. Many economists have called for such an approach (e.g., Stock, Chapter 5 in this book; Becker 2000; Colander and McGoldrick 2009). However, this argument has had little impact given the persistent narrow focus of most courses and textbooks.

Some of the major problems in contemporary economies that deeply interest students are climate change and the environment, labor markets and the future of work, inequality and the impact of race, gender and social class, consumer markets and efforts by huge firms to manipulate such markets, corporate power, and the appropriate role of government in markets. Unfortunately, most textbook-based Principles of Microeconomics courses give these topics short shrift.

Second, if an instructor decides to teach about contemporary policy debates, the best way to teach about controversial problems is to lay out clearly the different paradigmatic perspectives on each issue. Allgood and Bayer (2016, p. 97) include critical thinking as one of five core competencies that should guide learning outcomes in economics, and critical thinking is seen by most economics departments as the *most important competency*. Doing policy debates justice requires a pluralistic approach that describes the most relevant and important approaches to each problem. Indeed, the PPPP approach is an ideal way to achieve the critical thinking goal as articulated by Allgood and Bayer (ibid.):

> Students should be able to explain economic models as deliberate simplifications of reality that economists create to think through complex, nondeterministic behaviors; identify the assumptions and limitations of each model and their potential impacts; select and connect economic models to real economic conditions; explain economic data as useful but imperfect recordings of empirical realities; explain the strengths and limitations of economic data and statistical analyses; and think creatively and combine or synthesize existing economic ideas in original ways.

A pluralistic approach requires students to examine the assumptions behind each model and theory, giving them repeated practice in evaluating the applicability of theories, and seeing how variations in assumptions influence conclusions about policy effectiveness.

So, how exactly should a pluralistic approach be taught?

Much has been written about pluralistic approaches to teaching in the last few decades. Jack Reardon (2009, p. 7) argues that "pluralism should instill humility and a respective curiosity about alternative views" in which we "welcome [controversy, debate and disagreement] as a way of moving economics forward." However, we cannot allow pluralism to degenerate in "unworkable relativism" (Reardon, 2009, p. 6) or "anything goes" (Negru 2010, p. 188). The need is for "openness and tolerance of diversity, *and* engagement in critical conversation" (Negru 2010, p. 188).

Anyone who has taught contending economic perspectives in a class knows that it is usually ineffective to teach students a particular perspective while simultaneously criticizing it. Upon hearing the critique, students may immediately respond by asking why you wasted their time by asking them to learn something that is incorrect (Nelson 2009, p. 60). The highlights the importance of teaching each theory in a positive light, describing its most important contributions to the field.

Nelson (2009, p. 62) argues for framing core mainstream models as the "basic neoclassical model" of the consumer, producer or particular component of market behavior. "[T]he instructor need not show that traditional tools and concepts are wrong, but rather, by describing their highly restrictive assumptions, the instructor can enable students to understand the limited range of the models. And then, perfectly reasonably, one can segue on to explorations that cover other cases ... [or] pluralistic approaches" (Nelson 2009, p. 63).

Interestingly, while Nelson is advocating a multi-paradigmatic, pluralistic approach to teaching, she prefers to keep the different perspectives largely hidden under a "bigger toolbox" rubric. According to Nelson and Goodwin (2009, pp. 174–175), "extended discussions of competing theories, and extended examinations of the philosophy or history of economic thought, may be too subtle and abstract for some students' first course. Some may not yet be skilled enough in abstract and critical thought to be able to handle the ambiguity of a point-counterpoint approach." To avoid overwhelming introductory students, Negru (2010, p. 189) calls on instructors "to introduce parallel perspectives (in which no one view is correct), rather than competing views (where one view is assumed correct)." This is essentially the "bigger toolbox" approach with paradigmatic labels attached to perspectives and with the perspectives taught in parallel. In my experience, the paradigmatic approach promotes critical thinking, helps students to identify consistent perspectives and approaches, and, if framed around real-world data and a series of contemporary policy debates, grounds pluralist economic inquiry in a scientific approach while cultivating engagement.

Table 6.1   The most important contributions of heterodox paradigms

Economic paradigm	Most important contributions to the discipline
Feminist	Gender, household, well-being, patriarchy
Stratification/social	Racial stratification, inequality, ethics, good society
Institutionalist	Evolution, culture, institutions, power, growth, role of government
Post-Keynesian	Uncertainty, mark-up pricing, financial fragility, modern monetary theory, demand-side economics
Marxian	Class, power, exploitation, alienation, crises, growth, destructive side of competition
Austrian	Institutional foundations of markets, importance of information, dangers of overly intrusive government, focus on entrepreneurs
Supply-side	Incentives, deregulation, tax cuts, growth

Because mainstream economics is the approach taken by a majority of economists, and because mainstream economists dominate policymaking, it should occupy a majority of the material in the course. Students *must* understand the strengths and weaknesses of mainstream economics in order to understand modern debates, to progress further in their study of the field of economics, and to understand the differences between mainstream economics and heterodox schools of thought. About two-thirds of the material in my course (and textbooks) is mainstream.

Pluralism is incorporated by bringing in each major heterodox perspective where it has made the greatest contribution or had the greatest impact, as described in Table 6.1.[1] Brilliant, accomplished economists developed each of these paradigms in economics, and economists continue to adhere to these paradigms because they find the ideas useful for analyzing the economy. Furthermore, humility requires some degree of deference to the possibility that views with which we disagree might be correct at least some of the time. An effective, pluralistic approach that covers all major approaches fairly and frames ideas in a positive fashion also avoids the pitfall of the instructor being seen as "brainwashing" students, and as advocating a particular political perspective.

In addition to framing the different paradigmatic approaches to economics, it is important to lay out the political perspectives embodied in various policy debates. Given the types of policy debates in the modern United States (US), it is useful to delineate three main perspectives: laissez-faire, mixed market (markets featuring some regulation), and political economy (managed capitalist or socialist). On every main issue, it is possible to describe a laissez-faire, mixed market, and political economy perspective and to connect that approach to a particular paradigm. Austrian, supply-side, and conservative mainstream economists typically reflect the laissez-faire perspective. Moderate and liberal mainstream economists typically reflect the mixed market perspective, where markets are viewed as the central organizing structure of the economy but markets also require judicious regulation and intervention. The political economy perspective reflects progressive political economy variants including feminist, institutionalist, stratification/social, and post-Keynesian economists who argue for a more closely regulated, managed economy. And political economy also includes the radical political economy approach that is extremely critical of markets and argues for government control of key industries, as seen in Marxian economics and radical economists from the progressive political economy paradigms.

As an initial example of what the PPPP approach can look like, many students have worked low-wage jobs and are deeply interested in policy related to the minimum wage, making this an engaging topic to cover deeply. Presenting only the mainstream model of the market for labor, with the minimum wage as a price floor that causes unemployment, would be inappropriate given recent studies that increases in the US minimum wage have not tended to increase unemployment (Doucouliagos and Stanley 2009; Wolfson and Belman 2016). An effective way to teach the minimum wage is to lay out the standard mainstream labor model and its assumptions. Then, require students to explore three different perspectives: (1) the anti-minimum wage, laissez-faire perspective supported by most Austrian and conservative mainstream economists that increasing the minimum wage increases unemployment and harms the economy (Neumark and Wascher 2009; Neumark and Shirley 2021); (2) a moderate perspective that the minimum wage can be increased but only modestly (Rosalsky 2019); and (3) the political economy and liberal mainstream perspective that a much higher minimum wage would not tend to increase unemployment (Wolfson and Belman 2016), and would be beneficial to workers and the economy overall (Schneider 2019, pp. 493–495; Cooper et al. 2021). Students can then be asked to explain the best arguments from each perspective, and to offer their own critical analysis of the material. In the process, students compare and contrast the assumptions being made by economists from each perspective, and evaluate their relevance given the best available data.

To make sure that each perspective is outlined clearly, attention must be paid to developing paradigmatic perspectives on particular topics, and being explicit about the underlying assumptions of each approach. On each major subject, standard mainstream economic ideas should be taught alongside (parallel to) heterodox and contemporary theories, accompanied by descriptions of the best data and examples available related to the topic. In essence, this approach turns students into critical thinkers about economic ideas, and helps them to develop their own economic methodology and philosophy.

OPERATIONALIZING THE PPPP APPROACH

Teaching pluralistically requires motivating students to understand why it is important for them to understand multiple perspectives. This begins by sharing in the very first class and assignment that there are a variety of perspectives in economics, and that each perspective brings something different and useful to the table.

One possibility is to start by discussing different perspectives on consumer behavior in the first content-heavy class. All students have had some experiences as consumers, so they are able to think deeply about the subject right away. A particularly engaging example involves discussing how mainstream economists and political economists view Amazon's efforts to sell products to consumers. From a mainstream perspective, Amazon provides the best products (supported by reviews and extensive information) for the best price in a competitive marketplace featuring lots of sellers. Amazon is also convenient, providing one-stop shopping, and fast, inexpensive delivery. Consumers purchasing from Amazon are quite able to function as the quintessential "rational economic man," making well-informed purchases at the lowest possible price.

Political economists (including institutionalists, Marxian economists, and post-Keynesian economists) bring in additional factors to broaden students' understanding of consumer behavior. Amazon promotes impulse buying by encouraging consumers to purchase products which they might like based on sophisticated analytics designed to determine how consumers can be manipulated. Amazon promotes fads by telling consumers which items are "hot" or trending. Political economists also analyze the role of culture and trust in driving purchases, which in turn helps us to understand why companies pay for favorable reviews of their products and therefore manipulate the trust embodied in the posted reviews. Political economists also discuss how political, financial, and monopoly power give Amazon a huge advantage over competitors, because it gets subsidies to locate operations in particular locations, lower interest rates on financing, and can require producers to supply goods to Amazon for lower prices than they charge other retailers. Behavioral economics can be used to analyze how Amazon uses anchoring, cognitive bias, and nudges to manipulate consumers.

I then give students the following writing prompt:

> Consider the description of economic man in the reading, and the description of positive, scientific economics. Also consider how political economists study human behavior. Then reflect carefully on your own shopping habits. Do you usually make rational, calculated, fully informed purchases (like "economic man"), or do you tend to buy on impulse for a variety of reasons, or do you do both? Analyze how much of your purchasing behavior can be captured by "positive economics," and when the methods used by political economists would better reflect your behavior. How

much of your shopping behavior could be predicted scientifically? How much of it would be hard to predict?

Students come out of this discussion with a deep appreciation of the possibilities of the best work of mainstream economics and of heterodox economics, and a better understanding of their own purchasing behavior. Interestingly, most students tend to think that they lean more toward the rational side of consumer behavior until we study in more detail how culture and pecuniary emulation affect preferences later in the semester. This is one of the reasons why it is important for the PPPP approach to be sustained throughout the semester. Students develop an increasingly sophisticated understanding of the different perspectives, and even begin to anticipate how economists from different paradigms will approach various issues.

A key tension that emerges in pluralistic teaching is what to do with mainstream models. The supply and demand model is often viewed as the cornerstone of modern economics, and it certainly merits significant time and attention. However, prior to teaching the supply and demand model, it is worthwhile to explain to students the complex institutional foundations necessary to make markets work. Markets require stable property rights, which in turn require an effective legal system, to function efficiently. Property rights systems tend to foster investment, but they also contribute to inequality. Modern markets depend on laws to facilitate the aggregation of capital, such as the establishment of the limited liability corporation to encourage a larger size of operations and economies of scale. Markets require trust and contract laws to facilitate trust, or people will not have faith in market transactions. Markets require competition and a lack of coercion to function effectively. Infrastructure to reduce transaction costs and facilitate exchange is another core requirement of markets. This includes physical infrastructure (roads, buildings, ports, airports, and so on), market infrastructure (information, rules, regulations, laws, and internet services), and financial infrastructure (a stable currency and banking system), which are all necessary to make modern markets work effectively. Thus, the supply and demand model depends on a host of often invisible institutional structures which are all assumed to be present when we use the model. Understanding how important these institutional structures are to the functioning of markets can help students to recognize the government's essential role in establishing and facilitating markets, a point emphasized by political economists.

The mainstream model of the consumer and the law of diminishing marginal utility are core components of the law of demand, and a crucial topic. Feminist discussions of household decision-making offer an interesting contrast to the individualistic mainstream model (Schneider 2019, p. 226). Behavioral economic analysis of consumer behavior, including anchoring, cognitive bias, status quo bias, overoptimism, nudge, and loss aversion, is another rich vein to deepen student understanding of markets (Schneider 2019, pp. 228–230). Institutionalists note that cultural values and pecuniary emulation shape demand in fundamental ways (Schneider 2019, pp. 224–225). After studying these different perspectives, students can then assemble a very sophisticated analysis of modern consumer behavior featuring the supply and demand model and the insights from other paradigms.

The mainstream model of supply decisions involves firms with perfect information equating marginal cost and marginal revenue to maximize profits, with competition resulting in normal profits in the long run. Political and behavioral economists instead emphasize satisficing behavior, where firms do not have full information, and use rules of thumb to make decisions. Furthermore, the political economy emphasis on competition for profits as the essential feature of firm behavior results in a very different picture of decision-making, with firms competing to make breakthroughs and to establish monopoly power in order to maximize profits. It is also important to present some pluralistic models during the semester so that students understand that heterodox approaches can be qualitative or quantitative. After presenting the mainstream theory of the firm, it is useful to discuss the post-Keynesian model of mark-up pricing, and how the mark-up changes based on the degree of monopoly power and the firm's strategic decisions regarding short-term profit maximization versus market share.

Labor issues also present a rich topic for comparative analysis. Students are often disturbed to learn that many of the clothes they wear are produced in sweatshops. After learning about sweatshops via films and news articles about the Rana Plaza garment factory collapse in Bangladesh,[2] students confront a pro-sweatshop, laissez-faire perspective (Powell 2013) and an anti-sweatshop, political economy perspective (Miller 2013). Then, I ask them to respond to the following prompt:

> Write an essay in which you analyze the assigned film and articles on sweatshops. What do we learn about modern sweatshops from the film and the news articles? What are the strongest arguments that each economist (Powell, Miller) makes? Which arguments seem more ideological and less well supported by facts? How do these materials connect with the different perspectives we studied? Engage in substantive, nuanced critical analysis of the arguments, and add your own ideas on the topic. Be very careful to try to move beyond your own ideological biases in your analysis. Your essay should be at least three-quarters of a page (typed, single-spaced) in length.

The dualistic nature of the perspectives in this exercise provides a good opportunity for critical analysis, and students typically end up acknowledging the importance of the job-creating role of sweatshops, while questioning the ethics and exploitation inherent in the system.

This sets the stage for contrasting the Austrian, mainstream, and political economy views of the corporation later in the semester. Austrians argue that rivalrousness, property rights, and unregulated markets lead to optimal outcomes, including rapid growth and constant innovation that is a product of creative destruction. Mainstream economists focus on the benign profit maximization model which, in the absence of market failures, implies that markets result in optimally efficient outcomes. Political economists, however, argue that corporations are largely destructive entities which exploit workers and ruin the environment (Schneider 2019, pp. 389–390). Students are required to evaluate these perspectives to determine which views they find most compelling, and which assumptions are least valid.

Globalizing content also facilitates a pluralistic approach. Market-dominated economies (MDEs) such as the US and the United Kingdom, social market economies (SMEs) of Europe, and state-dominated economies (SDEs) such as China, offer alternative visions of how markets can be regulated and managed based on the ideas of different paradigms. Ignoring the various ways in which global economies are structured leaves students unprepared for navigating the complexities of the modern global economy. MDEs lean toward a laissez-faire philosophy and feature lower taxes, lower social expenditures, and higher poverty than SMEs, which incorporate more ideas from political economists while still employing markets (Schneider 2019, pp. 142–154). The Chinese SDE draws more from political economists while still featuring markets, and has had the most rapid growth rate in the world for more than 40 years (Schneider 2019, pp. 156–158). I ask students to compare and contrast MDEs, SMEs, and SDEs, by laying out: (1) the role the government plays in each type of economy; (2) the strengths and weaknesses of each economic system; and (3) how each type of economy reflects the perspectives we have studied. Acquainting students with the different types of economic systems and cultures that they will encounter as they interact in a global economic system is both engaging and useful in promoting critical thinking about economic approaches. The fact that growth rates do not tend to be higher in MDEs causes students to evaluate critically a number of assumptions in mainstream theories regarding taxation, investment, growth, and government intervention. The fact that MDEs, SMEs, and SDEs can all be successful or unsuccessful further complicates matters, nicely encapsulating the complexities surrounding economic debates regarding economic systems.

Inequality is another rich area for discussion and debate. Mainstream economists adhere to the marginal productivity theory of distribution, which implies that workers are paid exactly what they are worth. Conservative mainstream economist Gregory Mankiw (2013) argues that inequality is a necessary reward for risk-taking and entrepreneurship. Moderates treat inequality as a market failure that leads to social problems (crime, poverty, homelessness), and want to reduce it with social programs such as progressive taxation and a safety net. In political economic analysis of social class inequality, the employer's goal is to extract as much profit (surplus value) as possible from workers, which means that inequality and exploitation are essential features of capitalism. Only a socialist or communist system would truly eliminate inequality from this perspective. Stratification economists add another crucial feature to the analysis of inequality, by focusing on the systematic racial discrimination that characterizes the US economic system, and the extent to which this discrimination benefits whites while harming blacks. And feminist economists add essential analysis of gender inequality and the importance of patriarchal structures, gender roles, and occupational segregation. Each paradigm adds a compelling piece of the puzzle.

Contrasting how different countries approach inequality is also interesting for students. Nordic countries emphasize redistribution and the provision of high-quality public and quasi-public goods for all; whereas market-dominated economies such as the US tend to believe that obtaining most goods and services is the responsibility of private individuals.

Climate change is another topic that is both deeply interesting to students and crucial to frame pluralistically (Reardon, Chapter 8 in this book). Conservative economists who acknowledge climate change want to impose carbon taxes or cap-and-trade systems that are revenue-neutral, with all revenues returned to businesses or households. Moderate mainstream economists prefer to reserve some revenues from carbon taxes for investments in clean energy, and they argue for additional regulations on consumers and businesses to improve sustainability. Political economists question whether capitalism can be sustainable, and advocate a much greater role for government intervention, with stricter regulations of corporations and goods markets, high carbon taxes, and large investments in green industries (a Green New Deal). Students can then be asked to make an argument for how we should address these problems related to climate change, based on these perspectives.

Public goods are also better understood via multiple perspectives. Mainstream economists treat public goods as a market failure that requires government intervention, with the allocation of goods determined, in theory, by a political system that reflects society's preferences. Austrians such as Murray Rothbard argue that government provision of public goods is too inefficient and overbearing, and we are better off with private goods. Political economists – just as did John Kenneth Galbraith – argue that the US has a social imbalance with an oversupply of private goods and an inadequate supply of public goods due to the corporate growth lobby. Only with a system of countervailing power in which citizens and the government can rein in corporate power does Galbraith think the US will achieve an appropriate balance of private and public goods. After studying these perspectives, students can be asked for their own observations on the state of public goods, their critical analysis of the perspectives, and whether or not they think their country strikes the right balance of public and private goods.

CONCLUSION

A problem-based, positive, paradigmatic, pluralist approach can serve as an effective way to develop students' critical thinking and to acquaint them with the most important modern economic perspectives. It grounds the students in a mainstream theory while also examining the assumptions of the theory and providing additional perspectives from other relevant paradigms. Because issues and policy debates are framed positively around what each paradigm contributes to the discussion, students are encouraged to take each perspective seriously. In my experience, students find this approach engaging and empowering, and it inspires many of them to explore the discipline more fully in subsequent courses.

NOTES

1. A good source to become acquainted with the basic tenets of each perspective is Harvey (2020).
2. I like to use: (a) the classic documentary *Free Trade Slaves* (Films for the Humanities and Sciences 1999); (b) Ali Julfikar Manik, Steven Greenhouse and Jim Yardley, "Western Firms Feel Pressure as Toll Rises in Bangladesh", *New York Times*, April 25, 2013, http://nyti.ms/1ADZzv5; and (c) Julfikar Ali Manik and Jim Yardley, "Bangladesh Finds Gross Negligence in Factory Fire," *New York Times*, December 17, 2012.

REFERENCES

Allgood, S., and Bayer, A. (2016). Measuring college learning in economics. In R. Arum, J. Roksa, and A. Cook (eds), *Improving quality in American higher education* (pp. 87–134). Jossey-Bass.
Becker, W. (2000). Teaching economics in the 21st century. *Journal of Economic Perspectives 14*(1), 109–119.
Colander, D., and McGoldrick, K. (2009). The Teagle Foundation report: The economics major as part of a liberal education. In D. Colander and K. McGoldrick (eds), *Educating economists: The Teagle discussion on re-evaluating the undergraduate economics major* (pp. 3–39). Edward Elgar Publishing.
Cooper, D., Mokhiber, Z., and Zipperer, B. (2021, March 9). Raising the federal minimum wage to $15 by 2025 would lift the pay of 32 million workers. Retrieved January 12, 2022, from Economic Policy Institute: https://www.epi.org/publication/

raising-the-federal-minimum-wage-to-15-by-2025-would-lift-the-pay-of-32-million
-workers/.

de Muijnck, S., and Tieleman, J. (2022). *Economy studies: A guide to rethinking economics education.* Amsterdam: Amsterdam University Press.

Decker, S., Elsner, W., and Flechtner, S. (2018). *Advancing pluralism in teaching economics: International perspectives on a textbook science.* Taylor & Francis.

Doucouliagos, H., and Stanley, T. (2009). Publication selection bias in minimum-wage research? A meta-regression analysis. *British Journal of Industrial Relations 47*(2), 406–428.

Harvey, J.T. (2020). *Contending perspectives in economics: A guide to contemporary schools of thought.* Cheltenham, UK and Northampton, MA, USA: Edward Elgar Publishing.

Mankiw, N.G. (2013). Defending the one percent. *Journal of Economic Perspectives 27*(3), 21–34.

Miller, J. (2013, September/October). After horror, apologetics: Sweatshop apologists cover for intransigent U.S. retail giants. Dollars & Sense.

Negru, I. (2010). Plurality to pluralism in economics pedagogy: The role of critical thinking. *International Journal of Pluralism and Economics Education 1*(3), 185–193.

Nelson, J.A. (2009). The Principles course. In J. Reardon (ed.), *The handbook of pluralist economics education* (pp. 57–68). Routledge.

Nelson, J.A., and Goodwin, N. (2009). Teaching ecological and feminist economics in the Principles course. *Forum for Social Economics 28*(2–3), 173–187.

Neumark, D., and Shirley, P. (2021). Myth or measurement: What does the new minimum wage research say about minimum wages and job loss in the United States? NBER Working Paper Series, Working Paper 28388. Retrieved from: https://www.nber.org/papers/w28388.

Neumark, D., and Wascher, W.L. (2009). *Minimum wages.* MIT Press.

Perry, W. (1970). *Forms of intellectual and ethical development in the college years: A scheme.* Holt, Rinehard & Winston.

Powell, B. (2013, May 2). Sweatshops in Bangladesh improve the lives of their workers, and boost growth. Forbes.

Reardon, J. (2009). Introduction and overview. In J. Reardon, *The handbook of pluralist economics education* (pp. 3–16). Routledge.

Rosalsky, G. (2019, April 23). When does a minimum wage become too high? Retrieved from Planet Money: https://www.npr.org/sections/money/2019/04/23/716126740/when-does-a-minimum-wage-become-too-high.

Samuelson, Paul A. (1948). *Economics.* New York: McGraw-Hill.

Schneider, G. (2018). *The evolution of economic ideas and systems.* Routledge.

Schneider, G. (2019). *Microeconomic principles and problems: A pluralist introduction.* Routledge.

Schneider, G. (2022). *Economic principles and problems: A pluralist introduction.* Routledge.

Schneider, G. (forthcoming). *Macroeconomic principles and problems: A pluralist introduction.* Routledge.

Thoma, G.A. (1993). The Perry framework and tactics for teaching critical thinking in economics. *Journal of Economic Education 24*(2), 128–136.

Wolfson, P.J., and Belman, D. (2016). 15 years of research on US employment and the minimum wage. Tuch School of Business Working Paper No. 2705499.

PART II

Updating course content

7. Where is the "behavioral" in Introductory Microeconomics?

Simon D. Halliday and Emily C. Marshall

INTRODUCTION

In his provocatively titled piece "We're all behavioral economists now," Erik Angner (2019) argues that, far from being peripheral to economics, behavioral economics is now a central part of the field with the result that we are all behavioral economists. But if that is the case, we might ask, are all Introductory Economics classes Behavioral Economics classes now? The answer to that question would be an unequivocal, "No." How, then, should we think about the Introductory Economics classroom and the integration of behavioral economics into it? We highlight ways the main concepts in behavioral economics can be integrated into a Principles of Microeconomics classroom, demonstrating how certain principles-level ideas can be modified to include behavioral economics ideas either intuitively or with more formal introductory-level models.

The approach we take considers that behavioral economics is not in conflict with mainstream or neoclassical economics; rather, its integration into the mainstream of the discipline clarifies the usefulness of each. As Matthew Rabin (2002, pp. 658–659) has said, "[Behavioral economics] is not only built on the premise that mainstream economic methods are great, but also that most mainstream economic assumptions are great. It does not abandon the correct insights of neoclassical economics, but supplements these insights with the insights to be had from realistic new assumptions." Or, as Chetty (2015, p. 1) says, "[B]ehavioral economics represents a natural progression of (rather than a challenge to) neoclassical economic methods."

Our view, therefore, is one of integrationism: that behavioral economics has been incorporated into "mainstream" academic economic research and forms a fundamental means by which we can make more accurate predictions about behavior. However, many behavioral economics insights remain relegated to optional electives or additional chapters at the end of a standard Principles of Microeconomics course. Behavioral economics offers a way to try to answer questions that many students have after being introduced to microeconomics. Consider the following five questions that may arise:

- Are people always rational?
- Do people care only about themselves or do they also concern themselves with others?
- Can incentives fail or backfire?
- Are people consistent over time and in how they deal with risky choices?
- What is utility, and is it the same as happiness?

We highlight these questions as, in our experience, students can readily leave an Introductory Microeconomics class with the misunderstanding that economists assume people are always rational, self-regarding, time-consistent, expected utility-maximizing, and perfectly responsive to policy changes. By asking these motivating questions, we can demonstrate how economics engages with evidence and how economic ideas evolve. The answers also allow us to provide many real-world examples and applications, beyond utility maximization as shopping, or policy as merely the tweaking of prices.

These questions led us to identify five areas in which behavioral economics has contributed to economics:

- a nuanced understanding of rationality in the context of cognitive biases;
- a discussion of whether and to what extent people are self-regarding;
- an analysis of how people respond to choices over time and over risky outcomes;
- an application of behavioral economics to public policy and mechanism design (incentives backfiring and "nudges");
- an explanation of the relationship between utility, income, and happiness.

We summarize whether and to what extent these ideas are integrated into commonly used Principles of Microeconomics textbooks, and resolve that behavioral economics is sparsely covered in most. While our listed areas are not intended to be exhaustive, they offer areas in which behavioral economics can be integrated into the Introductory Microeconomics classroom, and we provide guidelines for their inclusion.[1] We encourage instructors who use these exercises or experiments to have students write about their participation to improve learning (Cartwright and Stepanova 2012).

BEHAVIORAL ECONOMICS COVERAGE IN INTRODUCTORY MICROECONOMICS TEXTBOOKS

In this section, we summarize the state of behavioral economics coverage in the most recent editions of ten commonly used Principles of (or Introductory)

Microeconomics textbooks.[2] Of the ten textbooks we assessed, seven do not include stand-alone chapters on behavioral economics and the content is distributed throughout the book sparingly. Of the textbooks with a chapter devoted to behavioral economics, the longest is Mateer and Coppock (2021) at about 23 pages. The next most exhaustive is Karlan and Morduch (2021) at about 11 pages. In large part, behavioral economics lacks coverage in popular Introductory Microeconomics material. While the amount of space devoted to the subject is not necessarily problematic, the brief treatment of the topic suggests cursory and superficial coverage, not integration with other economic concepts.

Another consideration of coverage is the placement in the curriculum: what knowledge do students need to understand the relevant concepts and how can learning behavioral economics enhance understanding of later material? Some textbooks (for example, Mankiw 2018) discuss behavioral economics at the end of the book. Stevenson and Wolfers (2020) include a section on behavioral economics, considering how people make mistakes around uncertainty, in the last part of the book. Most commonly, behavioral economics is discussed as a stand-alone chapter or part of a chapter on consumer choice and decision-making. Krugman and Wells (2021) include eight pages of coverage in the chapter "Decision making by individuals and firms." Similarly, Hubbard and O'Brien (2019) add a behavioral economics section to the chapter "Consumer choice and behavioral economics." Similarly, Greenlaw and Shapiro (2018) introduce behavioral economics in the chapter "Consumer choices" in a subsection, and they discuss rationality of consumer behavior in another section.

The final grouping of textbooks places behavioral economics in the context of consumer choice and as a stand-alone chapter. McConnell et al. (2021) include a separate behavioral economics chapter after "Utility maximization" and before "Microeconomics of product markets." Mateer and Coppock (2021) introduce behavioral economics as a chapter after "Consumer choice" and before "Health insurance and health care." Karlan and Morduch (2021) have a chapter positioned between "Consumer behavior" and "Game theory and strategic thinking." Bowles et al. (2017) consider behavioral economics content in the context of decision-making and the kinds of preferences people have—for example, altruism or inequality aversion—rather than individual limits to rationality.

Having diagnosed the problem of coverage, let us return to the content that could be covered in classes by teachers who wish to address the questions we articulated in the introduction.

BOUNDED RATIONALITY AND THE ENDOWMENT EFFECT

Almost all traditional Introductory Microeconomics courses begin by assuming that individual agents are rational, and this provides an opening to introduce behavioral economics. When economists say someone has rational preferences, formally we mean that a person has a preference relation (an ordering from least to most preferred) for different outcomes, and that the preference relation will correspond to a value in terms of utility.[3] A person who has reflexive, complete, and transitive (consistent) preferences is said to be "rational." A person with rational preferences will pursue, given their constraints, those outcomes which they would most prefer or that would maximize utility. Utility maximization is termed rational, and deviation from it is termed irrational (Becker 1962). We now explore how heuristics, biases, and the endowment effect demonstrate problems with rationality as taught in standard courses.

Heuristics and Biases

Work on rationality, heuristics, and biases has a long history in economics. Herbert Simon (Nobel laureate 1978), for example, argued for "bounded rationality" (people are rational for certain choices, but irrational for others) rather than rationality as we conceive it above (Simon 1956, 1979). Daniel Kahneman and Amos Tversky championed the "heuristics and biases" approach as an alternative to rational decision-making: a heuristic is a simple decision rule, and a bias is a consequence of a heuristic that leads to a suboptimal outcome (Tversky and Kahneman 1974). People use heuristics to facilitate decision-making in complex scenarios because they may not have the time or the ability to solve constrained utility-maximization problems.

Examples of heuristics include availability, representativeness, and anchoring. Anchoring is a heuristic where people tend to (typically, unconsciously) base their responses or decisions on the last piece of information they were primed with or they received. Availability bias refers to the tendency of people to make decisions or assess probabilities based on information that is easily recalled because it is recent, emotional, or vivid. Finally, representativeness bias occurs in situations where frequency and similarity are unrelated but people make judgments based on perceived closeness or matching.

The most straightforward approach to incorporating a discussion of biases in the principles framework is through interactive in-class examples from seminal behavioral economics work. We propose teaching examples for each of the three biases below.

Examples: availability bias

This heuristic is best demonstrated with some famous examples of mistaken probability estimates. Instructors can make the explanations more interactive by polling the class as each is introduced. One example includes the tendency of people to overestimate gun deaths due to homicides relative to suicides, because of media reporting. Another is that people tend to overestimate the probability of death due to events that prompt vivid imagery (for example, tornadoes) compared to those that do not (for example, asthma attacks) (Lichtenstein et al. 1978).

Examples: representativeness bias

We suggest interactive teaching examples of representativeness bias. The first is asking participants to predict the percentage of paths from top to bottom row that contain a certain number of X's and O's through a pre-designed matrix presented to them that contains five X's and one O in each row (Tversky and Kahneman 1973). Since X's appear far more frequently in the grid, students will likely assign a higher probability to paths that include 6 X's and no O's compared to 5 X's and 1 O, even though the latter is actually more frequent. In the second, profiles of individuals are distributed, and participants are asked to rank the probability of each individual's future outcome. One sample description is of Linda, a 31-year-old, single, outspoken, bright former philosophy student who was passionate about issues of discrimination and social justice. Participants are asked to rank the probability that she is currently involved in a variety of activities, including being active in the feminist movement (A), employed as a bank teller (B), and employed as a bank teller and active in the feminist movement (A and B). Here, students will likely rank the likelihood of each occurrence as A > (A and B) > B. However, statistically, the two combined outcomes have a lower probability of occurrence than the single outcomes (Kahneman and Tversky 1972). In both examples, students will see how people are subject to logical (and probabilistic) fallacies of judgments, made heuristically using proximity and similarity based on the visual or narrative representation.

Examples: anchoring

Consider conducting a simple in-class experiment that shows the anchoring bias.[4] First, ask students to write down the last two digits of their college/university ID number. Next, ask students to write down an estimate for the price of several goods shown through a PowerPoint presentation.[5] After the students have completed their estimates, the instructor can collect the pieces of paper and enter the results into a spreadsheet.[6] Typically, the results show that the estimated price is increasing as the ID number increases. Once students are primed with a particular number, they bias their estimates from value to the estimated target.[7]

Reference Dependence, Loss Aversion, and the Endowment Effect

Many instructors teach demand and supply as a fundamental aspect of microeconomics, but when people with non-standard preferences interact in markets, markets may not operate efficiently. The microeconomic foundation of demand and supply equilibrium with competitive markets and complete contracts is that sellers' willingness to sell (or "accept") and buyers' willingness to buy (or "pay") coincide, and result in the equilibrium price at which markets clear (quantity demanded equals quantity supplied). The endowment effect is a psychological phenomenon suggesting that when someone owns an object, their willingness to accept (or sell) is greater, and they must be paid more to part with the good. Consequently, mutually beneficial market transactions will not occur: the endowment effect impedes trade (Kahneman et al. 1990). The endowment effect may be driven by loss aversion: the proclivity that some people have to evaluate losses of a given amount as worse in utility terms than a gain of that same amount (compared to a given reference point). The endowment point relates to loss aversion because a person takes as a reference point their ownership of the good, and parting with the good feels subjectively worse than the equivalent gain of the value of the good at its price.

A student may ask if all people are victims of loss aversion and the endowment effect. Recent work shows that more experienced traders do not succumb to the endowment effect to the same degree as inexperienced traders. If the good being traded can be traded often and easily, then a person who regularly engages in the trade of that good will not experience an endowment effect (List 2003; Tong et al. 2016). This offers the instructor the opportunity to discuss markets in which the endowment effect is more likely to prevail and cause distortions. For example, durable goods that people do not exchange may often be more subject to the endowment effect than goods which are traded regularly.

Ask your students about goods that they buy and sell often (such as at the store) versus unique goods or those purchased in small quantities. For many, the "unique" good might be something like a trading card (Pokemon, Yu-gi-oh, and so on) or non-fungible tokens (NFTs). Do they "overvalue" the unique or seldom-traded goods versus commonly traded ones? Alternatively, if an instructor has the resources to do so, they could run a version of the original experiment using mugs and chocolate bars (Kahneman et al. 1990).

SOCIAL OR OTHER-REGARDING PREFERENCES

A fundamental contribution of behavioral economics over the past few decades has been to formalize the ways in which economists might think of "other-regarding" or "social" preferences, which contrast with the "self-regarding" preferences as taught in consumer theory. Other-regarding preferences include good and bad (or pro and con) feelings or sentiments about people who are not the "self": for example, neighbors, co-workers, and anonymous others. Adam Smith in the *Theory of Moral Sentiments* called such sentiments "sympathy" and "fellow-feeling" (Smith 1976 [1759]).

Theory of Social Preferences

Theories of social preferences emerged because of "anomalous" behaviors in experimental games: anomalous because the results contradicted the self-regarding Nash equilibrium of the game. Such anomalies have been observed, among others, in the Dictator Game to measure altruism; Ultimatum Games and the Trust Game to measure (strong) reciprocity and trust; and the social dilemmas (such as the Voluntary Contribution Mechanism and Common Pool Resource Game; with or without punishment) to measure conditional cooperation and punishment behaviors (Guth et al. 1982; Kahneman et al. 1986; Ostrom 1990; Hoffman et al. 1996; Falk et al. 2018).

Though the research initially looked at other-regarding preferences as including mainly prosocial behavior, a variety of research has also documented antisocial behavior. Prosocial behaviors help to sustain cooperation or coordination, such as when people punish others who do not cooperate in a Prisoners' Dilemma, thereby ensuring that the punished person cooperates. Antisocial behaviors, by contrast, include imposing a cost on oneself to cause costs to others that lead to worse outcomes for both. For example, stealing, antisocial punishment (punishment of people who cooperate), and the creation of vendettas in repeated games, are antisocial behaviors.[8] In both pro- and antisocial contexts, people are willing to bear a personal cost to alter the payoffs of other people, which is inconsistent with a theory of self-regarding behavior predicated merely on personal consumption.

In what ways can these insights be incorporated into the Introductory Microeconomics classroom? It is important to separate the idea of rationality from that of self-interest. That a rational person consistently pursues their ends imposes nothing on the contents of those preferences; that is, rationality does not imply self-interest. Therefore, students must, at a minimum, be taught that a person can consistently behave according to preferences that are reciprocal, conditionally cooperative, or altruistic. This reflects attitudes which a student might have about their own willingness to volunteer, donate money, or display kindness. Explanations of prosocial behavior should be accompanied by the antisocial aspects too: nastiness, spite, and antisociality. Students have often encountered these behaviors through basic prejudice, bullying, or gossip.

Activities to Teach Social Preferences

What are the best ways to incorporate an understanding of social preferences in the classroom?

1. Experimental games. Conduct a public goods game with and without punishment. A variety of resources exist to do this free of charge. Charlie Holt's VEconlab (http://veconlab.econ.virginia. edu/) offers a bare-bones way to run this experiment, with five rounds without punishment and five rounds with punishment. ClassEx (https://classex.de) offers another opportunity to run experiments and has a companion text with CORE's *Experiencing Economics* for specific experiments that illustrate economics ideas (https://www.core-econ.org/experiencing-economics/).[9]
2. Indifference curves. In the supplementary materials, we demonstrate how an instructor can contrast the behavior of two pairs of people in a Dictator Game: an entirely self-regarding person (A) paired with an anonymous other (B), and a somewhat altruistic person (C) paired with another (D). Person A gives nothing to B, whereas C shares some endowment with D.
3. Marginal benefits and marginal costs. If an instructor teaches with marginal benefits (MB) and marginal costs (MC), then considering a person (A) in a Dictator Game who has an endowment to allocate between themself (A) and a counterpart (B), a person will continue to allocate between themself and their partner until such time as the marginal benefits of doing so equal the marginal costs. This can be taught with a table of MB and MC.

With respect to the antisocial or cost-oriented aspects of social preferences, explain how behaviors we might otherwise consider "bad" have often helped to promote cooperation in small groups. For example, parochial altruism is altruism towards an in-group, but often at the cost of or antagonism toward out-groups. Students may themselves have engaged in gossip or sanctioning others who do not conform to behaviors they expect, and these behaviors promote cooperation or conformity within a group. The dark side of these kinds of behaviors pervade literature and movies: people developing vendettas for perceived slights, or undermined reputation, and so on. Ask students to provide examples from literature and movies to explain models of social preferences.

BEHAVIORAL MECHANISM DESIGN AND PUBLIC POLICY

Behavioral economics has had a significant impact on policy interventions, leading to the field of "behavioral mechanism design" or "behavioral public economics." Researchers highlight the role of behavioral economics in providing alternative policy tools, offering a pragmatic approach to policy design, and highlighting alternative welfare implications (Chetty 2015). We suggest two possible ways to incorporate behavioral policy topics. The prior material that an instructor has taught in their course will determine their preferred approach.

1. Choice architecture. If an instructor has taught the ideas of rationality, heuristics and biases, and time preferences, then they may want to focus on choice architecture and nudges, as these ideas show how these behavioral phenomena can translate to public policy.
2. Crowding out. If an instructor has taught the ideas of social preferences, then the idea of crowding out would be a good topic to teach as it is based on people having social preferences.

Choice Architecture and Nudges

As a consequence of limits on rationality and self-control problems, researchers have argued for understanding "choice architecture," meaning that the context in which people make choices can affect the resulting choices. For example, if the default is that a person is not enrolled in a retirement plan, then they may not realize their low savings rate; whereas if they are automatically enrolled in the retirement plan, they save more money. The approach thus offers "nudges" in a particular direction, the one the person would choose if they were aware of their own biases. Hence Thaler and Sunstein (2003) adopt the name "libertarian paternalism" for the idea behind nudging: to design the set of choices in such a way that the default is one the person themselves would prefer, while offering the same menu of choices. Chetty (2015) offers an alternative reason for using nudges in behavioral policy, based on model uncertainty rather than paternalism.

To demonstrate the importance of nudges, show students graphs that illustrate when a person is offered a new default and their outcome changes even though economics would predict that they should back switch to the behavior they otherwise "prefer." Chetty et al. (2014) shows the difference in behavior when workers switch from a job without a default level of savings into a job with a default level of savings. After the switch, the default policy changes the worker's savings rate, and the worker does not respond by electing to lower their savings rate voluntarily. They thus save more in the new job because of the differences in default policies.[10]

When discussing nudges or choice architecture with students, certain concerns or objections may arise: do nudges infringe on people's liberty, and who gets to decide what is "best"? Answering the first question, the person is always free to opt out of the default. Considering the second: when firms make choices about how they design choices or menus, they do so in a way to maximize their profits, not to choose that which is otherwise "best" for people; the democratic process (which leads to policy) is one means by which a citizen can voice what they would prefer a policymaker to do, but they have no such power over the decision of a firm, except not to frequent the firm's stores. To demonstrate this, consider two teaching examples.

First, consider the architecture of supermarkets. Ask students if the choice by the managers of supermarkets to put candy at or near the cashier is made "for the good of the customer" or because the managers or owners think they are able to take advantage of a customer's self-control problems. What would the choice architecture of an alternative store look like if the student were themself designing the store at which they planned to shop to benefit their health and well-being?

Second, an instructor can discuss social media, phone notifications, and individual behavior: ask students whether social media companies want people to spend more or less time on their platforms. The companies want people to spend more time using their applications, even though the evidence suggests tha doing so lowers subjective well-being, and that many people would rather spend less time on the platforms. Indeed, when offered the choice, people with social media accounts are willing to pay to give up access to their own accounts (Allcott et al. 2020, 2021).

Broadening these ideas, when surveying people about what they would intend to do, many people answer that they would like to save more, exercise more regularly, or eat more healthily. The point of nudges—anticipating people's own biases and self-control problems—is to design choices such that people do that which they would themselves prefer to do.

Incentives: Crowding Out and Crowding In

A standard refrain in introductory economics is that "incentives matter." The point that instructors make when they say this is that people respond to changes in prices. What this fails to teach is that, as a consequence of social or endogenous preferences, people may respond to material incentives in a way that is contrary to the policy goals of those incentives. When a policymaker changes prices or regulations, then they may fail to achieve the ends for which the policy was intended, because they failed to account for how people respond to the imposition of material incentives with an adequate understanding of the existing norms governing the interaction.

Behavioral economics changes our understanding of mechanism design by distinguishing between the situations in which people will respond in predictable and self-interested ways to prices and other incentives, and the situations in which designing mechanisms as if people were self-interested may cause them to behave self-regardingly and crowd out pro-social or other-regarding behavior.[11]

Consider the notorious Haifa daycare experiment. Uri Gneezy and Aldo Rustichini recount how an experiment in daycare centers in Haifa, Israel imposed a fine on parents who were late to pick up their children (Gneezy and Rustichini 2000a, 2000b).[12] Instead of the fine resulting in parents picking up their children on time, many parents instead began to pick up their children even later than before. Furthermore, once the fine system was rescinded, the behavior of parents did not return to the pre-experiment norm. Now the die-hard economist committed to material incentives might say that the initial fine was not high enough, but this is beside the point. The initial behavior adhered to a norm that "picking up your kids late is bad," and the creation of a material incentive undermined the norm and changed the locus of the exchange from one of social norms and social preferences to one of market exchange (and self-interest). The Haifa daycare centers changed the salience of parents' behavior so that it shifted from norms of the family and the community, to one of market exchange.[13]

RISK AND TIME PREFERENCES

Behavioral economists have long grappled with models of risk and time preferences to understand rational and consistent choices.

Risk Preferences

The basic intuitions of risk preferences can be taught in a variety of different ways that are comprehensible to introductory economics students. These methods include the following:

1. The ideas of risk aversion and risk neutrality can be taught without formalization alongside decreasing absolute risk aversion (Arrow 1971), that is, risk aversion decreasing with an individual's level of wealth (Binswanger 1980; Saha et al. 1994; Paravisini et al. 2017). This is also true for the intuitions of loss aversion and prospect theory, especially as they relate to the endowment effect discussed earlier.

2. If an instructor does not teach indifference curves, but does teach payoff or game tables, then they can teach the Assurance Game. Using the Assurance Game, they can show that the Pareto-inferior outcome can be a risk-dominant equilibrium (with risk-neutral agents). A student must learn how to compute an expected payoff, but the required algebra is consistent with that expected in many introductory courses.
3. If an instructor teaches indifference curves, then they can more formally teach how different risk preferences will result in different choices of risk and expected payoffs (or expected income/wealth) from a given risk–return schedule. This would include more formal explanations of what it means to be risk-averse or risk-neutral, and how a person can have decreasing absolute risk aversion.

We provide supporting material in the online appendix (https://www.e-elgar .com/textbooks/maier) for how to implement each of these ideas with suggested learning activities alongside graphs of experimental results. Students who make choices in an experimental decision setting can see their own choices mirrored in the decision spaces that are modeled by standard models and their behavioral counterparts.

Preferences Over Time: Self-Control Problems

The standard economic model of time preferences is one in which subjects are exponential discounters and are therefore time-consistent decision-makers: they have a consistent discount factor that does not change over time. Contrary evidence suggests two patterns of behavior, however: (1) many people have discount factors that vary over time such that they are less patient over shorter time horizons and more patient over longer time horizons (Thaler 1981; Benzion et al. 1989; Loewenstein and Prelec 1992); and (2) people have self-control problems and may reverse their decisions when arriving at a future period (Laibson 1997). This has resulted in the adoption of "present-biased" time preferences as an alternative model (O'Donoghue and Rabin 1999, 2015). How, then, can time preferences be taught in an introductory economics classroom?

First, varying levels of patience over time. If an instructor teaches the idea of compound interest, then they may comment on the intuition of a discounted present value, explaining the tradeoffs between choosing to consume now or soon versus later by discussing the role of interest rates and how money that is spent now for consumption could be a larger amount of money later to get more consumption later. They can introduce the intuition of hyperbolic discounting: people have different levels of patience depending on the span of time under consideration. They are less patient for events that are close to the present (next week or next month), and more patient for choices involving periods further in the future (two years or five years in the future).[14]

Second, present bias and self-control problems. People are present-biased in that they favor the present over the stream of future consumption, and this leads to procrastination: deferring costly actions to the future. An instructor can teach the intuition of present-biased preferences by commenting on empirically observed examples and their policy implications, by highlighting the role of self-control problems and procrastination.

How can an instructor illustrate these ideas? Survey students about choices with different amounts of money as an outcome, over various time frames, closer and further from the present. For example, ask students if they would prefer to receive $100 today or $110 tomorrow. Then, ask them if they would prefer to receive $100 in one year or $110 in one year and one day (Cartwright 2011). The amount of time between the two rewards is the same, one day, but one scenario is in the more distant future. The results can be compared to what people do in the published research (e.g. Benzion et al. 1989). Students who reverse their choices—for example, wanting $100 tomorrow but $110 in a year and a day—demonstrate that they are more impatient about near-future choices than further future choices.

The phenomenon of procrastination allows the instructor to teach present-biased preferences: preferences where, having decided, a person may reverse their choice in the future and continue to put things off. A person with standard time preferences will never procrastinate. If an instructor asks students whether they have procrastinated (and to provide examples), most students will give examples of procrastination such as deferring homework, chores, or similar (Cohen et al. 2020; Laibson 1997). Self-control problems are nearly universal.

What are the main takeaways from present-biased preferences?

1. Students should know that deadlines (a commitment device to have work done by a specific point in time) help a student to achieve better outcomes relative to if they are left free to make their own decisions about when to hand in work (Ariely and Wertenbroch 2002).
2. Many people make health choices without paying attention to their self-control problems, and commitment devices can assist in making decisions that a future self will value (Courtemanche et al. 2015).
3. Crucially for financial well-being in retirement, many people fail to save enough for retirement and commitment devices can increase a person's financial stability (Diamond and Koszegi 2003; Thaler and Benartzi 2004).

Choices over time also necessarily involve questions of limits on rationality. Firms take advantage of self-control problems by offering contracts to which they know people will not pay attention, as is the case with self-renewing health club memberships, life insurance, and vacation time shares (DellaVigna and Malmendier 2004; DellaVigna 2009). Simarly, Thaler and Benartzi (2004) design a retirement savings plan where individuals decide on lifetime contributions today, exploiting status quo bias (Samuelson and Zeckhauser 1988): a disposition to favor the status quo over changes to the status quo.

MONEY, UTILITY, AND HAPPINESS

Students often raise two concerns about economic thinking in introductory economics. First, what does "utility" measure, and does it correspond to happiness? Second, does money matter for happiness? The evidence suggests that happiness and utility do correspond to each other, and that money and happiness also correlate (with caveats).

When we talk about utility in economics we typically think of it as something more abstract than "happiness": it is that which we receive from achieving the ends we pursue. Utility may be positive (for goods, things we would prefer more of) or negative (for bads, things we would prefer to avoid).

To try to understand utility in a measurable way, Daniel Kahneman and other researchers have argued for a "hedonistic" (that is, pleasure and pain) measure of utility (Kahneman et al. 1997). To measure these pleasures and pains, research participants are exposed to uncomfortable experiences and asked to report their level of discomfort. For example, researchers have used mild electrical shocks and asked subjects to report their experience on a numerical scale, or asked them to put their hands into extremely cold water for as long as they can stand it and report their level of unhappiness having done so (Kahneman et al. 1993).

Outside of the laboratory, a variety of work internationally asks survey respondents to report on their life satisfaction and other measures of "subjective well-being" (Kahneman and Krueger 2006).[15] Almost all people surveyed like sex, socializing, relaxing, sharing meals with friends, praying, and exercising (these are "goods"). People do not like housework, childcare, commuting, or working (these are "bads"). People also report major changes in subjective well-being from painful events such as a sudden job loss, a death in the family, or divorce; or from joyful events such as marriage or the birth of a child (Kahneman and Krueger 2006; Lucas et al. 2003). Job security also affects happiness: the lower your job security, the lower your subjective well-being (Luechinger et al. 2010).

Measures of subjective well-being (SWB) are important for microeconomic theory because they may allow us to infer the tradeoffs between or among different feasible choices. For example, researchers have used subjective well-being data to infer marginal rates of substitution for residency choices among graduating doctors (Benjamin et al. 2014). A correspondence between SWB data and the microeconomic measures we care about help to provide students with motivations for why the theory is relevant to decisions that people make in the real world.

To teach these ideas, an instructor could ask students to keep a diary of their activities during one 24-hour day, and to rank their activities from most to least pleasurable. The instructor could do this with an anonymized online form. Students would themselves then infer the benefits of actions that incur disutility (a paid job or time spent studying) in order to get goods they want (money to spend on consumption or obtaining higher grades), or the tradeoffs they make among activities they value: for example, sleep and seeing friends both provide utility, but one cannot do both at the same time.

CONCLUSION

Behavioral economics is recognized as a core part of economic research, but it still remains excluded from many introductory textbooks and courses. Exploring five questions about economic ideas and their potential answers offers an instructor a variety of ways to engage with topics in behavioral economics and address misconceptions that arise in introductory economics courses. The instructor may engage with one or all of these questions, depending on their course. Many of the intuitions can be taught with cost–benefit analysis, discursive examples, experiments, or learning activities. Using graphs or data visualization from recently published papers means both that students can see how topical the content they learn in their economics classes is, while also providing an instructor with an accessible way to teach otherwise hard to grasp ideas.

NOTES

1. We also endeavored to include only ideas which have held up in replications, for example, the anchoring heuristic holds up in repeated replication in the Many Labs project (Klein et al. 2014), and the endowment effect is replicated in that project and others (Plott and Zeiler 2005; Isoni et al. 2011; Drouvelis and Sonnemans 2017).
2. These included Acemoglu et al. (2014), Bowles et al. (2017), Hubbard and O'Brien (2019), Karlan and Morduch (2021), Krugman and Wells (2021), Mankiw (2018), Mateer and Coppock (2021), McConnell et al. (2021), Greenlaw and Shapiro (2018), and Stevenson and Wolfers (2020). Please refer to the table in the supplementary materials for specific sections.
3. We provide the mathematical formalization of this in the supplementary materials at https://www.e-elgar.com/textbooks/maier.

4. A sample PowerPoint for this experiment is available in the online appendix. As with all in-class experiments, it is plausible that the results will not produce the anticipated outcome. Instructors should be prepared to discuss this if the situation arises.

5. Other versions or extensions of this experiment can be done where students are asked to guess the value of certain economic statistics.

6. Depending on the size of the class, results may need to be entered by a teaching assistant or discussed in the following class period to allow time for the data to be entered. While the instructor is entering the data, students can discuss in a think–pair–share format their hypothesis of the result and reasoning.

7. If the results do not show this perfectly, the class can engage in a discussion about the findings in the literature and why there might be variation in the class experiment (Wawrosz and Blahout 2020; Ariely et al. 2003).

8. To understand the antisocial aspects of other-regarding preferences, see Abbink et al. (2000), List (2007), Bardsley (2008), Herrmann et al. (2008), and Bolle et al. (2014).

9. There are other options for paid platforms for experiments. We do not comment on them here.

10. See Figure 1b in Chetty et al. (2014).

11. A variety of theories seek to explain how this happens and how to reconcile standard economic theories with psychological theories; see, for example, Bénabou and Tirole (2003, 2006) and Bénabou et al. (2018).

12. Numerous other examples exist in the literature (Gneezy et al. 2011; Bowles and Polania-Reyes 2012). The laboratory corroboration of the beliefs in and prevalence of norms is also widespread (Krupka and Weber 2013; Kimbrough and Vostroknutov 2016, 2018).

13. A replica of the graph is included in the online supplement.

14. Benzion et al. (1989) is especially helpful for this, as one can show how people compare debts (money owed) versus payments (money received).

15. We provide examples in the supplementary materials.

REFERENCES

Abbink, K., Irlenbusch, B., and Renner, E. (2000). The moonlighting game: An experimental study on reciprocity and retribution. *Journal of Economic Behavior and Organization 42*(2), 265–277.

Acemoglu, D., Laibson,D., and List, J. (2014). *Economics*. Pearson Education.

Allcott, H., Braghieri, L., Eichmeyer, S., and Gentzkow, M. (2020). The welfare effects of social media. *American Economic Review 110*(3), 629–76.

Allcott, H., Gentzkow, M., and Song, L. (2021). *Digital addiction*. Tech. rep. National Bureau of Economic Research Working Paper 28936.

Angner, E. (2019). We're all behavioral economists now. *Journal of Economic Methodology 26*(3), 195–207.

Ariely, D., Loewenstein, G., and Prelec, D. (2003). "Coherent arbitrariness": Stable demand curves without stable preferences. *Quarterly Journal of Economics 118*(1), 73–106.

Ariely, D., and Wertenbroch, K. (2002). Procrastination, deadlines, and performance: Self-control by precommitment. *Psychological Science 13*(3), 219–224.

Arrow, K.J. (1971). *Essays on the Theory of Risk Bearing*. Markham Publishing Co.

Bardsley, N. (2008). Dictator game giving: Altruism or artefact? *Experimental Economics 11*(2), 122–133.

Becker, G.S (1962). Irrational behavior and economic theory. *Journal of Political Economy 70*(1), 1–13.

Bénabou, R., Falk, A., and Tirole, J. (2018). Narratives, imperatives, and moral reasoning. National Bureau of Economic Research Working Paper 24798.

Bénabou, R., and Tirole, J. (2003). Intrinsic and extrinsic motivation. *Review of Economic Studies 70*(3), 489–520.

Bénabou, R., and Tirole, J. (2006). Incentives and prosocial behavior. *American Economic Review 96*(5), 1652–1678.

Benjamin, D., Heffetz, O., Kimball, M.S., and Rees-Jones, A. (2014). Can marginal rates of substitution be inferred from happiness data? Evidence from residency choices. *American Economic Review 104*(11), 3498–3528.

Benzion, U., Rapoport, A., and Yagil, J. (1989). Discount rates inferred from decisions: An experimental study. *Management Science 35*(3), 270–284.

Binswanger, H.P. (1980). Attitudes toward risk: Experimental measurement in rural India. *American Journal of Agricultural Economics 62*(3), 395–407.

Bolle, F., Tan, J., and Zizzo, D.J. (2014). Vendettas. *American Economic Journal: Microeconomics 6*(2), 93–130.

Bowles, S., Carlin W., and Stevens, M. (2017). *The Economy: Economics for a Changing World*. Oxford University Press.

Bowles, S., and Polania-Reyes, S. (2012). Economic incentives and social preferences: Substitutes or complements? *Journal of Economic Literature 50*(2), 368–425.

Cartwright, E. (2011). *Behavioral Economics*. Routledge Advanced Texts in Economics and Finance. Routledge.

Cartwright, E., and Stepanova, A. (2012). What do students learn from a classroom experiment: not much, unless they write a report on it. *Journal of Economic Education 43*(1), 48–57.

Chetty, R. (2015). Behavioral economics and public policy: A pragmatic perspective. *American Economic Review 105*(5), 1–33.

Chetty, R., Friedman, J.N., Leth-Petersen, S., Nielsen, T.H., and Olsen, T. (2014). Active vs. passive decisions and crowd-out in retirement savings accounts: Evidence from Denmark. *Quarterly Journal of Economics 129*(3), 1141–1219.

Cohen, J., Ericson, K.M., Laibson, D., and White, J.M. (2020). Measuring time preferences. *Journal of Economic Literature 58*(2), 299–347.

Courtemanche, C., Heutel, G., and McAlvanah, P. (2015). Impatience, incentives and obesity. *Economic Journal 125*(582), 1–31.

DellaVigna, S. (2009). Psychology and economics: Evidence from the field. *Journal of Economic Literature 47*(2), 315–372.

DellaVigna, S., and Malmendier, U. (2004). Contract design and self-control: Theory and evidence. *Quarterly Journal of Economics 119*(2), 353–402.

Diamond, P., and Koszegi, B. (2003). Quasi-hyperbolic discounting and retirement. *Journal of Public Economics 87*(9–10), 1839–1872.

Drouvelis, M., and Sonnemans, J. (2017). The endowment effect in games. *European Economic Review 94*, 240–262.

Falk, A., Becker, A., Dohmen, T., Enke, B., Huffman, D., and Sunde, U. (2018). Global evidence on economic preferences. *Quarterly Journal of Economics 133*(4), 1645–1692.

Gneezy, U., Meier. S., and Rey-Biel, P. (2011). When and why incentives (don't) work to modify behavior. *Journal of Economic Perspectives 25*(4), 191–210.

Gneezy, U., and Rustichini, A. (2000a). A fine is a price. *Journal of Legal Studies 29*(1), 1–17.

Gneezy, U., and Rustichini, A. (2000b). Pay enough or don't pay at all. *Quarterly Journal of Economics 115*(3), 791–810.

Greenlaw, S.A., and Shapiro, D. (2018). *Principles of Microeconomics* (2nd edition). OpenStax, Rice University.

Guth, W., Scmittberger, R., and Bernd Schwarze, B. (1982). An experimental analysis of ultimatum bargaining. *Journal of Economic Behavior and Organization 3*, 367–388.

Herrmann, B., Thöni, C., and Gächter, S. (2008). Antisocial punishment across societies. *Science 319*(5868), 1362–1367.

Hoffman, E., McCabe, K., and Smith, V.L. (1996). Social distance and other-regarding behavior in dictator games. *American Economic Review 86*(3), 653–660.

Hubbard, R.G., and O'Brien, A.P. (2019). *Microeconomics* (7th edition). Pearson.

Isoni, A., Loomes, G., and Sugden, R. (2011). The willingness to pay–willingness to accept gap, the endowment effect, subject misconceptions, and experimental procedures for eliciting valuations: Comment. *American Economic Review* 101(2), 991–1011.

Kahneman, D., Fredrickson, B.L., Schreiber, C.A., and Redelmeier, D.A. (1993). When more pain is preferred to less: Adding a better end. *Psychological Science 4*(6), 401–405.

Kahneman, D., Knetsch, J.L., and Thaler, R.H. (1986). Fairness as a constraint on profit seeking: Entitlements in the market. *American Economic Review 76*(4), 728–741.

Kahneman, D., Knetsch, J.L., and Thaler, R.H. (1990). Experimental tests of the endowment effect and the Coase theorem. *Journal of Political Economy 98*(6), 1325–1348.

Kahneman, D., and Krueger, A.B. (2006). Developments in the measurement of subjective well being. *Journal of Economic Perspectives 20*(1), 3–24.

Kahneman, D., and Tversky, A. (1972). Subjective probability: A judgment of representativeness. *Cognitive Psychology 3*(3), 430–454.

Kahneman, D., Wakker, P.P., and Sarin, R. (1997). Back to Bentham? Explorations of experienced utility. *Quarterly Journal of Economics 112*(2), 375–406.

Karlan, D., and Morduch, J. (2021). *Microeconomics: Improve Your World* (3rd edition). McGraw-Hill Education.

Kimbrough, E.O., and Vostroknutov, A. (2016). Norms make preferences social. *Journal of the European Economic Association 14*(3), 608–638.

Kimbrough, E.O., and Vostroknutov, A. (2018). A portable method of eliciting respect for social norms. *Economics Letters 168*, 147–150.

Klein, R.A., Ratliff, K.A., Vianello, M., Adams, R.B. Jr., ... and Nosek, B.A. (2014). Investigating variation in replicability: A "Many Labs" replication project. *Social Psychology 45*(3), 142–52.

Krugman, P.R., and Wells, R. (2021). *Microeconomics* (6th edition). Macmillan International Higher Education.

Krupka, E.L., and Weber, R.A. (2013). Identifying social norms using coordination games: Why does dictator game sharing vary? *Journal of the European Economic Association 11*(3), 495–524.

Laibson, D. (1997). Golden eggs and hyperbolic discounting. *Quarterly Journal of Economics 112*(2), 443–477.

Lichtenstein, S., Slovic, P., Fischhoff, B., Layman, M., and Combs, B. (1978). Judged frequency of lethal events. *Journal of Experimental Psychology: Human Learning and Memory 4*(6), 551.

List, J. (2003). Does market experience eliminate market anomalies? *Quarterly Journal of Economics 118*(1), 41–71.

List, J. (2007). On the interpretation of giving in dictator games. *Journal of Political economy 115*(3), 482–493.

Loewenstein, G., and Prelec, D. (1992). Anomalies in intertemporal choice: Evidence and an interpretation. *Quarterly Journal of Economics 107*(2), 573–597.

Lucas, R.E., Clark, A.E., Georgellis, Y., and Diener, E. (2003). Reexamining adaptation and the set point model of happiness: Reactions to changes in marital status. *Journal of Personality and Social Psychology 84*(3), 527.

Luechinger, S., Meier, S., and Stutzer, A. (2010). Why does unemployment hurt the employed? Evidence from the life satisfaction gap between the public and the private sector. *Journal of Human Resources 45*(4), 998–1045.

Mankiw, N.G. (2018). *Principles of Microeconomics* (8th edition). Cengage Learning.

Mateer, D., and Coppock, L. (2021). *Principles of Microeconomics* (3rd edition). W.W. Norton & Company.

McConnell, C.R., Brue, S.L., and Flynn, S.M. (2021). *Microeconomics: Principles, Problems, and Policies* (22nd edition). McGraw-Hill Education.

O'Donoghue, T., and Rabin, M. (1999). Doing it now or later. *American Economic Review 89*(1), 103–124.

O'Donoghue, T., and Rabin, M. (2015). Present bias: Lessons learned and to be learned. *American Economic Review 105*(5), 273–279.

Ostrom, E. (1990). *Governing the Commons: The Evolution of Institutions for Collective Action*. Cambridge University Press.

Paravisini, D., Rappoport, V., and Ravina, E. (2017). Risk aversion and wealth: Evidence from person-to-person lending portfolios. *Management Science 63*(2), 279–297.

Plott, C.R., and Zeiler, K. (2005). The willingness to pay–willingness to accept gap, the endowment effect, subject misconceptions, and experimental procedures for eliciting valuations. *American Economic Review 95*(3), 530–545.

Rabin, M. (2002). A perspective on psychology and economics. *European Economic Review 46*(4–5), 657–685.

Saha, A., Shumway, C.R., and Talpaz, H. (1994). Joint estimation of risk preference structure and technology using expo-power utility. *American Journal of Agricultural Economics 76*(2), 173–184.

Samuelson, W., and Zeckhauser, R. (1988). Status quo bias in decision making. *Journal of Risk and Uncertainty 1*(1), 7–59.

Simon, H.A. (1956). Rational choice and the structure of the environment. *Psychological Review 63*(2), 129.

Simon, H.A. (1979). Rational decision making in business organizations. *American Economic Review 69*(4), 493–513.

Smith, A. (1976 [1759]). *The Theory of Moral Sentiments. The Glasgow Edition of the Works and Correspondence of Adam Smith*. Oxford University Press (Liberty Fund).

Stevenson, B., and Wolfers, J. (2020). *Principles of Microeconomics*. Worth Publishers.

Thaler, R.H. (1981). Some empirical evidence on dynamic inconsistency. *Economics Letters 8*(3), 201–207.

Thaler, R.H., and Benartzi, S. (2004). Save more tomorrow™: Using behavioral economics to increase employee saving. *Journal of Political Economy 112*(S1), S164–S187.

Thaler, R.H., and Sunstein, C.R. (2003). Libertarian paternalism. *American Economic Review 93*(2), 175–179.

Tong, L.C.P., Ye, K.J., Asai, K., Ertac, S., … and Hortaçsu, A. (2016). Trading experience modulates anterior insula to reduce the endowment effect. *Proceedings of the National Academy of Sciences 113*(33), 9238–9243.

Tversky, A., and Kahneman, D. (1973). Availability: A heuristic for judging frequency and probability. *Cognitive Psychology 5*(2), 207–232.

Tversky, A., and Kahneman, D. (1974). Judgment under uncertainty: Heuristics and biases. *Science 185*(4157), 1124–1131.

Wawrosz, P., and Blahout, M. (2020). Anchoring bias and representative bias: Two classroom experiments. *Scientia et Societas 16*(3): 77–90.

8. Suggestions for incorporating sustainability into Principles of Microeconomics

Jack Reardon

INTRODUCTION

In 2021, *The Guardian* reported, "Our climate change turning point is right here, right now" (July 12, 2021), followed soon after by "We're on the brink of catastrophe" (August 7, 2021); at the time of writing, the years 2015 to 2021 had been the warmest on record. With warmer temperatures there is more evaporation, more water in the atmosphere, resulting in once-in-a-lifetime floods, heatwaves, and droughts. Our climate is changing, and humans are the preponderant cause. If we take no action and continue business as usual, these once-in-a-lifetime events will occur with greater frequency. Adding to this sense of urgency is the widespread scientific understanding that humanity must prevent global temperatures from rising more than 2°Celsius from their pre-Industrial Revolution level,[1] and preferably no more 1.5°C. If we are unsuccessful, the world will become increasingly inhospitable. Fortunately, we have a window of opportunity (albeit one that is shrinking) to effect change.

This chapter offers helpful suggestions for instructors to implement the concept of sustainability in the Principles of Microeconomics course. Students are very interested (and worried and anxious) about their future, and look to economics to help them understand the world they live in, learn how they can prepare, mitigate, and for some, gain the power to change. Incorporating the suggestions offered in this chapter will go a long way to help students better engage in their world.

After this brief introduction, the next section defines sustainability; subsequent sections offer specific teaching suggestions grouped by topics in the Principles of Microeconomics course; and the final section concludes.

DEFINING SUSTAINABILITY

Like the words "democracy" and "freedom," the word "sustainability" is multi-faceted and contested, meaning different things to different people. While several definitions of sustainability[2] exist, one that I prefer is: "Sustainability is enabling communities to thrive, across generations, in ways that maintain the ability of the larger environment (the containing system) to support this. [It is] living well for all (species), now and into the future, within the means of the environment" (Creative Change 2013, p. 6). In order to mitigate the worst effects of climate change, we must become sustainable, and that means emphasizing (as part of a cohesive whole) the economic, the social, and the environmental.

Adding a layer of complexity to sustainability is that it can be approached in one of three ways: business as usual, in which nothing substantive is done; solving within the current economic system; and radical change in which our modus vivendi fundamentally changes (Soderbaum 2008, pp. 14–15). Given the urgency of climate change which is already well underway, more and more people have recognized that business as usual is no longer viable, yet our infrastructure and institutions are locked into our current system. Thus, the best we can do in the immediate present is to reform within the current system. Analogously, for micro instructors we realize that teaching nothing about sustainability ignores the urgency of climate change, which does our students a disservice; yet, at the same time, given the current curricula constrained by degree requirements, fulfilling prerequisites, limited textbook choice, and assessment needs, we are locked into the current system. While this might very well change in the future, most instructors are interested in what we can now do within the given constraints.[3]

TOPIC ONE: INTRODUCTION TO MICROECONOMICS

Suggestion One: Introducing the Concept of Opportunity Cost with a Sustainability Twist

All microeconomics texts begin with the concept of opportunity cost. What better way to introduce students to this important concept than to discuss the opportunity cost of not taking measures to ensure that we stay within the 1.5°C threshold? Without measures to mitigate climate change, there will be longer and more prevalent heatwaves, higher average daytime (and nighttime) temperatures, more floods, and stronger storms; disease, drought, and viruses will become more rampant; agriculture will fail, especially in developing areas; and more people will die. This is the quintessence of opportunity cost. And yes, there is an opportunity cost for inaction.[4]

Here, it is important not to begin the semester with a doom and gloom sermon that the world is headed for disaster, but to highlight the role of education in creating and enabling the ability to solve problems. The goal is to instill students with a sense of optimism and empowerment.[5]

Suggestion Two: Discuss Sustainability

On opening day, I take the time to explain that economies are complex[6] and not easily understood, but nevertheless are ultimately (and fundamentally) comprised of individuals. As such, individual choices matter, not only in achieving the goals for our economy but also in setting an example, and in turn influencing the values and actions of others. I then ask students to form groups and list ten activities in their typical day involving external energy, from whatever source: fossil fuels, renewables, solar. Student responses include charging one's phone overnight, using the stove, refrigerator, microwave, driving/walking to class, preparing daily meals, watching TV, and so on. This activity serves as a helpful opening-day icebreaker emphasizing the role of listening/dialoging and getting the shy person to actively participate in a small group setting. Indeed, listening and dialogue are key ingredients on the road to sustainability and individual choice matters. I begin with my own example: As part of my job description, I teach microeconomics at our branch campus 60 miles away; and given the dearth of public transportation, I have no choice but to drive my car. But I drive at 65 mph, rather than 75/80 mph. By doing so I save 4 gallons of gas per week; and at 32 weeks for the academic year, I save three barrels of oil (one barrel contains 42 gallons). Although it is literally a drop in bucket in our nation's daily oil consumption of 19.7 million barrels, this example demonstrates that individual behavior matters. And it nicely segues into the concept of opportunity cost—what I could have done with the extra ten minutes (assuming I drove faster)—and, in addition, the importance of aligning one's values with sustainability.

I ask my students to continuously revisit their energy-intensive activities during the semester. Specifically, during my energy unit I ask about the energy source for each activity and any suggestions to conserve and change behavior.

Suggestion Three: Introduce the United Nations 17 Sustainable Development Goals (SDGs)

As a framework for the entire course and one that is quite amenable to "working within the current system" I suggest introducing the 17 United Nations (UN) SDGs[7] right off the bat. Published in 2015, the 17 SDGs offer initiatives for sustainable living that "underscore the point that sustainability involves a lot more than concern with the environment, emphasizing 'all,' inclusive, and 'urgent' [along with] the active verbs: end, ensure, achieve, promote, reduce, conserve, and revitalize. This is the language of the SDGs, this is the language of urgency" (Reardon et al. 2018, p. 18). The sense of urgency back then was palpable, which unfortunately has since redoubled.

Give a brief overview of the SGGs and have students form groups. Have them read the language carefully and discuss among themselves the specific wording, the action words used, and the sense of gender inclusion. Do the goals fit together cohesively, or do some contradict each other? Ask each student to adopt a single SDG and journal it during the semester, specifically focusing on how to effectuate and implement it, and the connections with the traditional topics of microeconomics. Depending on the time available at the semester's end, you could ask each student to make a five-minute video on their SDG and either present it to the class directly or post it on the class webpage.[8] Another variation is to make a class movie and/or write a newspaper article discussing the ideas of sustainability influenced by the UN SDGs developed by your class.[9]

Suggestion Four: Make the Connection Between Pluralism and Sustainability

To help students understand what pluralism means, I give my students the following example of when I was a first-year graduate student and rented a house with three other guys. (Given that many students live off-campus, this example will resonate.) Each of us had input into the rules or obligations that were set up, and each person's views and wishes were respected; no person's views were dominant. We listened, talked, and worked together. This is the quintessence of pluralism: respect for diversity, listening, and dialoguing (especially with those with whom we disagree). The antithesis of pluralism is monism, where only one view matters, with a dearth of listening and dialoguing.

While there are many good reasons why economics should become pluralist[10] in and of itself (Schneider, Chapter 6 in this book; Reardon 2015, 2017, pp. 11–13), probably the most pressing for our purposes is that sustainability cannot be understood or even conceptualized through a monist lens; it is inherently and intrinsically pluralist:

> It is absolutely impossible to discuss sustainability from one perspective. It is absolutely impossible to discuss sustainability without discussing justice, ethics, and power. And it is absolutely impossible to discuss justice and power without developing the skills to listen and dialogue. It simply cannot be done. Start teaching the UN 17 SDGs [with their emphasis on sustainability], and pluralism with its myriad

benefits becomes inevitable. Thus, recognizing and incorporating sustainability is a game changer. (Reardon 2021, 294)

Pandemics and climate change do not respect well-established intellectual silos, nor international borders. Workable solutions are not the prerogative of one discipline, as if only one discipline has the answer, since:

> the whole range of man's [*sic*] actions in society is too wide and too various to be analyzed and explained by a single intellectual effort. It is the duty of those who are giving their chief work to a limited field, to keep up close and constant correspondence with those who are engaged in neighboring fields. (Marshall 1890 [1946], p. 770)

Many instructors who accept the need for pluralism are nevertheless often at a loss as to how to incorporate it: should we teach every issue from every viewpoint? Of course not; this is a recipe for madness for both student and teacher. Rather, the instructor should encourage and foster (throughout the semester) listening, dialoguing, and the need to understand those we disagree with, and the humility to realize that no single discipline has all the answers. Here is a simple exercise involving the minimum wage that does not take long, and segues nicely into the traditional microeconomics topics: divide the class into two groups, with one group arguing in favor, and the other against. The goal is to reach a consensus and make a policy recommendation. This exercise teaches that the goal is not that everyone agrees, but we listen, dialogue, and comprise.

Suggestion Five: Present a Definition of Economics that Comports with Sustainability

The definition of the subject sets the tone for the whole course, and points to what will be emphasized throughout the course. The definition of economics is contested. Neoclassical economists largely prefer the means–end definition: economics is the study of how we allocate scarce resources to satisfy unlimited wants. But this definition has always been problematic. First, not all resources are scarce: for example, information and mental acuity are perfectly elastic, unlimited in potential, and the crucial resource needed to solve climate change, and "the kind of wealth that is not diminished or lost but is increased by being shared" (Dahl 1996, p. 120). Second, the assumption of unlimited wants is gratuitous and lacks empirical validation, and as such should not form the foundation of a scientific discipline. Third, scarcity is not inherent in any economic system, but is a function of the institutions of that society. So rather than blithely assume scarcity in all contexts, if a resource/product is scarce we must investigate the reason and then work to redress this. And fourth, the means–end calculus is applicable to any discipline and says nothing about the uniqueness of economics or its specific subject matter.

It is for this reason that heterodox or pluralist economists reject the means–end definition in favor of one of provisioning; that is, "economics is all about provisioning, or how societies organize themselves to sustain life and enhance its quality" (Nelson 2009, p. 61). And since this definition "does not focus on individual rational choice, [it] can encompass social and economic institutions, real human psychology, and the actual unfolding of historical events" (Nelson 2009, p. 61). And, needless to say, the provisioning definition is amenable to sustainability, whereas the means–end definition with its gratuitous assertion of unlimited wants is not.

Suggestion Six: Introducing Students to the Circular Flow

Many of us teaching microeconomics introduce students to the circular flow diagram sometime during the first week. However, I postpone this until later in the course, during the unit on energy.[11] The notion of a circular flow reso-nates with students, with the emphasis on producing goods and services, using energy, generating waste, and affecting the natural environment in other ways. Here, I ask students to return to their delineated energy activities and diagram their own circular flow, emphasizing especially their energy usage, and their environmental waste. This also can be used for students to estimate their own carbon footprint, which for many students can be quite an eye-opener. In my energy unit, I give the example of late 19th-century America, when horses were the primary means of transportation within cities. A draft horse working in New York City required almost 30 000 calories daily of oats and hay, which in turn required four acres of good farmland per year per horse (Rhodes 2018). And on the other end, one working horse produced about one gallon of urine daily and 30–50 pounds of manure (Rhodes 2018), mostly dumped on city streets. I also use this opportunity to briefly discuss the unlimited capacity of human ingenuity in solving immediate problems of the day, especially in the context of energy.[12]

TOPIC TWO: SUPPLY AND DEMAND, ELASTICITY

These topics form the central tools of microeconomics and are amenable at several points to introducing the concept of sustainability.

Suggestion One: Identifying Sustainable and Unsustainable Goods/ Services

Go back to the student lists of energy activities compiled on day one, and have them identify the goods and services as normal, inferior, luxury, necessity, and so on. And whether they are sustainable or unsustainable. This exercise underscores the inherent difficulty in explicitly defining a practical and work-able definition of sustainability, and the importance of group listening and dialoguing to reach a consensus. Have student groups recommend ways to increase demand for sustainable goods/services and decrease the demand for unsustainable goods.

Suggestion Two: The Availability and Price of Substitute Goods in Decreasing the Demand for Fossil Fuels

If we are to meet our global target of ensuring that the Earth's temperature does not rise above the 1.5°C threshold, we must systematically transition away from fossil fuels and adopt a regime of renewable energy. One of the factors affecting both supply and demand (of any good) is the price and availability of substitutes. Here, cross-elasticities could be estimated given data presented in class, and thus the class can determine which energy sources are substitutes or complements, as well as the degree of responsiveness between different sources. This need not be detailed; for example, you can look at the cost of electricity per kilowatt hour for different sources such as coal, nuclear, solar, wind, and natural gas. Divide the class into groups, with each group focusing on one energy source. Have each group give a brief, yet balanced, presentation on the viability of their respective resource. In addition to fostering listening and dialogue—key to sustainability—this exercise segues nicely into dis-cussing the role for government in encouraging the production and use of the available substitutes to fossil fuels, and government's role in providing the basic infrastructure for substitutes to become viable.[13]

TOPIC THREE: TAXES, TRADE, TARIFFS

A primary role of the government is creating the right incentives for successful provisioning, while avoiding or minimizing disincentives. This objective is becoming increasingly important in order to keep global temperatures under the 1.5°C ceiling.

Suggestion One: Incorporating Lessons from the Collapse of Previous Societies

An important lesson from Jared Diamond's (2005) book *Collapse* is that even in the face of environmental collapse and destruction, there are several explanations for inaction/denial which can prevent the implementation of and even the need to adopt solutions. Even though Diamond discusses non-market societies, the lessons resonate for market societies: the role of power, elites, denial of impending disaster, and continuing obliviousness to the increasing disaster. Pick one society that Diamond discusses (say Easter Island, which is well known) and ask students to identify actions that could have been taken to prevent the collapse, and what type of government intervention would have been necessary. A tax, perhaps? And if such a situation were to occur today, how would we react?[14] This activity works well either to promote in-class discussion or as a homework assignment.

Suggestion Two: Externalities

All students can relate to the topic of externalities[15] because of their everyday experience living with their family or roommates. Public goods and externalities are becoming increasingly important on the road to sustainability. In class, have each student turn to their neighbor and exchange descriptions of a negative externality that they have been involved with, either as a perpetrator or a recipient, and the best way to solve it. This exercise allows the opportunity to scale beyond two individuals to a neighborhood, region, nation, and even between generations. As we scale up, voluntary negotiations (for example, the Coase theorem[16]) become less and less viable or practical as transaction costs increase. A good class exercise is to investigate the negative externalities of gasoline consumption, a product with which everyone is familiar, although the negative externalities resulting from gasoline go largely unrecognized.[17] I also have students read selections from Ronald Coase's (1960) article (the full article at 40 pages is a tad ponderous) to explore the concept of externalities. Coase discusses simple examples which students can easily understand, enabling the discussion to segue into more realistic externalities in situations that are inherently more complex. The resulting treatment of externalities is far more nuanced and honest than that in most economics texts. The goal of this analysis is not to make our students experts in welfare economics—after all, this is an introductory course—but merely to underscore the nuances in understanding and offering solutions.

Suggestion Three: Discuss a Tax on Carbon

Have students read the "Economists' Letter" (2019) published in the *Washington Post* that recommends a Pigouvian tax as the most effective instrument to quickly and efficiently arrest the progress of climate change. Is this the best instrument to nudge us away from unsustainable behavior? Of course, the government would not need to undertake this *ex post* action if society could internalize the necessary sustainable values so that sustainability becomes an automatic modus vivendi; but how is this to be done? The traditional theory of an imposition of a tax uses welfare economics to ascertain whether society is better off with or without a Pigouvian tax, and assumes both a redistribution and a distortion, that is, a deadweight loss). If we reduce the production and consumption of carbon—an unstainable product—then rather than a deadweight loss we have a societal gain. The neoclassical theory of taxation assumes that a tax will reduce output, thereby increasing deadweight loss. But if we reduce the production of a product that is instrumental in causing global warming, then this is a societal gain. This is a good opportunity to discuss the conceptual meaning of a deadweight loss and its relevance (or lack thereof) to a carbon tax, and who really benefits/loses from a carbon tax.

Suggestion Four: Have a Class Discussion on Goal #14 of the 17 UN SDGs, "Conserve and Sustainably Use the Ocean, Seas, and Marine Resources"

How does one conserve? How to use goods and services sustainably? Which is the appropriate unit of action: the individual, the firm, the region, the nation, or the world? Or a combination of all? For helpful active learning exercises in illustrating the sustainable use of common resources, see Lewis (2018) and Fisher (2019).

Suggestion Five: Trade

The current system of global trade, abetted by cheap fossil fuels, is both inefficient and unsustainable. While lower prices and a greater array of goods increase consumer surplus, they also decrease societal surplus due to negative effects of more global warming gases and more fossil fuel use. As a suggested exercise, sketch out a scenario in which carbon is priced; that is, a negative externality is internalized. Have students discuss how pricing carbon would affect trade (this exercise is a function of how much time is devoted to the topic). Specifically, add a carbon fee to imports from countries where carbon is not priced (for example, the European Union's proposed border carbon tax) and then estimate the reduction in quantity demanded due to the price increase.

Who benefits from such a fee? Are the societal benefits greater than the cost? What are the estimated elasticities of demand?[18]

TOPIC FOUR: THE FIRM

If we are to become sustainable, then the firm must play an increasingly important role. Given its centrality in a capitalist economy, the firm must be the key driver toward sustainability. But the unit on the firm in neoclassical texts is overly deductive and ahistorical, so after finishing the unit students have a good understanding of the logic of the firm, but little if any understanding about what actual firms do, never mind whether actual firms are sustainable.[19]

Suggestion One: Have Each Student Research a Particular Firm

I ask my students to research any firm of their choice, suggesting a firm that is close to their field of concentration, one for which they might want to work upon graduation. (Obviously, the bigger the firm, the more information is available.) What does this firm produce? How does it compete? Which are its rivals? Does this business offer anything on its web page about its commitment to sustainability?

Suggestion Two: Examine Gender Inequality

As a society, if we are to become sustainable, then Goal #5 of the 17 UN SDGs is critical: "Achieve gender equality and empower all women and girls." This is a powerfully evocative statement, and no explicit activities are needed beyond class discussion. And, based on my experience, the discussion can become quite visceral. What is gender equality? How does one go about achieving it? How to empower? What does gender equality really mean? Since we spend a lot of time at work, how can the firm effectuate gender equality? Is the firm the best instrument for promoting gender equality? (For additional ideas on how to consider gender issues in the Principles of Microeconomics course, see Joshi Rajkarnikar, Chapter 11 in this book.)

Suggestion Three: Get to Know the Largest Firms

Take a look at the largest 50[20] firms as listed in the Fortune 500. What do they produce? How large are they are? What industries do they operate in? On their web pages, what do they say about sustainability, if anything?

Suggestion Four: Assign the book *Cradle to Cradle: Remaking the Way We Make Things* (Braungart and McDonough 2009) for Students to Read During the Course

The book can be assigned as a semester-long journaling exercise. It is a short, easy read, peppered with provocative ideas on how technology can make firms more sustainable, and need not be incorporated directly into the lecture material, although I do so when I make the distinction between *ex ante* and *ex post* solutions to negative externalities. The authors suggest that instead of producing an automobile with zero emissions (still a long way away) why not produce an automobile with positive emissions that stores carbon and reuses water vapor? And make a running shoe that absorbs ground particulates. The secret is mimicking nature; in doing so, the firm becomes part of a living, breathing ecosystem and produces a product not for obsolescence, but which can be reused and circulated with the ecological system. Reading this book will stimulate interest in what firms do, and what they can do better.

TOPIC FIVE: THE CONSUMER

Central to any capitalist economic system is the consumer. In the United States, consumption accounts for 69 percent of gross domestic product. In order to construct a workable theory of sustainable consumption it is necessary that we understand exactly how the sustainable consumer consumes, and how such a consumer differs from the non-sustainable consumer commonly assumed in the neoclassical approach. And that we understand how the sustainable consumer interacts with the sustainable firm.

Suggestion One: Have a Class Discussion on Goal #12 of the 17 UN SDGs, "Ensure Sustainable Consumption and Production"

What is meant by sustainable consumption and production? Why the word "and"? How does one go about ensuring this? How would one go about implementing this? How does one go about differentiating unstainable from sustainable consumption? Once again, the goal is not to reach any resolution at this level, but to expose students to the nuances of debate, and to emphasize the critical role of dialogue, listening, and debate: central ingredients in becoming sustainable.

Suggestion Two: As a Class Engage in Meatless Mondays

Consuming and producing meat is unsustainable. It consumes an inordinate amount of land and energy, while contributing significantly to climate change, especially vis-à-vis a plant-based diet. Reducing meat consumption is an easy exercise that everyone can do. As a class exercise, invite students to consider a Meatless Monday (or Meatless Tuesdays if the class meets Tuesday to Thursday). And devote five minutes once a week to having a student group report on the world's major meat producers, where the meat is produced and consumed, and the effect of meat on sustainability. For helpful resources in learning about the history of Meatless Mondays and getting started, see Meatless Monday Global (2021), and the Monday Campaign (2021). Examining their meat consumption could be part and parcel of each student's estimation of their climate footprint.

CONCLUSION

Out for a recent early morning walk I was stunned at a huge red sun rising through thick smoke. A huge rising ball of fire impressed on me that nature reigns supreme, reminding me how precious life is, and how delicate the balance is here on Earth. If nature had ever given us a warning that she was tired, that she had reached her limits, it was now, amidst these so-called once-in-a-lifetime weather events that are happening with increasing frequency all over the globe. But we continue to ignore her, hoping for a return to normalcy, keeping an ever-present eye on the price of gasoline as if this was our only connection to the environment. Nature is sustainable; humankind is not.

The confluence of climate change and Covid-19 (sadly, a precursor of future viruses unless we radically change our way of living) is presenting our moment for change and action much sooner rather than later; it is "a rare opportunity to change course [which] we should make the most of" (Ord 2021, p. 93). Economists should engage in such work and dialogue as social scientists; for if, as Alfred Marshall wrote, "Political economy or economics is a study of mankind [*sic*] in the ordinary business of life" (Marshall 1890 [1946], p. 1), and if our ordinary business is changing, then so should the discipline of economics—or so one would think.

If we are to live sustainably, guided by the UN's 17 SDGs, or some other recipe, then we need a 21st-century pluralistic and sustainable economics, one that can guide the debate and help to inform policy-makers. We need to construct a sustainable theory and jettison the deadwood that has continued to clutter. For, as Jevons wrote, "the best works should ever be open to criticism [and] no body and no school nor clique must be allowed to set up a standard of orthodoxy which shall bar the freedom of scientific inquiry" (Jevons 1871 [1931], pp. 275, 276).

   This chapter offers active suggestions to instructors of microeconomics for incorporating sustainability. Doing so is one way to ensure that this course is "an intellectual adventure of the first order" (Frank 2012, p. 411).

NOTES

1. This prescription dovetails with Lovelock's Gaia hypothesis, whereby a complex and intricate relationship exists between "the Earth's biosphere, atmosphere, oceans, and soil; the totality constituting a feedback or cybernetic system which seeks an optimal physical and chemical environment for life on this planet" (Lovelock 1979 [2000], p. 10). Failing to abide by the 2°C prescription could irrevocably destroy this complex and intricate relationship.
2. For a discussion of the concept of sustainability, see Reardon et al. (2018, pp. 13–19). Also see Creative Change (2013, pp. 6–8) for a discussion of competing definitions.
3. For those instructors interested in a more long-term, radical approach to reconceptualizing the entire economics curriculum, see Reardon (2012).
4. For invaluable resources to effectuate this suggestion, see Buis (2018) and Carbon Brief (2021).
5. See Reardon et al. (2018, pp. xvi–xx) and Boyd and Reardon (2020, pp. 3–25) for a practical discussion of empowering/enabling with a sense of optimism/hope.
6. While many of feel obligated to spend the bulk of the opening day on the syllabus, Underwood (2020) makes a compelling case to jump right in and actively engage in the course subject. To do so sets the tone of active learning for the rest of the course, and increases class engagement and student interest.
7. For a listing and exposition of the SDGs see United Nations (2015). For an expanded discussion see Reardon et al. (2018, pp. 17–19).
8. For helpful hands-on advice see Andrews (2019).
9. I did a similar class project on suggestions to reduce the federal budget deficit, publishing in the *Minneapolis Star Tribune* (Reardon 2011)
10. For a discussion of pluralism, the arguments for and against, and its different levels of complexity, see Negru (2009), Reardon (2015, 2017, 2021), and Heise (2017).
11. Few textbooks offer a chapter on energy, perhaps forgetting that energy (and its production and distribution) is fundamental to economic activity and economic systems. I sandwich my energy lectures (one or two) between the chapters on public goods and externalities.
12. See Rhodes (2018) for a plethora of examples.
13. For example, one reason why the electric automobile lost out to the internal combustion engine during the automobile's infancy was the lack of a supporting infrastructure (Rhodes 2018, pp. 233–234). Today we are in a similar situation: while the supporting infrastructure for the internal combustion engine (run on gasoline) is ubiquitous, that of hydrogen and renewables is scarce to non-existent. Hence the need for investment.
14. A central theme of Diamond's *Collapse* is how vested interests use their power to protect the status quo. However, the use of power is largely absent from neoclassical texts, and is only discussed in the narrow context of monopoly/monopsony. For a helpful primer on power and its use, see Reardon et al. (2018, pp. 59–64).

15. Even the word "externality" is value-laden and troubling, suggesting that environmental damage should be subservient to production.
16. Coase's solutions are only applicable if three assumptions hold: absence of power, absence of transaction costs, and perfect information; assumptions that are seldom if ever met in the real world.
17. For a helpful prototype, see Harris and Roach (2018, pp. 44–46).
18. See United States Environmental Protection Agency (2021) for how to calculate a carbon footprint, and Treehugger (2021) to calculate an ecological footprint.
19. To understand how a firm can restructure to become sustainable, see Boyd and Reardon (2020, pp. 360–378).
20. There is nothing magical or compelling about this number; I have done it with the top ten.

REFERENCES

Andrews, T. (2019). Econ FilmMaking: An experiential, problem-based, multimedia project for Microeconomics. *International Journal of Pluralism and Economics Education 10*(3), 288–302.

Boyd, G., and Reardon, J. (2020). *Rebuild the economy, leadership, and you: A toolkit for builders of a better world.* Evolutesix.

Braungart, M., and McDonough, W. (2009). *Cradle to cradle: Remaking the way we make things.* Vintage Books.

Buis, A. (2018). A degree of concern: Why global temperatures matter. NASA's Global Climate Change Website. https://climate.nasa.gov/news/2865/a-degree-of-concern -why-global-temperatures-matter/. Accessed October 30, 2021.

Carbon Brief (2021). The impact of climate change at 1.5 C, 2 C, and beyond. https:// interactive.carbonbrief.org/impacts-climate-change-one-point-five-degrees-two -degrees/. Accessed October 31, 2021.

Coase, R. (1960). The problem of social cost. *Journal of Law and Economics 3*, 1–44.

Creative Change: Educational Solutions (2013). Educating for sustainability: A framework of essential knowledge, skills, and dispositions 30 2008–13. www .creativechange.net. Accessed July 31, 2021.

Dahl, A.L. (1996). *The Eco principle: Ecology and economics in symbiosis.* Zed Books.

Diamond, J. (2005). *Collapse: How societies choose to fail or succeed.* Penguin.

Economists' Letter (2019). This is not controversial: Bipartisan group of economists calls for carbon tax. *Washington Post*, January 17. https://www.washingtonpost .com/business/2019/01/17/this-is-not-controversial-bipartisan-group-economists -calls-carbon-tax/. Accessed February 1, 2019.

Fisher, W. (2019). Teaching the tragedy of open access: A classroom exercise on governing the commons. *International Journal of Pluralism and Economics Education 10*(3), 278–287.

Frank, R.H. (2012). Less is more: The perils of trying to cover too much in Microeconomics Principles. In G. Hoyt and K. McGoldrick (eds), *International handbook on teaching and learning economics* (pp. 403–412). Edward Elgar Publishing.

Harris, J.M., and Roach, B. (2018). *Environmental and natural resource economics: A contemporary approach* (4th edition). Routledge.

Heise, A. (2017). Defining economic pluralism: Ethical norm or scientific imperative? *International Journal of Pluralism and Economics Education 8*(1), 18–41.

Jevons, W.S. (1871 [1931]). *The theory of political economy.* Ibis Publishing.

Lewis, C. (2018). What the fishing boats have in common: A classroom experiment. *International Journal of Pluralism and Economics Education 9*(1–2), 192–203.

Lovelock, J. (1979 [2000]). *Gaia: A new look at life on earth.* Oxford University Press.

Marshall, A. (1890 [1946]). *Principles of Economics* (8th edition). Macmillan & Co.

Meatless Monday Global (2021). https://meatless-monday.hivebrite.com/#:~:text= The%20Meatless%20Monday%20Global%20Platform%20is%20a%20c. Accessed October 1, 2021.

Monday Campaign (2021). About Meatless Mondays. https://www.mondaycampaigns .org/meatless-monday/about. Accessed October 31, 2021.

Negru, I. (2009). Reflections on pluralism in economics. *International Journal of Pluralism and Economics Education 1*(1–2), 7–21.

Nelson, J. (2009). The Principles course. In J. Reardon (ed.), *The handbook for pluralist economics education* (pp. 57–68). Routledge.

Ord, T. (2021). We must heed the pandemic's warning. *The Economist*, special issue: The World in 2021, 93–94.

Reardon, J. (2011). Budget deficit reduction 101: Advice from college freshmen. *Minneapolis Star Tribune* June 1, p. A9.

Reardon, J. (2012). A radical reformation of economics education: Towards a new beginning. *Real-World Economics Review 62*(December), 2–19.

Reardon, J. (2015). Roundtable: Dialogue on pluralism. *International Journal of Pluralism and Economics Education 6*(3), 272–308.

Reardon, J. (2017). Editorial: When will economics become pluralist? *International Journal of Pluralism and Economics Education 8*(1), 7–13.

Reardon, J. (2021). Improving pluralism in economics education. In A. Hermann and S. Mouatt (eds), *Contemporary issues in heterodox economics: Implications for theory and policy action* (pp. 282–298). Routledge.

Reardon, J., and Madi, M. (2020). Suggestions for incorporating sustainability into the macroeconomics course. In S. Decker, W. Elsner and S. Flechtner (eds), *Principles and pluralist approaches in teaching economics* (pp. 152–168). Routledge.

Reardon, J., Madi, M., and Cato, M.S. (2018). *Introducing a New Economics.* Pluto Press.

Rhodes, R. (2018). *Energy: A human history.* Simon & Schuster.

Soderbaum, P. (2008) *Understanding sustainability in economics.* Earthscan.

Treehugger (2021). What is an ecological footprint? Definition and how to calculate it. https://www.treehugger.com/what-is-ecological-footprint-4580244. Accessed October 31, 2021.

Underwood, D.A. (2020). Welcome to Macroeconomics! *International Journal of Pluralism and Economics Education 11*(1), 96–106.

United Nations (2015). UN Sustainable Development Goals. https://sustaianbled evelopment.un.org?menu=1300.

United States Environmental Protection Agency (2021). Household carbon footprint calculator. https://www3.epa.gov/carbon-footprint-calculator/. Accessed October 31, 2021.

PART III

Inclusive teaching

9.   Promoting inclusivity in Principles of Microeconomics

Jennifer Imazeki

With its focus on individual choices and tradeoffs, and with potential for application to myriad public policy issues, the Principles of Microeconomics course can be integral for inviting students from a range of backgrounds into the discipline. However, the way it is taught in many institutions can instead turn students away from the discipline. Ensuring that it actually is inviting may require many economics instructors to re-imagine what and how they have been teaching in this foundational course.

My own college experience provides an illustration. I took my first economics course, which happened to be Microeconomics, because it was required for my intended major (International Relations). Although I liked the math part, I found very little appealing about the content, which I perceived as being all about business and completely unconnected to my interests in social issues and helping people. If I had not been required to take a second course (Macroeconomics), where I discovered that some economists study things such as income distributions and how poor countries develop, I likely would not have ended up an economics major. Even then, I somehow made it to my senior year before taking a class in Public Economics and discovering that economists also study things such as education, which is what led me to even consider graduate programs in economics.

While my story has a happy economics ending, there are many other students who would never have made it beyond that first Microeconomics course at all. When I began teaching economics myself, I was determined to offer a Microeconomics Principles course that reflects all the things I love about the field. I had to rearrange the chapters in the traditional textbook, and I selected my examples carefully, so that social issues were surfaced much earlier. When I began to learn more about the scholarship of teaching, and then became Director of my institution's Center for Teaching and Learning, I discovered that this approach is entirely consistent with the literature on attracting and retaining students like me (that is, non-white and female). And as I have continued to explore strategies for inclusive teaching in my current role supporting campus diversity efforts, I am even more convinced that the Microeconomics

Principles course lends itself well to many of those best practices. In this chapter I discuss why it is important for instructors to work intentionally to build inclusive Principles of Microeconomics classrooms, and provide some suggestions for how to go about that work.

CREATING AN INCLUSIVE CLASSROOM

What is an inclusive classroom? At the risk of stating the obvious, an inclusive classroom is one where all students feel included. So what does it mean for students to feel included? In a learning setting, feeling included generally means that students are not just able to learn and contribute, but they feel that their contributions are invited and valued. This requires that students feel safe, so when they speak up they know that they will be heard and respected.

Whether or not a student feels included in our classes matters not just for student learning in our one class, but for the larger picture of how students experience college overall. Numerous studies have documented the negative impact of a "marginalizing" course climate (that is, a classroom that is not inclusive), not only on cognitive development (Pascarella et al. 1997) and academic performance (Sandler and Hall 1986), but also on retention and graduation (Astin 1997; Seymour and Hewitt 1997).

Unfortunately, feeling included is not necessarily the default experience for all students. While some students will walk into their classes and feel included from the beginning, automatically, without any special action on the part of the instructor, many other students will not, and for reasons that may or may not be obvious. A classroom does not have to be blatantly hostile or exclusive to be "marginalizing"; the reasons why a given student feels excluded may be quite subtle and invisible to the instructor. This is why ensuring that our classroom is inclusive requires intentional thought and effort.

Identity Matters

One important reason why a student may not feel included right away is because they hold certain social identities that have historically been marginalized (Tajfel and Turner 1979). In general, people tend to become more aware of their own identities when those identities are different from others around them; for example, an American who only speaks English may never think about their nationality or their language skills until they travel to other countries where English is not the primary language (or, as was the case for the author, a native Californian may not even realize that "Californian" is an identity until moving to Wisconsin for graduate school). When one then comes across someone else who shares one's identity (for example, that American tourist encounters another American), there is a tendency to feel a sense of connection, enhanced by that shared difference.

In discussions of social identities, one may naturally think first of race and gender; this is particularly true in economics, given that the discipline (as with much of the academy in general) is predominantly white and male (Bayer and Rouse 2016). However, economists are also overwhelmingly straight, cis-gender, Christian, neurotypical, able-bodied, and not military-affiliated. And whatever one's upbringing might have been like, anyone teaching economics in a college classroom is highly educated, and will almost always present as educated and well-off to our students. Thus, for many students from histor-ically underrepresented backgrounds, walking into an economics classroom can be akin to that American tourist walking down a foreign street: they are not expecting to find someone with shared experiences. This does not necessarily mean that they will feel excluded, but the chances are higher that they will not automatically expect their instructor to understand them, or to welcome and value them.

WHAT DOES AN INCLUSIVE INTRODUCTORY MICROECONOMICS CLASSROOM LOOK LIKE?

So how does one go about creating an inclusive classroom? In many ways, inclusive teaching is simply good teaching, and good teaching is inclusive teaching; so following the guidance found in many of the pedagogy chapters of this volume, particularly promoting more interaction (Chapter 14) and making content more relevant (Chapters 5, 8, 10, 11, and 16), will help promote an inclusive environment as well. While there are many resources on inclusive pedagogy for instructors in any discipline (for example, see Oleson 2020; Center for New Designs in Learning and Scholarship, 2021; or your own institution's Center for Teaching and Learning), I want to focus here on three pillars of inclusive teaching that may be the most unfamiliar for those who have received traditional training in economics: being self-reflective, being identity-conscious, and being relational.

Be Self-Reflective

The first pillar of inclusive teaching is less about pedagogical or curricular strategies and more about one's mindset. By mindset, I mean the beliefs and expectations that we all hold, not only about our students but also about our-selves and our role as instructors. Whether we are aware of them or not, these beliefs influence the pedagogical choices that we make and, in turn, impact the experience students have in our classes. For example, Leslie et al. (2015) show that among economists, a higher than average share of faculty believe that success is a function of raw intellect (for example, higher levels of agreement with statements such as "Being a top scholar of [discipline] requires a special aptitude that just can't be taught"), and a lower than average share of doctoral degrees go to women and African Americans. Within courses, Canning at al. (2019) find much larger racial achievement gaps when faculty have a "fixed mindset," meaning that they believe ability and intelligence are fixed qualities, in contrast to a "growth mindset" that believes ability can be developed and nurtured.

These beliefs translate into expectations about how "good students" should act in our classrooms, what they should know before they walk into class, and what they should be doing outside of class to contribute to their own learning. Some of these expectations are explicit—things we outline in our syllabus, for example—but many are simply assumptions that we hold implicitly, and may not even be aware of. We also have beliefs about what we are "supposed to do" as instructors. For example, do you see your role as delivering and explaining content, or as guiding students to discover ideas? As judging students or supporting them? Is your Principles course a gatekeeper or a gateway?

Here are some general questions to consider:

- What do you believe students should look like? How should they dress, wear their hair? How should they talk? When should they talk?
- How should they act, with each other and with you?
- What should they know before your class begins? For Microeconomics Principles in particular, what prior exposure to math or economics are you expecting them to have?
- What is required for a student to succeed in your classes?
- What should students be doing outside of class?
- To what extent are your expectations embedded in your own experience (for example, what sort of student were you as an undergraduate), and how might your experience be different from that of your students?
- To what extent are your expectations connected to identities such as race, gender, sexual orientation, and so on (more about this in the "Be Identity-Conscious" section below)?

Whether we are aware of them or not, these beliefs influence virtually every aspect of our courses, manifesting in our course policies, our assignments, the examples we use, the topics we include, and our interactions with students. As you reflect on your answers to the questions above, consider how these beliefs influence how and what you teach. For example, when students first walk into your classroom, do you assume that they know how to manipulate the equation for a line, or that they have studied (and remember how to do) calculus? If so, the methods you use to teach basic supply and demand are likely to look quite different from those of an instructor who does not make these assumptions. Do you assume that your students always do the reading before class? If so, you may be more likely to jump straight into material that builds on that reading, rather than doing some review first. Do you assume that students who do not speak up in class are unprepared or uninterested? If so, you may interact differently with those students than if you assume that quiet students are shy, or intimidated by you.

As you think through how your assumptions influence your pedagogical choices, also consider what the repercussions are for students if they do not meet your assumptions. This can highlight where you may want to adjust, or to learn more about whether students actually do match your expectations. For example, there are many different ways to teach deadweight loss: from simply showing things graphically, to calculating algebraic equations, to using calculus. If you overestimate the math skills of your students, you may find that students who do, in fact, grasp the concept are unable to show you their knowledge because they struggle with the math. Using a different approach, or providing students with multiple ways to think about a concept, can make your class more inclusive for more students. You can also give students early assessments to gauge their math skills directly, and then provide extra support to those who need it (see the section below on being proactive).

Be Identity-Conscious

Another pillar of inclusive teaching is to be identity-conscious. This goes back to the identity discussion above, recognizing that identity matters, and taking proactive steps to invite students from a range of identities to engage with you and your course. Here are some specific strategies that you may want to consider.

Include topics that are likely to feel more relevant for marginalized groups
Bansak and Starr (2010) suggest that one explanation for the gender gap among economics majors may be that while women are more likely to be interested in learning about topics with a social dimension (for example, poverty, discrimination), they are less likely to believe that economics will be relevant and useful for them, and instead see economics as being about business and making money. Thus, a stronger emphasis on applied topics such as inequality, the environment, healthcare, education, and so on, can help students from historically underrepresented groups better understand that our field has much to contribute to social welfare and policy. Chapter 5 in this book discusses one approach that makes these issues the primary focus of the course. Another approach is to reconsider the order in which you discuss market failures, and/

or how much time you spend on different types of failures; that is, many Microeconomics courses spend a great deal of time on imperfect competition (monopoly, oligopoly, monopolistic competition), while public goods, externalities and imperfect information are relegated to the optional chapters (or rushed through at the end of the semester). Even without a direct focus, applications that are more interesting to a broader range of students can be incorporated through the problems and examples used for foundational concepts. For example, what markets do you use for examples of monopoly, oligopoly, and monopolistic competition? Who is most, and least, likely to be interested in those markets? While the Organization of the Petroleum Exporting Countries (OPEC) has long been the classic example of an oligopoly in introductory economics courses, most students are likely to be more engaged if you talk about the media or tech industries instead. You can also let students know that economics applies to a range of issues by explicitly sharing the source of external readings and materials; for example, the United States-based National Bureau of Economic Research (NBER) has many research summaries written at a level accessible to Principles students, and when you assign a reading from the NBER Retirement and Disability Research Center, or reports from the programs in Economics of Education or Children, you are indirectly letting students know that these are topics which economists study.

When possible, talk about current research being done by a diverse range of economists, and make their identities visible

No matter what your own identity might be, you can still show students that economics is "for them" by sharing the work of people who look like them (Bettinger and Long 2005). If you discuss the research of an economist from an underrepresented community, include their picture on the slide so that students can see who you are talking about. Use full author names, not just initials, in your reading lists so that students can see when authors are women. Unsure who is doing what? Subscribe to the newsletters and listservs for the Committee on the Status of Women in the Economics Profession, and the Committee on the Status of Minority Groups in the Economics Profession, so that you can receive information on the recent work of economists in these groups. Traore (2020), the Women in Economics podcast series from the Federal Reserve Bank of St Louis, Missouri (https://www.stlouisfed.org/timely-topics/women-in-economics), and the American Society of Hispanic Economists' (ASHE) Latinx Economists series (https://asheweb.org/past-latino-economists-highlights/), are also useful sources.

Analyze your materials to ensure that they are relevant and relatable to students from a wide range of backgrounds and cultures
Even if you do not change any of the topics you have been teaching, you can review the examples you use in lectures, the names and contexts you use in assignments and exam questions, and the images in your slides. If you typically use humor in your presentations, think about whether students from other cultures are likely to understand the jokes; this may be particularly important if you have international students in your classes who may not only be unfamiliar with American references, but also whose English skills may not be advanced enough to grasp the nuance that can be critical for some forms of humor.

Learn about your own implicit biases
Implicit bias is "the attitudes or stereotypes that affect our understanding, actions, and decisions in an implicit manner. Activated involuntarily, without awareness or intentional control. Can be either positive or negative. Everyone is susceptible" (Kirwan Institute 2016, p. 14). It is important to remember that everyone has implicit biases; they are a natural result of interacting in a social world. What matters is acknowledging our biases and recognizing how they may manifest in our actions so that we can disrupt them before they cause harm. Taking an implicit association test, available from Harvard's Project Implicit (https://implicit.harvard.edu/implicit/), is a good place to start. Going back to the questions in the "Be Self-Reflective" section above, many of the expectations we have—and the opinions we form of students when they do not meet those expectations—are based in our implicit biases, so a better understanding of our own biases can be an important tool for understanding and reflecting on those expectations and opinions.

Understand what microaggressions are and try to avoid committing them
A common way that implicit bias manifests in our interactions with others is in the form of microaggressions, which Sue et al. (2020) define as "brief and commonplace daily verbal, behavioral, or environmental indignities, whether intentional or unintentional, that communicate hostile, derogatory, or negative slights" because of a person's marginalized status in society. Women and people of color in economics experience microaggressions all the time (Daly 2018; Wu 2018; Bayer et al. 2020), but in addition to race and gender, microaggressions can be based on socio-economic status, sexual orientation, religion, and any number of other social identities. Some common microaggressions in education include assuming that Black students are athletes, or that Asian or Latinx students are not American; scheduling exams on Jewish holidays (assuming everyone is Christian); using the wrong names and pronouns for transgender students; asking a student from a particular social group

to speak for all members of that group; and calling on male students far more often than female students. See Sue et al. (2020) and University of Denver (2013) for additional examples; by learning more about common microaggressions, you can take steps to avoid committing them yourself (also see below, on planning ahead).

When microaggressions do happen, intervene
It is not uncommon for students to experience microaggressions coming from other students. This can be particularly problematic in online forums (such as discussion boards) and spaces where the instructor is absent (such as when students work in small groups or breakouts). As soon as you are aware of these sorts of incidents, it is important to respond in a way that reinforces your support for the targeted students. While this can be uncomfortable for many instructors, you have the advantage of being in an educational setting in the first place, and you can approach this as a learning opportunity (see Sue et al. 2020 for guidance). Intervening is also significantly easier if you have been proactive in establishing ground rules for the class and setting clear expectations about acceptable behavior (see the suggestions for creating community in the next section).

Plan ahead to manage potential issues
Many of the same strategies that can make your class more inclusive can also increase the potential for a well-intentioned instructor to inadvertently cause harm. For example, the earlier suggestion to ensure that your materials are relevant to students from diverse backgrounds can backfire if you rely on biased stereotypes to create your examples (for example, if you only include Latinx names in examples about tacos, that will not make your Latinx students feel included). And teaching applied topics such as inequality and discrimination can open the door for discussions that end up microaggressing students from particular communities. This is why being self-reflective and understanding your own biases are so important, as is getting to know your students. Recognizing where these challenges may arise will allow you to plan ahead. Consider asking trusted colleagues to review your content. Think ahead about how you will frame discussion of potentially controversial topics. And be prepared to be humble enough to apologize when you realize you have made a misstep.

Be Relational

A third pillar of inclusive teaching is to be relational; that is, remember that your students are fellow human beings who are looking for connection and positive relationships. While establishing supportive interpersonal relationships with students is one of the most fundamental tenets of effective teaching, it can be particularly important for students from traditionally underrepresented backgrounds.

Get to know your students

Many instructors ask students to fill out a form on, or prior to, the first day of class, gathering basic information (for example, preferred name and correct pronunciation, hometown, year in school, major/minor, participation in any activities that may impact attendance) as well as some personal information. The latter may include anything from favorite things (music, movies, and so on), hobbies or special interests, or postgraduation plans, to questions more specific to the course and their learning such as, "What are your expectations/ concerns for this class?" or "What can I do to help you succeed?" Given that many Microeconomics topics revolve around the individual consumer, students' responses to these questions can be particularly useful for tailoring content, such as examples used in lectures or the context for exam questions. Getting to know your students is also an important way to begin assessing whether the assumptions you make about them are justified (see the "Be Self-Reflective" section above).

Give students opportunities to share their perspectives and experiences

You can also get to know your students as part of the learning process itself, by creating assignments that invite students to connect course material to their own lives. For example, a common type of problem in a Principles of Microeconomics course is to give students a scenario and ask them to graph the impact on a specified market; for example, in American football, "Show how the Super Bowl win impacted the market for Los Angeles Ram jerseys." Such questions may or may not resonate with all of your students. An alternative that assesses the same knowledge and skills might ask students to come up with the scenario themselves; for example, "Select a good or service of your choice where you have noticed a change in price. Explain what might have caused that price change and show this using a supply and demand graph." Although grading such a question will likely take more time and effort, it also is likely to give you a better view of students' true level of understanding of concepts, and help students to see the relevance of concepts to their own lives, as well as give you insights about what markets students actually care about.

Let your students get to know you

Just as you need to get to know your students, so you should let them see that you are a human being too. Many students, no matter what their background, can view their professors as intimidating figures whose job is primarily to judge students. Sharing some of your own story can reduce that intimidation factor, to help students feel more comfortable in coming to you with questions. It can be particularly effective to share aspects of your own identity (to the extent that you feel comfortable doing so) that may not be immediately obvious, such as being part of any historically marginalized group, or overcoming adversity in your own educational journey. My students are often surprised to hear that I did not start out as an economics major, but switched, in part, because a professor told me I was not cut out to be an international relations major as I originally planned. Sharing that story not only allows me to explain to them why I fell in love with economics, but gives them a glimpse of me as a relatable human being who was not always a straight-A student.

Build community within the class

Everything that an instructor does to create an inclusive classroom can be undermined by students who mistreat their classmates, so it is important to engage the whole class in co-creating a welcoming learning environment. Take some time on the first day of class to establish ground rules: that is, a community agreement about how students and the instructor will treat one another; see University of Michigan's *Guidelines for Classroom Interactions* (https://crlt. umich.edu/examples-discussion-guidelines) for resources and suggestions. Establishing this agreement serves two important purposes: most directly, you will have a list of behaviors that you can remind students of whenever needed, plus you will indirectly signal to students that you care about (and intend to enforce) having a classroom where everyone can feel comfortable participating.

Use the syllabus to signal your values

Your syllabus is often the first introduction students have to you and your course, and is an opportunity to set a positive tone for everything that follows. Including a diversity and inclusion statement can be an important signal of your commitment to supporting all of your students; see San Diego State's guide on *Diversity and Inclusion Statements* (https://sacd.sdsu.edu/cie/cie -resources/syllabus-statements) for resources and suggestions. Beyond an inclusion statement, you should consider the overall tone of the syllabus and consider how students will feel about you as they read it. Is your syllabus an invitation or a contract? Does it focus on opportunities to learn, or policies and punishments? As discussed in Palmer et al. (2014), a learner-centered syllabus is one where the tone is positive and inviting, addressing the student as a competent, engaged learner. One very simple change that can make a big difference is in the choice of personal pronouns; that is, by using first or second person (I, you, we, us) language; rather than using third-person language (the course, the students). Another simple change is to present your course schedule as questions that pique interest rather than just a list of topics; for example,

"Why does the price of gas go up in the summer?" instead of "Supply and Demand," or "Do offers to match competitors' prices mean you actually pay less?" instead of "Monopolistic Competition."

Be proactive in offering support

There are myriad reasons why students are reluctant to ask for help, but there are several ways in which you can make it easier for them. Pay attention to early warning signs that students may be struggling, and reach out proactively. Have they missed class or assignments without any indication to you about why? Are they logging into the learning management system regularly? Did they fail the first midterm exam? Consider sending a short note that lets them know you have noticed, and encourages them to come see you, or lets them know where to find additional resources, such as tutoring services, your institution's learning center, help sheets you have put on the course site, and so on. Of course, intervening early may require making changes that allow you to see those warning signs in the first place. If you typically have only a few big high-stakes assessments (for example, a couple of mid-term assessments and a final), consider breaking those up into smaller, more frequent quizzes or in-class "clicker" questions (see Salemi 2009).

CONCLUSION

Creating a classroom where all students feel welcome, safe to participate, and supported in their learning, requires intentional effort and reflection on the part of the instructor. For economics instructors, this intentionality may be particularly important, given that economics can sometimes be seen as a discipline dominated by privileged groups, valuing self-interest and innate intelligence over social consciousness and development. However, the Microeconomics Principles course offers a special opportunity to show students with diverse backgrounds, identities, and beliefs that economics is relevant for all of us. While some students will walk into Principles of Microeconomics simply because it fulfills a graduation requirement, there is the potential for this to be the course that causes them to change majors and puts them on a path to eventually teach the class themselves. If we want to put more students on that path, particularly students who are currently underrepresented in the discipline, we must make sure that what and how we teach is welcoming and supportive for all students.

REFERENCES

Astin, A.W. (1997). *What matters in college?* Jossey-Bass.

Bansak, C., and Starr, M. (2010). Gender differences in predispositions towards economics. *Eastern Economic Journal 36*(1), 33–57.

Bayer, A., Hoover, G.A., and Washington, E. (2020). How you can work to increase the presence and improve the experience of Black, Latinx, and Native American people in the economics profession. *Journal of Economic Perspectives 34*(3), 193–219.

Bayer, A., and Rouse, C.E. (2016). Diversity in the economics profession: A new attack on an old problem. *Journal of Economic Perspectives 30*(4), 221–242.

Bettinger, E.P., and Long, B.T. (2005). Do faculty serve as role models? The impact of instructor gender on female students. *American Economic Review 95*(2), 152–157.

Canning, E.A., Muenks, K., Green, D.J., and Murphy, M.C. (2019). STEM faculty who believe ability is fixed have larger racial achievement gaps and inspire less student motivation in their classes. *Science Advances 5*(2), eaau4734.

Center for New Designs in Learning and Scholarship (2021). *Inclusive pedagogy toolkit*. Retrieved from https://cndls.georgetown.edu/inclusive-pedagogy/ip-toolkit/introduction/.

Daly, M.C. (2018). Getting from diversity to inclusion in economics. *FRBSF Economic Letter 2018*, 15.

Kirwan Institute (2016). *State of the science: Implicit bias review.* Retrieved from https://kirwaninstitute.osu.edu/research/2016-state-science-implicit-bias-review.

Leslie, S.J., Cimpian, A., Meyer, M., and Freeland, E. (2015). Expectations of brilliance underlie gender distributions across academic disciplines. *Science 347*(6219), 262–265.

Oleson, K.C. (2020). *Promoting inclusive classroom dynamics in higher education: A research-based pedagogical guide for faculty*. Stylus Publishing.

Palmer, M.S., Bach, D.J., and Streifer, A.C. (2014). Measuring the promise: A learning-focused syllabus rubric. *To Improve the Academy: A Journal of Educational Development 33*(1), 14–36.

Pascarella, E.T., Whitt, E.J., Edison, M.I., Nora, A., Hagedorn, L.S., et al. (1997). Women's perceptions of a "chilly climate" and their cognitive outcomes during the first year of college. *Journal of College Student Development 38*, 109–124.

Salemi, M.K. (2009). Clickenomics: Using a classroom response system to increase student engagement in a large-enrollment principles of economics course. *Journal of Economic Education 40*(4), 385–404.

Sandler, B.R., and Hall, R.M. (1986). The campus climate revisited: Chilly for women faculty, administrators, and graduate students. Retrieved from https://files.eric.ed.gov/fulltext/ED282462.pdf.

Seymour, E., and Hewitt, N.M. (1997). *Talking about leaving*. Westview Press.

Sue, D.W., Calle, C.Z., Mendez, N., Alsaidi, S., and Glaeser, E. (2020). *Microintervention strategies: What you can do to disarm and dismantle individual and systemic racism and bias*. John Wiley & Sons.

Tajfel, H., and Turner, J.C. (1979). An integrative theory of intergroup conflict. In W.G. Austin and S. Worchel (eds), *The social psychology of intergroup relations* (pp. 33–37). Brooks/Cole.

Traore, F. (2020). 19 Black economists to celebrate and know, this Juneteenth and beyond. *Fortune.* Retrieved from https://fortune.com/2020/06/19/black-economists-fixing-systemic-racism-juneteenth/.

University of Denver Center for Multicultural Excellence (2013). *Microaggressions in the classroom*. Retrieved from http://otl.du.edu/wp-content/uploads/2013/03/MicroAggressionsInClassroom-DUCME.pdf.

Wu, A.H. (2018, May). Gendered language on the economics job market rumors forum. *AEA Papers and Proceedings 108*, 175–179.

10. Creating an anti-racist pedagogy in Principles of Microeconomics

Mary J. Lopez and Fernando Lozano

INTRODUCTION

The marginalization of women and historically underrepresented racial/ethnic groups in the economics profession is a significant concern. The diversity problem of economics stems partly from the discipline's inability to be relevant and relatable to students from diverse backgrounds. For many students, Introductory Microeconomics is their first contact with the discipline. In the leading Principles of Microeconomics textbooks, students are introduced to the discipline with some version of Lionel Robbins's definition of economics as "the distribution of scarce resources" (Backhouse and Medema 2009). With this definition of economics, which is now considered self-evident, an Introductory Microeconomics course will follow a conversation of "normative" versus "positive" approaches to science. From the first moment we are in the classroom, we frame economics as a field that encompasses society's most important choices under a veil of scientific rigor and unbiasedness. Students then segue to a discussion of the utility or profit maximization paradigm. In the first weeks of a Principles of Microeconomics course, little is mentioned about economic inequality, discrimination, hegemonic violence, or racism; issues that are salient to the personal histories of marginalized students. As the course progresses into demand theory (consumer preferences, rationality, budget sets) and supply theory (firm theory), the emphasis is on the efficiency of markets and competitive equilibria. However, taking students down a long road of profit maximization and well-functioning markets where violence, racism, or exploitation often play no role is often at odds with the world that marginalized students experience.[1] By the time students reach the often inadequate coverage of labor market discrimination, many will have already decided whether or not the discipline is relevant and relatable. It is not surprising that first-generation, low-income students, students of color, women, and students who identify with a non-binary gender, may feel alienated and unable to identify with economics.

The data certainly suggest that the failure of introductory economics courses to represent the personal histories of marginalized students may be discouraging them from pursuing degrees in the discipline. Since 1995, the percentage of bachelor's degrees awarded in economics to African American, American Indian, and women students has declined. According to the American Economic Association's (AEA) recent report of the Committee on the Status of Minority Groups in the Economics Profession (CSMGEP), only 5.16 percent of undergraduate degrees in economics were awarded to Black or African American students in 2018–2019, 12.14 percent of degrees were awarded to Hispanic students, and only 0.2 percent of degrees were awarded to American Indian students.[2] The greatest underrepresentation occurs among women from underrepresented racial/ethnic groups, with white male undergraduate students majoring in economics at roughly five times the rate of women from underrepresented racial/ethnic groups (Bayer and Wilcox 2019).[3] STEM (science, technology, engineering, mathematics) fields such as chemistry, mathematics, statistics, and engineering, have seen larger increases in majors from historically underrepresented groups over the past decade than economics (Avilova and Goldin 2018; Bayer and Rouse 2016). The lack of diversity at the undergraduate level carries forward to the graduate level. During the 2018–2019 academic year, 1225 PhDs were granted in economics, of which 13 were awarded to African Americans, 27 to Hispanics, and none were awarded to American Indians.[4]

There are several benefits to increasing diversity in the economics profession. First, research shows that diversity among individuals who work together can lead to higher-quality outcomes (Bayer and Rouse 2016). Applied to a classroom setting, diversity has the potential to improve the academic success of all students. Second, economists have an opportunity to influence the policy process. A more diverse profession broadens the range of problems and proposed solutions that are deemed important to society (Bayer and Rouse 2016; Bayer and Wilcox 2019). If the profession explores issues that are relevant for society, this can also lead to further diversity within the discipline. Finally, diversity is a step toward addressing the systemic disadvantages that marginalized students have experienced in gaining access to resources and opportunities in the field.

Textbooks often provide students with the most salient image of the field, and there have been some encouraging additions to the catalogue available to microeconomics instructors. Cassidy (2017) argues that the discipline needs to rethink how it teaches economics. Using CORE's (Curriculum Open-Access Resources in Economics) (see Chapter 4 in this book) free, online textbook as an example, Cassidy suggests that while traditional economics courses emphasize principles such as "trade makes everyone better off" or "markets are usually a good way to organize economic activity," CORE frames economics as "perfect competition is a special case and not the norm" and addresses topics that are of greater interest and relevance to students, such as distribution and fairness, justice, and exploitation. Betsey Stevenson and Justin Wolfers's (2020) *Principles of Economics* textbook also attempts to make introductory economics more relevant to the lives of students, particularly those from diverse backgrounds. The authors include topics that are of interest to a diverse group of students, such as economic inequality, climate change, social costs of unemployment, and implicit bias. Both books reference a diverse set of names, individuals, and examples that avoid stereotypes and reduce implicit bias. Although both textbooks are a good starting point in making economics more relevant and relatable, we argue that the best way to make economics more inclusive and representative of the personal histories of marginalized students is for introductory economics instructors to engage in anti-racist pedagogies. Not only is an anti-racist pedagogy necessary to create a more diverse profession, it is essential if we want to develop a more informed profession.

In this chapter we illustrate what an anti-racist pedagogy might resemble in a Principles of Microeconomics course. We begin with a discussion of the three different elements that embody an anti-racist pedagogy, and then discuss the ways in which instructors can adjust course content to make it more relevant and relatable to marginalized students. We provide examples of how instructors can expand the narrative of discrimination, from one that emphasizes the elimination of discrimination via well-functioning markets, to one that emphasizes the role that race and racism play in creating and maintaining economic inequality. We also illustrate how instructors can include new topics such as the racial wealth gap to explore how historical and contemporary structures preserve privilege for some groups. Finally, we discuss the importance of exposing students to alternative fields within economics so they are aware that alternative paradigms exist that may provide better context for their personal histories.

AN ANTI-RACIST PEDAGOGY IN ECONOMICS

What constitutes an anti-racist pedagogy in economics? There are three basic elements that embody an antiracist pedagogy. First, instructors should set clear and equitable rules so that all students can thrive on the course. Second, instructors should implement strategies that can reduce differences in student achievement and attainment. Finally, instructors should adjust course content so that it aligns with students' interests, backgrounds, and personal histories. The first two focus more on how we teach, and the third, which is the focus of this chapter, addresses what we teach.

Implementing an anti-racist pedagogy begins with self-awareness and reflection on the part of the instructor. It is not possible to begin to establish a set of clear and equitable rules for the course unless instructors first examine the assumptions they have about their students' interests, motivations, and abilities, and the role that the instructor plays in helping students thrive. In reflecting on their assumptions, it is important for instructors to acknowledge the position of privilege which they occupy in the classroom, as well as to understand how students' academic experiences are shaped by their lived experiences. Identifying the unique attributes of students and gaining a better understanding of who they are will allow instructors to mitigate their own biases and think more deeply about their role as an instructor and their expectations for students. Jennifer Imazeki (Chapter 9 in this book) provides a deeper discussion of the importance of instructor self-awareness and reflection in creating an inclusive learning environment.

The course syllabus, which outlines the rules, policies, expectations, and objectives that govern the course, is an indicator of the instructor's commitment to creating an inclusive learning environment where all students have an equal opportunity to succeed. Upon examining our own assumptions and expectations of students, instructors will be in a better position to develop the course syllabus. Taylor et al. (2019) provide an excellent toolkit for creating an inclusive and equitable syllabus. The syllabus should provide concise rules for equitable grading, rationale for the high expectations you have for your students and the ways in which you will support them, and guidelines for creating inclusive and safe class discussions (for example, outlining the ways in which hostility and exclusion will be addressed). It should also provide detailed course objectives that emphasize growth in learning—as opposed to outcomes or content—and that are achievable by all students in the class (Taylor et al. 2019). If the course is challenging, the syllabus should validate feelings of anxiety that students may have about the course, and reference academic resources provided by the instructor and the institution to ensure academic success (Taylor et al. 2019). It is also important to use language which conveys to students that they are active participants in knowledge generation and that power within the course does not reside with the instructor (Taylor et al. 2019). Instructors can also implement these strategies in their assignments. For example, instructors should provide clear and detailed instructions, list any challenges that students might expect to encounter with the assignment, and provide guidance for where students can seek help. Instead of emphasizing deadlines and penalties for late submissions, instructors should emphasize the rationale for assignments, the ways in which assignments build upon or connect with each other, and the ways in which assignments or exams promote growth mindset versus fixed mindset (Taylor et al. 2019). Assignments should include questions that guide student critical thinking and allow students to connect course content to their own experiences (Kishimoto 2018). Finally, students should also be provided with rubrics or other criteria for grading before assignments are due, to ensure that all students have an equal opportunity to succeed.

An anti-racist pedagogy can be expanded with strategies to reduce racial and gender differences in achievement and attainment. Students enrolled in introductory economics courses should have an equal opportunity to complete and do well in the course. Instructors can attenuate racial and gender disparities in achievement and attainment by reducing stereotype threat and impostor syndrome. Stereotype threat refers to the way in which performance is inhibited by negative stereotypes about the cognitive abilities of a group that an individual identifies with (Aronson et al. 2002).[5] Lower academic achievement and attainment among marginalized students is often mistakenly attributed to weaker academic backgrounds or preparation. However, stereotype threat causes marginalized students to underperform relative to their capabilities because of the pressure of not wanting to conform to stereotypes (Darity and Aja 2014).[6] Failure to understand the role that stereotype threat plays in achievement and attainment may result in instructors discouraging marginalized students from pursuing economics, because they believe that they are not academically prepared to do so. One strategy to address stereotype threat is to employ an assets-based approach to student learning. An assets-based approach involves validating marginalized students' identities, skills, and experiences (Rendón 2014). To accomplish this, instructors can create spaces and assignments that allow students to share and connect their personal histories or experiences, with the goals of helping students to see that they have the ability to succeed and bring value to the classroom. Instructors can also provide students with a variety of learning pathways where their potential can be fully realized even when course expectations are high. Impostor syndrome can also cause marginalized students to doubt whether they should be taking an introductory economics course or majoring in economics, even when they are performing well in the course or the major. One way to address impostor syndrome is to create a strong sense of community among those studying economics. This can be accomplished in the classroom with group activities and guest speakers or outside of the classroom with economics student associations.[7] Bayer et al. (2019) find evidence that a greater sense of belonging is associated with enhanced student performance in introductory economics classes, and greater likelihood that students will pursue economics as a major.

The final element of an antiracist pedagogy in Introductory Microeconomics is to develop a curriculum that speaks to the personal histories of marginalized students. Bayer et al. (2020) show that when students perceive economics course material to be relatable and relevant to their own lives, they develop greater interest and perform better in the discipline. In the next section, we provide instructors with several examples of how to modify existing topics covered in Introductory Microeconomics, as well as incorporate new topics and fields to make economics more relevant and relatable for marginalized students. Specifically, we argue that breaking the profession's silence on race and racism is a meaningful and necessary way to make the discipline more relevant.[8]

INCORPORATING RACE AND RACISM INTO PRINCIPLES OF MICROECONOMICS

The economics profession's silence on race and racism is evident in the absence of any meaningful discussion of the topic in the leading introductory economics textbooks (Koechlin 2019). When race inches its way into the narrative—usually via discussions of labor market discrimination—bestselling textbooks such as Gregory Mankiw's *Principles of Microeconomics* teach students that profit motive is the "natural antidote" to employer discrimination (Mankiw 2020, p. 393) and that "business owners are usually more interested in making profits than in discriminating against a particular group" (Mankiw 2020, p. 391). Koechlin (2019) states that the narrative used in the leading introductory economics textbooks leaves students with an understanding that profit motive and well-functioning markets eliminate discrimination, and that intergroup disparities are the result of differences in productivity driven by individual choices and behavior. In addition, Bayer (2018) shows that just 1 percent of economics journal articles mention the word "racism." Such a narrative may leave students to infer that race, racism, and discrimination are not important topics in economics. In addition, students who have experienced or witnessed racial discrimination may be unable to make a connection between economics and their own lives.

For economics to be relevant and relatable, the discipline needs to acknowledge the existence and persistence of racial discrimination in equilibrium, the ways in which historical and contemporary discriminatory policies and institutional practices contribute to racial inequality, and the structural factors that preserve the economic and social status of dominant groups. Yet, expanding the narrative is not an easy feat. There is no low-cost way to incorporate race and racism into a Principles of Economics course, and the strategies outlined below require instructors to rely on a significant number of resources outside the teaching materials associated with leading introductory economics textbooks. However, as explained in the previous section, failure to implement an anti-racist pedagogy in economics has significant implications for the diversity of the field.

Demonstrate and Contextualize the Persistence of Racial Disparities in Economic Outcomes

Most introductory textbooks rarely display economic outcomes by race. When racial disparities are shown, the data are typically displayed for the most recent year only and exclude any discussion of the factors driving the disparity. Mankiw's introductory textbook shows poverty rates by race and ethnicity for 2017, but only mentions that "Poverty is correlated with race. Blacks and Hispanics are more than twice as likely to live in poverty as whites" (Mankiw 2020, p. 401). Failure to contextualize racial disparities leaves the door open for students to infer that Blacks and Hispanics are poorer than whites because of individual choices or deficiencies unique to people of color, and not because of historical and contemporary racism. Instructors can expand the narrative of how race and racism determine economic outcomes by using the following strategy.

First, instructors can use data from the Federal Reserve Economic Data (FRED), the United States (US) Census Bureau Historical Tables, or the Economic Policy Institute's (EPI) State of Working America Data Library to display racial disparities in economic outcomes over time. All three sources provide up-to-date, historical data on several economic outcomes by race, and have easy-to-use platforms for downloading and displaying data. Racial differences in education, income, wages, unemployment, and poverty can be incorporated into chapters covering earnings, income inequality and poverty, human capital, economic mobility, or the labor market. Historical data allow students to observe how racial disparities in economic outcomes remain largely unchanged or widen over time. For example, instructors can illustrate how the median income gap between Black and white households has changed very little since the 1960s.[9] Or, instructors can show that even during years when unemployment was at its lowest, Black workers were more likely to be unemployed than white workers.[10] Historical data also allow students to observe the cumulative disadvantage that has impacted the economic position of Blacks and Hispanics. Presenting the data in this manner is a first step to prepare students to discuss the structural sources of racial economic inequality and the historical and contemporary advantages that have been afforded to whites.[11]

Second, when displaying historical data on racial disparities in economic outcomes, it is important to demonstrate that factors associated with individual productivity, such as education, are not the main drivers of racial economic inequality. Many racial disparities persist and, in some instances, worsen among those with college degrees (Hamilton et al. 2021; Darity et al. 2018). Instructors can use data from the EPI's State of Working America Data Library to illustrate how Black workers are more likely to be unemployed and have lower wages than white workers at every level of educational attainment. A unique feature of the EPI's data library is that it also provides data for both the unadjusted and regression-adjusted racial wage gap, which allows students to observe how much less Black workers earn on average relative to white workers, holding gender, ethnicity, education, age, and geographic division constant. Observing racial disparities across all levels of degree attainment will allow students to begin to understand that the economic returns to education are not the same for all groups (Hamilton 2017). That is, although education is important, it is not sufficient to eliminate racial economic inequality (Hamilton and Darity 2017).[12] It is also important for students to understand that cultural factors are not a driving force behind racial disparities in economic outcomes. For example, lower educational attainment among Blacks and Hispanics is not due to a culture where parents and students of color devalue education. In fact, Nam et al. (2015) find that Black parents with limited resources show greater support for their children's education than white parents.

The third and final step is for instructors to contextualize racial disparities in economic outcomes. The most meaningful way for instructors to do this is to expose students to articles from economists who have placed racial disparities in their historical and structural contexts. Students could read and discuss articles that address the following topics: (1) the impact of historical racial animus on racial disparities in labor market outcomes and voting behavior (Williams 2021, 2022; Williams et al. 2021); (2) the relationship between racial violence and racial residential segregation (Cook et al. 2018); (3) the extent to which racial segregation diminishes upward economic mobility (Derenoncourt 2022; Andrews et al. 2017);[13] (4) race-neutral programs aimed at eliminating racial inequality (Darity and Hamilton 2012); (5) the relationship between violence and African American patents (Cook 2014);[14] (6) the impact of discrimination on Asian entrepreneurship (Amuedo-Dorantes et al. 2021); (7) the contemporary and historical ways in which institutions, policies, and practices have devalued the lives of people of color (Darity and Mullen 2020; Cook and Logan 2020);[15] and (8) the case for economic reparations (Darity and Mullen 2020).[16]

Adding the Racial Wealth Gap to the Curriculum

Studying the racial wealth gap is one of the most direct ways for students to begin to understand the role that race and racism play in determining economic outcomes. However, few leading Introductory Microeconomics textbooks include coverage of the topic. Instructors can expand the narrative by adding the racial wage gap to the introductory curriculum. For instructors who are concerned about time constraints, one option to free up space is to follow the approach found in the CORE and Stevenson and Wolfers texts which examine market structure by means of a general model of the firm's price and output strategies, as opposed to separate units for perfect competition, monopoly, oligopoly, and monopolistic competition. Alternatively, instructors could find ways to minimize coverage of cost curves or calculation of the price elasticity of demand.

First, instructors can begin with a discussion of how income differs from wealth and the importance of wealth for economic mobility. Wealth allows families to make investments in their health, homes, and education without having to accumulate new debt; opens pathways for entrepreneurship; provides financial reserves during illness or job loss; allows families to relocate to different neighborhoods; generates political and social power; and makes it easier to navigate the criminal justice system.[17] Emphasizing the intergenerational transmission of wealth is also important. Wealth provides support, opportunity, and the ability to create more wealth for future generations through inheritances, gifts, down-payments for homes, or tuition support. However, people of color have been largely excluded from intergenerational transfers of wealth because structural factors have denied or made it challenging for them to access capital (Hamilton and Darity 2017).

Second, instructors can present historical data on wealth by race using the Federal Reserve's Survey of Consumer Finance. The Interactive Chartbook linked to the Fed survey data allows instructors to create tables or graphs that display racial differences in wealth dating back to 1989. It is also important for instructors to emphasize that the racial wealth gap exists at all levels of educational attainment, at all levels of employment (full-time, out of the labor force, unemployed), and across income quintiles (Darity et al. 2018).[18] Black households where the head of the household graduated from college have less wealth than white households where the head of the household dropped out (Hamilton 2020).

Third, once students have examined the empirical evidence on the persistent and extreme nature of the racial wealth gap, they can segue to a discussion of the underlying causes of the racial wealth gap. It is important to steer students away from a narrative that attributes wealth accumulation only to savings, savings behavior, or financial knowledge. Wealth is also acquired through intergenerational transfers, such as inheritances or family support for tuition and housing. Instructors can present Williams's (2017) wealth privilege model, which explains how current wealth and racial status determine opportunities for wealth accumulation. Wealth functions as a source of power for its owners through an ever-growing expansion of choices and opportunities, and as a result can preserve and widen the racial wealth gap. According to Williams (2017), structural factors such as the United States' racialized history and its contemporary discrimination generate wealth privilege for dominant groups, and that privilege is maintained as wealth grows over time (through returns to assets owned) and across generations (through family inheritances and support). Instructors might also find it useful to reference redlining in the discussion of the racial wealth gap. The Federal Reserve Bank of St Louis has an excellent teaching tool for redlining which includes a detailed lesson plan that incorporates FRED data. Instructors might also want to supplement coverage of the income tax system with a discussion of the ways in which tax policies exacerbate racial wealth inequalities. The Urban Institute has a feature where students can examine how the federal income tax code promotes existing racial inequality.[19] Finally, instructors can engage students in a conversation on ways to eliminate the racial wealth gap (Darity et al. 2018).

Exposing Students to Alternative Fields in Economics

The most meaningful way for instructors to expand the narrative of race and racism in Principles of Microeconomics courses is by exposing students to alternative fields in economics. Introductory economics textbooks are dominated by the mainstream narrative. However, Koechlin (2019) argues that the narrative emphasizes education, productivity, and choices as the main determinants of income/wages, and not historical and contemporary racism. Furthermore, race only becomes part of the narrative through our ability to prove that discrimination exists in the labor market. As a result, the discussion centers mainly on measurement issues, and on identifying which actors (employers, customers, or employees) are responsible for the discrimination. However, if we are aiming for a meaningful discussion of the roles that race and racism play in determining economic outcomes and opportunity, then we will need to move outside the mainstream narrative.

Instructors can begin by introducing students to stratification economics (SE). Incorporating theories from economics, sociology, and social psychology, SE provides a framework for understanding how relative group position creates and maintains racial disparities in economic outcomes (Darity et al. 2017; Hamilton and Darity 2017; Darity 2022). For example, mainstream theory assumes that discriminators act independently of others. However, Darity et al. (2017, p. 50) argue that discriminators act as members of a group with "a common interest in preserving or extending the relative status of the group," especially when their relative position is threatened by another group. Thus, for members of the dominant group, engaging in discriminatory actions to preserve their relative status in the social or economic hierarchy is both a rational and a functional strategy (Darity et al. 2017; Hamilton 2020).[20] In other words, in the process of establishing or maintaining relative status, the dominant group sets the basis for how other groups will be treated (Darity et al. 2017).[21] The idea that discrimination is both rational and functional is the reason why it can persist, which is contrary to what mainstream economics predicts.[22]

In the field of SE, the social hierarchy determines the functioning of the economy (Davis 2019). As groups engage in efforts to maintain their social and economic statuses, the economy moves toward an equilibrium of unequal outcomes (Davis 2019). To illustrate further, SE provides a highly relevant framework for understanding the racial wealth gap. The racial wealth gap is not due to poor financial choices or saving behavior among persons of color, but rather due to structural factors that determine the initial endowment of wealth and the intergenerational transfer of wealth, which allows the dominant group to maintain its status in the distribution of wealth (Darity 2005; Hamilton and Darity 2017). Efforts to improve education, financial literacy, or even entrepreneurship will not be enough to close the racial wealth gap. Hamilton and Darity (2017) argue that policies that address "the long-standing consequences of slavery, the Jim Crow years that followed, and ongoing racism and discrimination that exist in our society today" can eliminate the racial wealth gap.

One additional field that instructors can draw on to create a more expansive narrative is feminist economics (FE). FE takes an intersectional approach to the labor market. An intersectional approach examines the interconnectedness of race, gender, identity, and/or class in creating unique labor market experiences (Brown and Misra 2003; Brewer et al. 2002). Instructors can use intersectionality to discuss the various identities that individuals have such as Latinx women and lesbian, gay, bisexual, transgender and queer (LGBTQ) people of color.[23] For individuals who have multiple identities, the sum of the components of discrimination may not always equal the total amount of discrimination. Kim (2009) and Paul et al. (2018) find that the total earnings penalty for Black women (relative to white men) is greater than the sum of discrimination on account of separate gender and race components. In other words, discrimination is not additive, but unique to an individual's multiple identities. The EPI's State of Working America Data Library allows instructors to easily complement their discussions of intersectionality and discrimination with data on several economic outcomes by race and gender.

CONCLUSION

The contributions of the economics profession to society rest on the profession's ability to be more inclusive. This chapter has argued that to create a more diverse and inclusive discipline, anti-racist pedagogies should be adopted in economics courses, particularly at the Principles of Microeconomics level, which is often students' first exposure with the discipline. We highlighted the importance of making economics more relevant and relatable to students who have typically been marginalized in economics. Engagement and interest in economics can be strengthened if students see their own personal histories reflected in the course content. We discussed ways for instructors to create opportunities for students to share their personal histories, and to help students realize the value they bring to the classroom. Expanding the narrative on racial disparities in economic outcomes and exposing students to alternative schools of thought are two important ways in which instructors can create spaces for students who have experienced marginalization to engage more deeply with economics. The strategies we suggest require instructors to invest additional time and effort beyond what is found in the ancillary materials that accompany the leading textbooks. However, adopting an anti-racist pedagogy is essential if the discipline wants to make economics relevant and relatable.

NOTES

1. See Dani Rodrik's presentation on "Doing and teaching economics in the real world" found at https://www.youtube.com/watch?v=xGcKbu0dnpsandt=260s, which emphasizes moving away from a single economic model and instead adopting multiple models and theories to explain complex social reality. See also Raj Chetty's discussion on rethinking the way we teach economics so that it more closely aligns with how economists practice economics, and is more relevant and relatable for students, at https://www.vox.com/the-highlight/2019/5/14/18520783/harvard-economics-chetty. Finally, works by Kvangraven and Alves (2019, 2021), Kvangraven and Kesar (2020), Alves and Kvangraven (2020), and Koechlin (2019) provide greater insights into alternative economic models and theories that allow economists and students to explore important economic issues more thoroughly.
2. See the 2020 Report of the Committee on the Status of Minority Groups in the Economics Profession at https://www.aeaweb.org/content/file?id=13728.
3. The link to Bayer and Wilcox (2019) and to many other resources mentioned in this chapter can be found in the online supplement to this chapter at https://www.e-elgar.com/textbooks/maier.
4. See https://www.aeaweb.org/content/file?id=13728.
5. For further discussion of stereotype threat in economics and strategies for addressing it, see https://diversifyingecon.org/stereotype-threat/.
6. See also Alston et al. (2022).
7. Instructors can reduce the impostor syndrome by bringing diverse speakers to class. The focus of seminars does not need to be related to race or racism. Instead, economists from diverse backgrounds in any field can speak of their own personal histories (for example, how they developed interest in economics, challenges and obstacles they faced in the field). See the Research Seminar Speaker Database for Marginalized Economists at https://econspeakerdiversity.shinyapps.io/EconSpeakerDiversity/.
8. We focus on the role that race and racism play in determining economic outcomes. However, there are other ways to make the discipline more relevant for students from diverse backgrounds, such as including topics related to climate change or behavioral economics.

9. The US Census Bureau provides historical income tables at https://www.census.gov/data/tables/time-series/demo/income-poverty/historical-income-people.html.

10. See https://www.epi.org/blog/racism-and-the-economy-fed/ for an example of how unemployment data from the EPI's State of Working America Data Library can be displayed for students.

11. As an alternative to presenting the data to students, instructors can have students graphically display the data themselves, in a short assignment in which they are asked to use data from the sources listed to illustrate racial differences in one or more economic outcomes over time, and identify whether differences have narrowed, widened, or remained constant. Instructors can also ask students to identify 3–5 factors that they believe are responsible for the racial disparities they observe in their graphs.

12. Instructors can also assign a short article by Hamilton et al. (2015) that can help students to gain a better understanding of why higher levels of education and effort are not the solutions to eliminating racial economic inequality.

13. Short videos where Ellora Derenoncourt explains her work at a level pitched for students taking Introductory Microeconomics can be found at https://www.youtube.com/watch?v=br3cvVU3_Dkandlist=PLMR7YToRbjlZ-RP8ydOuD4gO14eYc8VNkandindex=2 and https://www.youtube.com/watch?v=O72aDX-rmmIandlist=PLMR7YToRbjlZ-RP8ydOuD4gO14eYc8VNkandindex=3.

14. A podcast on this topic can be found at https://www.econtalk.org/lisa-cook-on-racism-patents-and-black-entrepreneurship.

15. See also Cook and Logan (2020) for a discussion of how violence against Blacks impacted entrepreneurship, voting, and ownership of property.

16. The Washington Center for Equitable Growth also has a summary of research on racial violence and exclusion in the US which includes several of the studies listed above. The summary can be found at https://equitablegrowth.org/elevating-economic-research-on-racist-violence-and-exclusion-in-the-united-states/.

17. Instructors can ask students to generate a list of the ways in which wealth creates opportunity. Students can also read about the importance of wealth in providing economic opportunity, and about factors contributing to the racial wealth gap, at https://www.americanprogress.org/issues/economy/reports/2021/03/19/497377/eliminating-Black-white-wealth-gap-generational-challenge/.

18. See https://www.stlouisfed.org/on-the-economy/2021/january/wealth-gaps-white-black-hispanic-families-2019 for an example of how racial differences in wealth are displayed by education and income.

19. The feature can be found at https://apps.urban.org/features/race-and-taxes/#capital-gains-and-dividends.

20. https://kirwaninstitute.osu.edu/article/building-equitable-recovery-role-race-labor-markets-and-education-read-report suggest that racial discrimination may be more pronounced at higher levels of education because educated persons of color pose the greatest threat. Instructors could connect SE and this prediction back to the presentation of data that shows racial economic disparities at all levels of degree attainment.

21. Instructors can also have students read Ards et al. (2015), which finds that racial stereotypes lead to creditworthy Blacks avoiding applying for loans because of the "socially generated self-misperception of not being creditworthy." The SE field draws on the theory of stereotype threat from social psychology. The premise is

that to preserve group status, the dominant group determines what the widely held social beliefs about a non-dominant group will be.

22. To prepare students for discussion, instructors can assign a 20-minute video where Darrick Hamilton explains the field of stratification economics, found at https://www.youtube.com/watch?v=2fN-2rElsVo.

23. The Williams Institute has several publications that provide economic data on LGBT people of color found at https://williamsinstitute.law.ucla.edu/publications/black-lgbt-adults-in-the-us/. Instructors can also discuss the need for better data collection on LGBTQ communities of color. Instructors can highlight the high rates of poverty and lower incomes for LGBTQ people of color, and discuss how intersectionality can help us to better understand the extent of discrimination they face in the labor market. See also https://www.americanprogress.org/article/black-lgbtq-individuals-experience-heightened-levels-discrimination/. Instructors can also emphasize the lack of research and reliable data in this important area.

REFERENCES

Alston, M., Darity, W., Eckel C., McNeil, L., and Sharpe, R. (2022). The effect of stereotypes on Black college test scores at a historically Black university. *Journal of Economic Behavior and Organization 194*(2), 408–424.

Alves, C., and Kvangraven., I.H. (2020). Changing the narrative: Economics after COVID-19. *Review of Agrarian Studies 10*(1), 147–163.

Amuedo-Dorantes, C., Borra, C., and Wang, C. (2021). Asian discrimination in the coronavirus era: Implications for business formation and survival. IZA Working Paper 14182.

Andrews, R., Casey, M., Hardy, B.L., and Logan, T. (2017). Location matters: Historical racial segregation and intergenerational mobility. *Economics Letters 158*, 67–72.

Ards, S., Ha, I.S., Mazas, J., and Meyers, S.L., Jr (2015). Bad credit and intergroup differences in loan denial rates. *Review of Black Political Economy 42*(1–2), 19–34.

Aronson, J., Fried, C.B., and Good, C. (2002). Reducing the effects of stereotype threat on African American college students by shaping theories of intelligence. *Journal of Experimental Social Psychology 38*(2), 113–125.

Avilova, T., and Goldin, C. (2018). What can UWE do for economics? *American Economic Association Papers and Proceedings 108*, 186–190.

Backhouse, R.E., and Medema, S.G. (2009). Defining economics: The long road to acceptance of the Robbins definition. *Economica 76*(1), 805–820.

Bayer, A. (2018). The economics profession's unique problem with diversity. *Minority Report 10*, 17–19.

Bayer, A., Bhanot, S.P., and Lozano, F. (2019). Does simple information provision lead to more diverse classrooms? Evidence from a field experiment on undergraduate economics. *AEA Papers and Proceedings 109*, 110–114.

Bayer, A., Bhanot, S.P., Bronchetti, E.T., and O'Connell, S.A. (2020). Diagnosing the learning environment for diverse students in Introductory Economics: An analysis of relevance, belonging, and growth mindsets. *American Economic Association Papers and Proceedings 110*, 294–298.

Bayer, A., and Rouse., C.E. (2016). Diversity in the economics profession: A new attack on an old problem. *Journal of Economic Perspectives 30*(4), 221–242.

Bayer, A., and Wilcox, D.W. (2019). The unequal distribution of economic education: A report on the race, ethnicity, and gender of economics majors at US colleges and universities. *Journal of Economic Education 50*(3), 299–320.

Brewer, R., Conrad, C., and King, M. (2002). The complexities and potential of theorizing gender, caste, race, and class. *Feminist Economics 8*(2), 3–17.

Brown, I., and Misra, J. (2003). The intersection of gender and race in the labor market. *Annual Review of Sociology 29*, 487–513.

Cassidy, J. (2017). A new way to learn economics. *The New Yorker*, September 11.

Cook, L.D. (2014). Violence and economic activity: Evidence from African American patents, 1870–1940. *Journal of Economic Growth 19*, 221–257.

Cook, L.D., and Logan, T.D. (2020). Racial inequality. Research Brief, Economics for Inclusive Prosperity.

Cook, L.D., Logan, T.D., and Parman, J. M. (2018). Racial segregation and southern lynching. *Social Science History 42*(4), 635–675.

Darity, W.A., Jr (2005). Stratification economics: The role of intergroup inequality. *Journal of Economics and Finance 29*, 144–153.

Darity, W.A., Jr (2022). Position and possessions: Stratification economics and intergroup inequality. *Journal of Economic Literature 60*(2), 400–426.

Darity, W.A., Jr, and Aja, A. (2014). Why we're wrong about affirmative action: Stereotypes, testing and the "soft bigotry of low expectations." *Huffington Post: The Blog*, July 28.

Darity, W.A., Jr, and Hamilton, D. (2012). Bold policies for economic justice. *Review of Black Political Economy 39*(1), 79–85.

Darity, W.A., Jr, Hamilton, D., Mason, P., Price, G.N., Davila, A., et al. (2017). Stratification economics: A general theory of intergroup inequality. In A. Flynn, S. Homberg, D. Warren, and F. Wong (eds), *The hidden rules of race: Barriers to an inclusive economy*. Cambridge University Press.

Darity, W.A., Jr, Hamilton, D., Paul, M., Aja, A., Price, A., et al. (2018). What we get wrong about closing the racial wealth gap. Samuel DuBois Cook Center on Social Equity and Insight Center for Community Economic Development.

Darity, W.A., Jr, and Mullen, A.K. (2020). *From here to equality: Reparations for Black Americans in the twenty-first century.* University of North Carolina Press.

Davis, J.B. (2019). Stratification economics as an economics of exclusion. *Journal of Economics, Race, and Policy 2*, 163–172.

Derenoncourt, E. (2022). Can you move to opportunity? Evidence from the Great Migration. *American Economic Review 112*(2), 369–408.

Hamilton, D. (2017). Post-racial rhetoric, racial health disparities, and health disparity consequences of stigma, stress, and racism. Working Paper, Washington Center for Equitable Growth.

Hamilton, D. (2020). The moral burden on economists: Darrick Hamilton's 2017 NEA Presidential Address. *Review of Black Political Economy 47*(4), 331–342.

Hamilton, D., Biu, O., Famighetti, C., Green, A., Strickland, K., and Wilcox, D. (2021). Building an equitable recovery: The role of race, labor markets, and education. Institute on Race and Political Economy Report, The New School, February.

Hamilton, D., and Darity, W.A. Jr (2017). The political economy of education, financial literacy, and the racial wealth gap. *Federal Reserve Bank of St Louis Review 99*(1), 59–76.

Hamilton, D., Darity Jr, W., Price, A.E., Sridharan, V., and Tippett, R. (2015). Umbrellas don't make it rain: Why studying and working hard isn't enough for Black Americans. The New School. https://socialequity.duke.edu/wp-content/uploads/2019/10/Umbrellas_Dont_Make_It_Rain_Final.pdf.

Kim, M. (2009). Race and gender differences in the earnings of Black workers. *Industrial Relations 48*(3), 466–488.

Kishimoto, K. (2018). Anti-racist pedagogy: From faculty's self-reflection to organizing within and beyond the classroom. *Race Ethnicity and Education 21*(4), 540–554.

Koechlin, T. (2019). Whitewashing capitalism: Mainstream economics' resounding silence on race and racism. *Review of Radical Political Economics 51*(4), 562–571.

Kvangraven, I.H., and Alves., C. (2019, May 8). Why so hostile? Busting myths about heterodox economics. *Developing Economics*. https://developingeconomics.org/2019/05/08/why-so-hostile-busting-myths-about-heterodox-economics/.

Kvangraven, I.H., and Alves, C. (2021). Does economics need to be decolonized? *Economics Observatory*, January 20.

Kvangraven, I.H., and Kesar. S. (2020, August 3). Why do economists have trouble understanding racialized inequalities? Institute for New Economic Thinking. https://www.ineteconomics.org/perspectives/blog/why-do-economists-have-trouble-understanding-racialized-inequalities#:~:text=The%20economics%20discipline's%20lack%20of,and%20a%20lack%20of%20diversity.

Mankiw, N.G. (2020). *Principles of Economics*. Cengage.

Nam, Y, Hamilton, D., Darity, W.A., Jr, and Price., A.E. (2015). Bootstraps are for Black kids: Race, wealth, and the impact of intergenerational transfers on adult outcomes. Research Brief, Insight Center for Community Economic Development. http://www.insightcced.org/wp-content/uploads/2015/07/Bootstraps-are-for-Black-Kids-Sept.pdf.

Paul, M., Zaw, K., Hamilton, D., and Darity, W.H., Jr (2018). Returns in the labor market: A nuanced view of penalties at the intersection of race and gender. Working Paper, Washington Center for Equitable Growth. https://equitablegrowth.org/working-papers/intersectionality-labor-market/.

Rendón, L.I., Nora, A., and Kanagala, V. (2014). *Ventajas/assets y conocimientos/knowledge: Leveraging Latin@ strengths to foster student success.* Center for Research and Policy in Education, University of Texas at San Antonio. https://www.utsa.edu/strategicplan/documents/2017_12%20Student%20Success%20_Ventajas_Assets_2014.pdf.

Stevenson, B., and Wolfers, J. (2020). *Principles of Economics*. Macmillan Press.

Taylor, S.D., Veri, M.J., Eliason, M., Hermoso, J.C.R., Bolter, N.D., and VanOlphen, J.E. (2019). The social justice syllabus design tool: A first step in doing social justice pedagogy. *Journal Committed to Social Change on Race and Ethnicity 5*(2), 133–166.

Williams, J.A. (2021). Confederate streets and Black-white labor market differentials. *American Economic Association Papers and Proceedings 111*, 27–31.

Williams, J.A. (2022). Historical lynchings and the contemporary voting behavior of Blacks. *American Economic Journal: Applied Economics 14*(3), 224–253.

Williams, J.A., Logan, T.D., and Hardy, B.L. (2021). The persistence of historical racial violence and political suppression: Implications for contemporary regional inequality. *Annals of the American Academy of Political and Social Science 694*(1), 92–107.

Williams, R.B. (2017). Wealth privilege and the racial wealth gap: A case study in economic stratification. *Review of Black Political Economy 44*(3–4), 303–325.

11. Feminist approaches in the Introductory Microeconomics course

Pratistha Joshi Rajkarnikar

INTRODUCTION

A feminist approach to economics refers to creating a gender-aware and inclusive approach to evaluating economic processes and outcomes. Looking at economic processes through a gender lens might help us to notice things that we would otherwise miss. For example, a gendered analysis of differences in poverty levels between male- and female-headed households would shed light on the specific constraints faced by female-headed households, such as limited access to markets or lack of asset ownership, that would be imperceptible in a gender-blind analysis. This might suggest different policy interventions for addressing poverty for each kind of household. Thus, a feminist approach to economic analysis would draw more attention to inequalities based on gender and other social categories.

This chapter discusses ways to integrate gender issues in an Introductory Microeconomics course, highlighting the reasons why gender matters in the economy and in economic theory. It starts by examining some of the limitations of the gender-blind approach in the mainstream theory and describing key contributions of the feminist approach. It then suggests specific ways to make an Introductory Microeconomics course more inclusive by revising the definition and the traditional model of the economy. The final section discusses how the changes suggested would provide students with a more realistic and comprehensive understanding of economic issues and improve their critical thinking skills. While this chapter focuses exclusively on gender inequality, many of the issues discussed here also apply to other social identities, such as race, discussed in "Creating an anti-racist pedagogy in Principles of Microeconomics" (Chapter 10 in this book).

THE NEED FOR A FEMINIST APPROACH

The Mainstream Model

The mainstream microeconomic model of the economy is a model of market exchange, where the world is simplified into two kinds of economic actors—households and firms—and economic activity is described in terms of the circular flow of goods, services, labor, capital, and money (wages, profits, rents, interest, and payment for goods and services) among these economic actors (Figure 11.1). In this model, all economic agents are assumed to be driven by self-interest, and have well-defined preferences and complete information about all their choices. Based on additional assumptions of non-satiation and free disposal, a rational economic agent is assumed to choose an optimizing outcome where households maximize their utility (satisfaction) levels, and businesses maximize their profits.

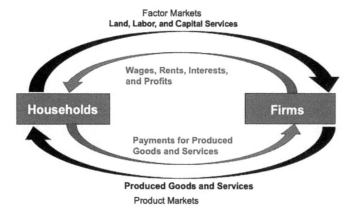

Note: The mainstream model portrays market activities between households and firms.
Source: Goodwin et al. (2018).

Figure 11.1   Basic neoclassical model of the economy

Mainstream economics has a very limited treatment of gender. This model, focused largely on markets, neglects the importance of gender norms; historical, political, social, and cultural aspects; and environmental factors in influencing economic outcomes. There is only a small role for the government in this model, and unpaid work as well as the use of environmental amenities are often ignored. The notion of a "rational economic man" primarily motivated by self-interest—a central construct of the neoclassical model—is also unre-alistic, as revealed by the evolving field of behavioral economics. A feminist approach to understanding the economy addresses many of these limitations and provides a more comprehensive and realistic view of the economy, as I will argue in this chapter.

Non-Market Work

One of the defining characteristics of feminist economics is the inclusion of the non-market sphere in economic analysis. The non-market sphere includes households and communities, as well as the non-profit sector and the state. Economic activities that are essential to sustaining the economy and enhancing human well-being are provided through the non-market sphere. This includes activities such as raising children, maintaining homes, preparing meals, caring for the ill, and maintaining social relationships that improve one's psycho-logical well-being. These activities largely constitute the care economy. The non-market sphere also includes social services provided by the non-profit or community organizations, such as skills-based training, or initiatives for envi-ronmental protection. Many of these services directly contribute to economic output and would be counted in national accounting if they were provided through the market. But when these services are provided through mostly unpaid work in the non-market sphere, they are assumed to have no economic value.

Activities in the non-market sphere also create economic value through the generation and the maintenance of human capital and social capital, that are essential for markets to function effectively. Human capital includes knowledge and skills gained through shared knowledge within households and communities, and social capital includes cultural norms, and values of trust, honesty, fairness, and concern for the common good. Such values facil-itate market transactions by minimizing the need for extensive contracts and policing that involve high transaction costs. More importantly, they strengthen social relationships and contribute to creating healthy and vibrant societies. Societies with inadequate care labor are likely to suffer economically and socially, for example, due to low productivity levels, higher crime rates, and lack of trust.

A 2018 report from the International Labour Organization finds that globally about 76 percent of non-market work is carried out by women, and that women spend an estimated three times more time than men per day on unpaid care work (Figure 11.2). Given that the burden of unpaid non-market work falls disproportionately on women, the neglect of the non-market sphere in main-stream economics makes women's work invisible and undervalues women's contribution to the economy. A feminist approach to economics addresses this by emphasizing the need to count non-market work within national account-ing, and raising awareness about the gendered division of labor.

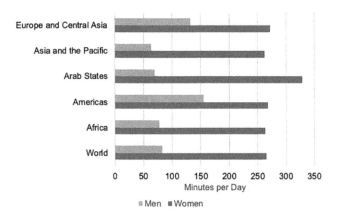

Note: Women spend more time in unpaid work than men almost everywhere in the world.
Source: International Labour Organization (2018).

Figure 11.2   Time spent in unpaid work by women and men

One of the key implications of the exclusion of non-market work in main-stream economic analysis is that women are only seen as productive members of the society when they take up market work. A reduction in paid work to take up more care responsibilities is perceived as inefficient and welfare-reducing. A feminist analysis would provide a more accurate analysis of this change by valuing work done in the care sector. This is specifically relevant for under-standing the issue of the double burden of work that women engaging in both market and household work might experience. Participation in market work might be more stressful than empowering for women if taking up market work without a reduction in household work intensifies their workday (de la Rocha 1994).

Power Relations

Feminist economists also emphasize the importance of gender relations—relations of power between men and women—in influencing economic opportunities and outcomes. Mainstream microeconomic analysis focuses on economic processes at the household level, where the head of the household (usually a man) is assumed to make decisions considering the well-being of the entire family (see, e.g., Becker 1981). It is assumed that allocation of household resources, distribution of market and non-market work, and decisions on consumption and savings, are all based on achieving optimal outcomes maximizing productivity, income, or utility levels for the household as a whole.

A feminist view questions these assumptions by considering the importance of socio-cultural forces, gender norms, and power relations within the household. Intra-household power relations are shaped by cooperation from emotional ties and mutual dependence between men and women as well as conflicts from sharing work responsibilities and distributing household resources (Hartmann 1981; Sen 1990). Often women take up a large share of unpaid domestic work, receive fewer resources, and have a smaller say in household decision-making. Mainstream models mask women's disadvantaged position within the household, by taking the households as the unit of analysis. Extending our microeconomic analysis to consider the power relations that shape household decisions can provide us with important insights into inequalities that exist within a household.

Institutional Context and Gender Norms

The neoclassical assumption of self-interest being the key motivating factor in individual decision-making is a huge oversimplification of human behavior. Social factors, such as cultural norms, feelings of concern for others, social and cultural biases, perceptions about fairness, or care for the environment, often influence economic decisions. Additionally, socially constructed characteristics that assume men to be more rational and independent, and women to be more emotional, altruistic, and dependent, may also influence individual behavior (Urban and Pürckhauer 2016). There is ample research showing differences in the ways that men and women make decisions. For example, studies show that women are generally more risk-averse than men (Charness and Gneezy 2012), female migrants are likely to send more remittances home (Goff 2016), and female-headed households spend a greater proportion of income on children (Handa 1996).

Note that these differences may not be due to biological differences between men and women. Gender norms and institutional structures play an important role in motivating men and women to behave differently. For example, in societies where women's participation in public spaces might be restricted due to patriarchal norms in which women's role is limited to the domestic sphere and informal economy, women's decision to take up market work may be heavily dependent not on their own calculations about the benefits of market work, but on how the society may perceive their presence in public spaces. Economist Jayati Ghosh argues that such norms rooted in patriarchy explain the low labor market participation for women in India (around 35 percent) despite the country's growth experience. Idealized notions of femininity being associated with generosity and altruism, and social expectations on women's roles, often influence women's choices and behavior (Rashid 2013; Pickbourn 2011). By considering the institutional contexts and gender norms that influence economic decisions, a feminist approach helps explain gender-based inequalities more widely.

Implications for Policy-Making

In the mainstream neoclassical model, the only things of value are profits and utility. Based on the assumptions of optimization, this model claims to produce ideal economic outcomes by prioritizing economic growth and efficiency, while neglecting issues of distribution and sustainability. Hence, the policy implications drawn from this theory largely fail to address social and gender-based inequalities. In contrast, because the feminist approach to economic analysis focuses on the power relations and different institutional and social constructs for men and women, it brings to light the need for addressing gender-based inequalities in policy-making.

Take, for example, the Covid-19 pandemic. A gender-blind analysis of the economic impacts of the pandemic would fail to recognize that the pandemic is disproportionately hurting women more than men, and exacerbating gender inequality related to work and family. This is partly because women are overrepresented in the industries that have been hardest hit by the pandemic, such as leisure, hospitality, education, food, and retail services. Additionally, closures of childcare centers and schools have increased women's childcare responsibilities and prompted many women to leave the workforce or cut down their work hours. Also, given that more women are employed in the healthcare sector, they have had to bear the double burden of working longer hours at care institutions, while also taking on additional responsibilities at home. A 2020 report from McKinsey Global Institute estimates that women's jobs are 1.8 times more vulnerable to the crisis than men's jobs, based on survey data from the United States (US) and India (Madgavkar et al. 2020). In the US, about 80 percent of those who left work between March 2020 and 2021 were women (Gersh 2021). Given such disparities, it is essential to analyze the impacts of the pandemic through the gender lens. Accordingly, policies to address the crisis must also be gender-sensitive. For example, committing more support and resources to care work, providing universal safety nets and decent pay to care workers, committing to reduce gender gap in wages, and setting targets for women in leadership and management positions, might help to address some of the gender-based inequalities (Miambo-Ngcuka 2021).

More broadly, feminist economics emphasizes the importance of the care economy and advocates for public policy to address the issue of inadequate care services. It argues that the state must design a system that guarantees access to basic care services to meet a society's demand for care (Rodríguez Enríquez 2005). This would help to relieve the double burden of work for women to some extent. In addition, the focus on addressing issues of inequalities based on the division of labor in the market as well as non-market spheres could encourage policy measures that help to close the gender pay gap. For example, policies advocating for family-friendly workplaces, equal pay for equal work, protection of women's reproductive rights, and safety from domestic violence, all help to improve women's material circumstances (Bartlett 2017). Hence, a feminist approach to economic policy is much more likely to address issues of inequality than the mainstream approach.

REFORMING THE MICROECONOMICS CURRICULUM

Having discussed the importance of a feminist approach to microeconomic analysis, I now present specific ideas on how gender issues can be integrated in an introductory economics course. These ideas are based on my work with colleagues Neva Goodwin, Julie Nelson, Brian Roach, and Jonathan Harris to develop contextual teaching materials and Introductory Economics textbooks that emphasize the role of social and environmental issues in economic analysis (see Goodwin et al. 2018).

Changing the Definition of Economics

The starting point for addressing the problems discussed above is changing the way we define economics. The most common definition of economics is that it is the discipline that helps people to make optimal choices under conditions of scarcity. This definition primarily focuses on optimization to increase efficiency and growth. While these goals may be important, especially in societies with inadequate resources, they might compete with other goals such as equality, fairness, and sustainability, all of which might be equally if not more important for human well-being (Nelson and Goodwin 2005). Hence, we suggest a much broader definition, defining economics as the study of how people manage their resources to meet their needs and enhance their well-being.

In this definition, the term "well-being" broadly refers to a good quality of life, and goes beyond just meeting the basic needs. Improvements in well-being could come from higher growth and efficiency levels, but factors such as dignified work, more equality, better work–life balance, improved social relations, freedom to express one's opinions, access to good education and healthcare, and a clean environment, also increase well-being. This broader definition includes enhancing the well-being of individuals in all their roles, not just as consumers and producers, but also as family members, care givers, and citizens. Considering these broader goals helps to integrate social and environmental concerns in our economic analysis, and highlights the value of non-market work.

Changing the Economic Model

The neoclassical model of the economy, presented in Figure 11.1, needs to be replaced with a model that is more inclusive and realistic. Such a model is presented in Figure 11.3, where the market activities of the basic neoclassical model are presented within the business sphere, and two additional spheres— core and public purpose—are added to account for all non-market economic activities. The core sphere includes households, families, and community groups, where economic activity takes place without exchange of money, and mainly out of love and concern for others. The public purpose sphere includes government and other local, national, and international organizations, and accounts for the benefits of public goods and services. These three spheres are placed within the social and environmental contexts to account for the important roles that factors such as gender norms; cultural, political, and historical settings; and natural environment play in influencing economic processes and outcomes.

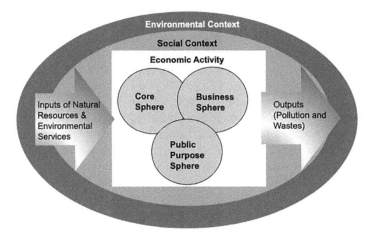

Note: The contextual model portrays the economy as existing within the social context and natural environment with market and non-market spheres of activity.
Source: Goodwin et al. (2018).

Figure 11.3   The contextual model of the economy

This model allows us to account for work done in the non-market sphere that contributes to economic well-being. For example, estimates of value produced in the core sphere show that the size of the core sphere is about 14 percent of the gross domestic product (GDP) in South Africa and in Canada (Ferrant and Thim 2019), about 25 percent of the GDP in Sweden, and about 31 percent of that in Denmark (Folbre 2018). The market-exclusive focus of the traditional economics ignores the core sector work and therefore fails to account for the full range of activities that human beings engage in. The inclusion of public purpose sphere in this model allows us to account for the role that the government can play in improving economic well-being through public provisioning of care services and creation of an institutional framework for addressing gender-based inequalities. Finally, embedding all economic activities within the social and environmental context highlights the important role that social norms, historical and political factors, and environmental aspects play in understanding economic processes.

Including Inequality and Discrimination

As discussed above, the mainstream theory places excessive focus on growth and often neglects distributional issues. Large inequalities could hurt the social fabric and be harmful for overall well-being. Historically, gender discrimination has been rooted in sexist beliefs that women are innately inferior to men. Based on social beliefs that men are primary breadwinners while women can rely on their husbands for financial support, better-paying jobs are reserved for men, while women are limited to low-paying or unpaid domestic work (Goodwin et al. 2018). Data from the World Economic Forum (2021) shows that in 2020 the wage gap (the ratio of the wage of women to that of men in a similar position) was about 37 percent, illustrating the pervasiveness of gender gap globally. Additionally, gender norms regarding educating girls, occupational choices for women, and disruptions in women's careers as they take time to care of their families, influence economic outcomes for women.

Including issues of inequality in a microeconomic curriculum involves examining the role of historical and institutional factors in influencing economic opportunities and outcomes for people from different races/ethnicities and genders. For example, discussions on the labor market should go beyond looking at patterns in unemployment solely based on demand and supply of labor. Specific issues of discrimination and biases must be addressed to provide an accurate description of labor market outcomes.

This could include presenting data on unemployment rates, median wages, or other labor market outcomes disaggregated by gender, race and ethnicity, and other social categories. Introducing data from time use surveys to illustrate the division of labor in the market versus non-market spheres would also be helpful in illustrating inequalities in the distribution of work. Additionally, discussions on occupational segregation in the labor market and the value generated in the care economy would provide important insights into the issues of gender inequality. For the United States, most of the data on labor market outcomes disaggregated by various social groups as well as the time use survey is available through the Bureau of Labor Statistics. Time use surveys have also been conducted in various other countries, including Canada, Australia, the United Kingdom, Japan, and Mexico. These are valuable resources for estimating the value generated in non-market spheres.

Of equal importance is the need to discuss the role of the government in designing social policies that affect the provision of care, access to basic services, and tax policies that directly affect distributional issues. Countries with more progressive tax policies and better provision of public services are likely to have lower gender inequality, while those with gender-blind policies end up deepening existing inequalities (see, e.g., Babayan and Nicholas 2020; Rodríguez Enríquez and Itriago 2019). Including these examples might shed light into the important role that the public purpose sphere plays in addressing inequalities based on gender and other social categories.

Including Insights from Behavioral Economics

Given the problems with the portrayal of human beings as rational agents in the neoclassical world, it is critical to introduce insights from behavioral economics that provide a more realistic framework to understand complex human motivations. Behavioral economists use insights from numerous disciplines, including psychology, sociology, anthropology, biology, economics, and neuroscience, and have devised creative experiments to explore how people make decisions. The key findings from this field show that people's decisions are heavily influenced by their biases and the institutional contexts, including social and cultural forces (see Chapter 7 in this book, "Where is the 'behavioral' in Introductory Microeconomics?").

This is especially important for understanding gender issues, since social and cultural norms directly influence economic opportunities and outcomes for women. Austen and Jefferson (2008) argue that there is potential to apply many of the concepts from behavioral economics to existing feminist analyses. For example, the concept of availability heuristic—where people make decisions based on mental shortcuts or familiar facts—could explain gender differences in decision-making. Since these mental shortcuts are influenced by gender norms that portray women as being altruistic and subservient, women might be more likely to resist decisions that are selfish. Behavioral economists also recognize that cognitive processes motivate humans to categorize individuals and attribute to them specific stereotypical behaviors. Based on this concept, Reskin (2003) argues that gender discrimination in the labor market might be explained by intuitive thoughts and stereotyping behavior.

One interesting finding from behavioral economics is that while economic behavior is often irrational, it is not always random. This means that our decision-making process is systematic and predictable (Ariely 2010). Our behavior is often guided by our habits and influenced by the way information is presented to us. Hence, it is possible to influence people's behavior through policy "nudges" that encourage people to make certain decisions (Thaler and Sunstein 2008). Recent research has shown that such nudges can be useful to influence policies to close the gender gap. For instance, in her 2017 book *What Works: Gender Equality by Design*, behavioral economist Iris Bohnet suggests a variety of strategies for decreasing gender bias. She argues, for example, that not using gendered language in job ads (for example, "caring" that attracts women, or "assertive" that attracts men) would create a more balanced applicant pool. Other studies have shown that findings from behavioral economics might be helpful for fostering diversity and gender equality (Waylen 2018), and reducing the gender pay gap (Heilman and Kusev 2017). Using such insights from behavioral economics can provide a better understanding of human behavior and shed light on policy approaches to address gender inequality.

Inclusion of the topics suggested above, along with an expanded discussion of power, including evolving social customs and gender norms, will enhance the teaching of the Introductory Microeconomics course and should provide students with a much better and deeper understanding of gender issues in economics. This also helps to create policies that are more gender-sensitive.

IMPLICATIONS FOR STUDENT LEARNING

Instructors often find that students are apprehensive of Introductory Economics courses. A 2002 study based on a survey of 399 students in a large public university finds that perceptions about economics courses as being heavily focused on quantitative skills is one key reason for the apprehension (Benedict and Hoag 2002). Students might also find the theoretical expositions based on assumptions of rationality too abstract, unreasonable, and uninteresting. This might discourage them from pursuing further studies in economics.

There is also evidence of a gender gap among students who study economics as well as those who go on to pursue careers in this field. For example, about 58 percent of all undergraduates in the United States are women but only one-third of economics majors are women, compared to about 50 percent of female graduates in science, technology, engineering, and mathematics (STEM) and business fields (Ceci et al. 2014). Part of this gender gap in economics could be because the curriculum excludes topics and methods that appeal to women and students from underrepresented backgrounds more generally. Hence integrating alternative paradigms that address issues of inequality might help close this gap and make the field more appealing to students from diverse backgrounds (Feiner and Roberts 1995).

A feminist approach to teaching economics as proposed in this chapter should provide students with a comprehensive understanding of the real world and help to develop their critical thinking skills. Not limiting their understanding to the narrow models focused on optimization and markets, and exposing them to complex realities due to unpredictability, irrational behavior, and the influence of socio-cultural, historical, political, and ecological factors, helps them to attain a more sophisticated understanding of real-world issues. Most of the suggestions for reforming the Principles of Microeconomics course discussed above should appear as commonsense modifications to make economic analysis more realistic. A feminist approach to Introductory Microeconomics, that focuses on human well-being goals, should provide students with an opportunity to question their own values and become critical thinkers and creative learners (Shackelford 1992).

Often, Introductory Economics courses are taught with a focus on preparing students for the intermediate courses in the major, instead of helping them to understand how economics can be relevant to their everyday lives. Given that less than 2 percent of the students who take an Introductory Economics course go on to major in the field, the focus of the current curriculum should be shifted from formal modeling and statistical testing, to discussions of ethical and moral issues and civic engagement activities (Colander and McGoldrick 2009). A feminist approach to economics education is necessary today, given the complex and evolving challenges that modern societies face, including persistent and rising income disparities, and the different ways that gender, race, and other demographic factors interact to produce various forms of inequalities. A forward-thinking economics curriculum should equip students to consider questions of well-being, ethics, equity, and sustainability.

REFERENCES

Ariely, D. (2010). *Predictably irrational: The hidden forces that shape our decisions.* Harper Perennial.

Austen, S., and Jefferson, T. (2008). Can behavioural economics contribute to feminist discussions? Women in Social and Economic Research, Working Paper No. 23, Curtin University of Technology, Perth Western Australia.

Babayan, M., and Nicholas, A. (2020, January 30). Progressive taxation can advance gender equity. Washington State Budget and Policy Center. https://budgetandpolicy .org/schmudget/gender-equity/.

Bartlett, K.T. (2017). Feminism and economic inequality. *Minnesota Journal of Law and Inequality 35*(2), 265–287.

Becker, G.S. (1981). *The treatise on the family*. Harvard University Press.

Benedict, Mary E., and Hoag, John (2002). Who's afraid of their economics classes? Why are students apprehensive about introductory economics courses? An empirical investigation. *American Economist 46*(2), 31–44.

Bohnet, Iris (2017). *What works: Gender equality by design*. Harvard University Press.

Ceci, S.J., Ginther, D.K., Kahn, S., and Williams, W.M. (2014). Women in academic science: A changing landscape. *Psychological Science in the Public Interest: A Journal of the American Psychological Society 15*(3), 75–141.

Charness, G., and Gneezy, U. (2012). Strong evidence for gender differences in risk taking. *Journal of Economic Behavior and Organization 83*(1), 50–58.

Colander, D., and McGoldrick, K. (2009). The economics major as part of a liberal education: The Teagle Report. *American Economic Review: Papers and Proceedings 99*(2), 611–623.

de la Rocha, M.G. (1994). *The resources of poverty: Women and survival in a Mexican City*. Blackwell Publishers.

Feiner, S., and Roberts, B. (1995). Using alternative paradigms to teach about race and gender: A critical thinking approach to Introductory Economics. *American Economic Review 85*(2), 367–371.

Ferrant, G., and Thim, A. (2019). Measuring women's economic empowerment: Time use data and gender inequality. Policy Paper 16, OECD Development Policy Papers. https://www.oecd-ilibrary.org/development/measuring-women-s-economic-empowerment_02e538fc-en.

Folbre, N. (2018). Developing care: Recent research on the care economy and economic development. Research Report, International Development Research Center. http://www.iaffe.org/media/cms_page_media/788/Folbre_Nancy.pdf.

Gersh, K. (2021). Opinion: Women are leaving the workforce at a disturbing rate – Here's what leaders can do about it. *Market Watch*, July 8.

Goff, M.L. (2016). Feminization of migration and trends in remittances. *IZA World of Labor*. https://wol.iza.org/uploads/articles/220/pdfs/feminization-of-migration-and-trends-in-remittances.pdf.

Goodwin, N., Harris, J., Roach, B., Nelson, J., Joshi Rajkarnikar, P., and Torras, M. (2018). *Principles of Economics in context*. Routledge.

Handa, S. (1996). Expenditure behavior and children's welfare: An analysis of female headed households in Jamaica. *Journal of Development Economics 50*, 165–187.

Hartmann, H.I. (1981). The family as the locus of gender, class, and political struggle: The example of housework. *Signs 6*(3), 366–394.

Heilman, R.M., and Kusev, P. (2017). The gender pay gap: Can behavioral economics provide useful insights? *Frontiers in Psychology: Opinion*. https://doi.org/10.3389/fpsyg.2017.00095.

International Labor Organization (ILO). (2018). Care work and care jobs: For the future of decent work. Geneva. https://www.ilo.org/wcmsp5/groups/public/---dgreports/---dcomm/---publ/documents/publication/wcms_633135.pdf.

Madgavkar, A., White, O., Krishnan, M., Mahajan, D., and Azcue, X. (2020). COVID-19 and gender equality: Countering the regressive effects. McKinsey Global Institute, July 15.

Miambo-Ngcuka, P. (2021). World leaders must put women at center of COVID-19 recovery. *World Economic Forum*. https://www.weforum.org/agenda/2021/06/countries-must-close-economic-gender-gaps-for-a-fair-covid-19-recovery/.

Nelson, Julie A., and Goodwin, Neva (2005). Teaching ecological and feminist economics in the Principles course. Global Development and Environment Institute Working Paper, Tufts University.

Pickbourn, L.J. (2011). Migration, remittances and intra-household allocation in Northern Ghana: Does gender matter? Unpublished doctoral dissertation, University of Massachusetts Amherst.

Rashid, S.R. (2013). Bangladeshi women's experiences of their men's migration: Rethinking power, agency, and subordination. *Asian Survey 53*(56), 883–908.

Reskin, B. (2003). Rethinking employment discrimination and its remedies. In M. Guillen, R. Collins, P. England, and M. Meyer (eds), *The new economic sociology* (pp. 218–244). Russell Sage.

Rodríguez Enríquez, C. (2005). La economía del cuidado: un aporte conceptual para el estudio de políticas públicas. Documento de trabajo número 44, Interdisciplinary Centre for Public Policy Research (Ciepp).

Rodríguez Enríquez, C., and Itriago, D. (2019). Do taxes influence inequality between women and men? *Oxfam Research Report*. Oxfam International.

Sen, A. (1990). Gender and cooperative conflicts. In I. Tinker (ed.), *Persistent inequalities: Women and world development* (pp. 123–203), Oxford University Press.

Shackelford, Jean (1992). Feminist pedagogy: A means for bringing critical thinking and creativity to the economics classroom. *American Economic Review 82*(2), 570–576.

Thaler, R.H., and Sunstein, C.R. (2008). *Nudge: Improving decisions about health, wealth, and happiness.* Penguin Books.

Urban, J., and Pürckhauer, A. (2016). The perspectives of pluralist economics. *Exploring Economics: Feminist Economics.* https://www.exploring-economics.org/en/orientation/feminist-economics/.

Waylen, G. (2018). Nudges for gender equality? What can behavior change offer gender and politics? *European Journal of Politics and Gender 1*(1–2), 167–183.

World Economic Forum (2021). Global gender pay gap index. https://www3.weforum.org/docs/WEF_GGGR_2021.pdf.

12. Promoting gender diversity in Introductory Microeconomics

Martha Olney

Women are underrepresented in economics at all levels: the introductory classroom, the undergraduate major, PhD programs, and the professoriate (Chevalier 2021). While other fields, notably physics and other science, technology, engineering, and mathematics (STEM) fields, have increased the representation of women over recent decades, the situation in economics is stagnant (Bayer and Rouse 2016).

The low proportion of undergraduate women studying economics is not new, nor is it unique to the United States. Overrepresentation of men in the economics major, relative to their numbers in the college or university, grew in the United States in the 1980s and showed no improvement from the 1990s forward (Avilova and Goldin 2018a). Underrepresentation of women students in economics has also been documented in the United Kingdom (Crawford et al. 2018). In China, women students are underrepresented in STEM majors generally (Duoduo 2018). Auriol et al. (2021) looked at the situation in Europe, and Duval-Hernández and Villagómez (2011) studied Mexico. The literature exploring the extent of the problem, its causes, and possible strategies for change, is large and growing. Bayer and Wilcox (2019), Avilova and Goldin (2018a, 2018b), and Buckles (2019) are a tiny sample of many articles that provide a good overview.

This chapter focuses on one small slice of the problem: Introductory Microeconomics. What can faculty do to improve representation of women? Two broad considerations are relevant: encouraging enrollment in the first economics course, and encouraging continued study of economics after the first course.

Resources and strategies that instructors can implement are offered below. Granted, some instructors have little classroom autonomy. Advanced Placement (AP) economics teachers are expected to quite literally "teach to the test," especially when local school rankings reflect how many students receive a score of 4 or 5 on AP exams. Many faculty work in community or four-year college settings in which the introductory curriculum is determined by committee, sometimes without their input. While some of the strategies offered in this chapter may not be feasible for those with little autonomy, others can be implemented by anyone.

COLLECTIONS OF RESOURCES

Three general resources in addition to the many excellent chapters in this book should be bookmarked. *Diversifying Economic Quality* (*Div.E.Q.*), provided by Amanda Bayer and the American Economic Association's (AEA) Committee on the Status of Minority Groups in the Economics Profession (CSMGEP, https://www.aeaweb.org/about-aea/committees/csmgep) contains a great series of resources to "promote inclusive, innovative, and evidence-based teaching practices in economics" (https://diversifyingecon.org/). Spending an hour exploring *Div.E.Q.* as you plan the semester is sure to pay off. This is a rich and practical resource.

The second general resource is the AEA's website, *Best Practices for Economists: Building a More Diverse, Inclusive, and Productive Profession* (https://www.aeaweb.org/resources/best-practices). The section "Working with Students" offers five strategies:

- Use outreach to counter stereotypes about economics and close other information gaps
- Offer course content that is relevant for diverse students
- Use effective and inclusive classroom techniques
- Build a sense of belonging for all students
- Help your students to understand and enjoy the learning process

For each strategy, there are three to five suggestions for implementation plus a bibliographic essay.

Third, the website *Starting Point: Teaching and Learning Economics* contains "a comprehensive array of research-based instructional strategies aimed at promoting student learning in economics" (https://serc.carleton.edu/econ/index.html). This site explicitly includes a section for those teaching at two-year community colleges. Although the focus of *Starting Point* is not promoting diversity per se, it fleshes out in detail diversity-promoting classroom techniques.

TWO CAUTIONS BEFORE WE BEGIN

In doing any work to improve diversity, it is important to keep two things in mind: stereotypes and biases. The resources and strategies offered here are not intended to reinforce stereotypes, but to recognize that in some matters, for whatever reason, there are differences in distributions by gender.

Faculty doing this work must be mindful of what we say and to whom in order to avoid seeming to stereotype. As social scientists, we are well aware that citing an observed difference between two populations in the mean of some variable is absolutely not the same as asserting that all or nearly all members of one population have a higher value of that variable than do those of the other population. That was a cumbersome sentence; as social scientists, we take that cumbersome sentence and shorthand it: women tend to be more sensitive to grades than men. Unfortunately, the typical student in an introductory economics course, perhaps also just starting their first statistics course, does not hear the cumbersome sentence; when we use shorthand, they hear a gender stereotype.

It can be helpful to students to draw some normal distributions and explore with them the difference between a stereotype and a statement about a distribution. Draw two sets of two bell curves. In each set, the means should differ by the same amount. Draw tight distributions with low variance in the first set; the two curves should barely overlap. In the second set, depict the same difference in the means but much larger variances, therefore providing greater overlap between the two curves. Now initiate a conversation about when it is and is not misleading to refer only to population means. When the variance is small and there is little overlap of the two distributions (the first set), broad-brush statements about differences in the means do a fine job of describing the differences between the two populations. But when there is more than minimal overlap of the two distributions (the second set), statements relying just on the difference in the means can easily become stereotypes.

This chapter, focused on gender differences, is solidly in the situation depicted in the second set of bell curves. Without denying that there is a great deal of overlap in many regards between male and female students, studies have identified areas in which there are differences—on average—by gender. Awareness of these differences informs the strategies offered here.

The second caution relates to our own biases. None of us is free of bias. To be effective in our diversity efforts, it pays to be aware of what biases we bring to the table. Are we implicitly assuming girls do not like math? Do we ever think, "She's good at math, for a girl"? Students are savvy; they can often identify our biases long before we do. We must be mindful of our implicit biases so that we do not undermine our efforts. One popular site for identifying our own biases is Harvard's Project Implicit (https://implicit.harvard.edu/implicit/takeatest.html).

PROMOTING ENROLLMENT IN INTRODUCTORY MICROECONOMICS

Promoting gender diversity in economics involves two considerations: enrolling a more diverse group of students in our introductory courses, and encouraging more students to continue beyond that first class. Enrollment is the focus of this section. Improving enrollment of women in Introductory Microeconomics requires attention to those students who have not yet graced our doors: high school students, newly admitted students who have not yet arrived on campus, and students already in residence but not in our courses.

An extensive literature addresses the question of how students choose courses and majors. Stock and Stock (2018) find that personal interest, parental preferences, potential income, potential for success, and high school experience were cited by economics majors at a central Texas college as the top factors influencing their choice of major. But in an experimental design conducted in Germany, Müller (2021) finds that high school girls are more sensitive than boys to parental pressure and preferences. And Quadlin (2020) finds distinct gender differences in the factors influencing major choice, with earnings more salient for men than for women, and altruistic rewards more likely to be key for women.

What Is Economics?

Bringing new students into our field is essentially about marketing a product: economics. Step back and consider what we are selling. What is economics?

Introductory Microeconomics is likely the first economics class that a student ever takes. Many students begin by thinking that economics is finance, whether that is personal financial literacy or corporate finance. However, when students and their parents believe that economics is primarily a pathway to a career in finance, this belief can skew the interested population. Careers in corporate finance tend to be less appealing to women students (Avilova and Goldin 2018a), who are more drawn than men to majors and professions that address societal problems and social injustice (Crawford et al. 2018).

If economics is not synonymous with finance, then what is economics? Trained on years of standard principles textbooks, many faculty have a canned answer: "Economics is the study of the allocation of scarce resources." As a marketing strategy, that is a non-starter. Consider this instead: "Economists use data and economic principles to try to solve social and economic problems."

More narrowly, what are your learning outcomes for Introductory Microeconomics (Allgood and Bayer 2017)? Does the class take a literacy approach (Stock, Chapter 5 in this book; Hansen et al. 2002; Benjamin et al. 2020)? Do you explicitly or implicitly incorporate ethical questions (Page 2021)? Is the emphasis on developing economic intuition or on rote application of mathematical tools? Is the primary takeaway that markets are perfect, or imperfect? How extensive is the flow between the material and policy issues in students' home communities? Introductory courses that feature social issues prominently, consider ethical questions carefully, and emphasize economic intuition over rote mathematical applications, can attract more women to study economics.

Outreach to High School Students

High school students, and their parents, often know little about economics. Many have a vague sense that economics is about money or about finance more broadly. In many states, economics is required in the high school curriculum (Council for Economic Education 2020). But the curriculum of these required economics classes varies considerably, with some state standards heavily focused on financial literacy, feeding into the false notion that economics equals finance. So even when there is an economics requirement in place, there is no guarantee that high school students will learn what economists do.

An outreach program to local high schools can be effective. Current economics majors or recent college graduates can visit high school classrooms to talk about their experiences with the many fields within economics. Such programs are often organized by a college's student organizations, especially those with a focus on improving diversity in economics. The student organization Women in Economics at the University of Wisconsin-Madison, for instance, has a high school outreach program (https://www.linkedin.com/company/uw-we). Whether this initiative would require a light touch or something more from the faculty member will depend on the student organization leadership. Because student leadership changes every year or two, it may be the organization's faculty sponsor who over time maintains the connections with local high schools.

For teachers, there are also outreach programs coordinated by some of our colleagues. The Center for Economics Education at Northern Kentucky University connects with high school teachers and students (https://www.nku.edu/academics/cob/centers/cee.html). The Eller College of Management at the University of Arizona hosts the Office of Economic Education, which also provides resources and workshops for high school teachers (https://eller.arizona.edu/programs/non-degree/economic-education). There are many more, scattered around the country.

The AEA Task Force on Outreach to High School and Undergraduate Students in Economics is, as of early 2022, offering free wall posters to high school teachers, each portraying a diverse group of students, featuring the message "Economists change the world with data," and including a QR code that links to the AEA's website for high school students (https://www.aeaweb.org/about-aea/committees/task-force-student-outreach).

Outreach to Newly Admitted Students

Turning to community and four-year colleges, does the college have a spring visit day for newly admitted students? On many campuses, this day offers departments a chance to market themselves. While some students and their parents will walk up to the economics table or booth already knowing what economics is, others will arrive with a firmly embedded "economics equals finance" fallacy. Your goal is to broaden their perspective.

Take a look at the fliers available to new students. Do they implicitly assume that students know what an economist does and what an economics major learns? Many of us make exactly that error, focusing our visit day fliers on "requirements for the major" or "course offerings." Start instead by selling what economists do. A flier can highlight recent graduates and their jobs. Include photos, too. Maryam is now an analyst with the state department of transportation. Jamil is an analyst for a local health insurance company. Monique is a research assistant at the nearby Federal Reserve Bank. Ray is in law school. Chen is working with the city on a project to address homelessness. If a recent graduate is working in finance, include them but do not lead with that profile. Lead and conclude with the alumni profiles that will cause someone to say, "Wow, I didn't know you could do that with an economics major!"

A poster session featuring research projects of the department's undergraduate students is also a good sell. Posters by undergraduate students working as research assistants for graduate students or faculty in the department are another great option for a visit-day poster session. Current undergraduate students should be available to talk about their research experiences with prospective students. Here again, pay attention to the diversity of topics. Learning what questions economists address—it is not all finance—goes a long way.

Outreach to Students in Residence

College advisors are another potential source of new students, both from the recently admitted group and from students already in residence. Most advisors on college campuses are stretched thin. Their knowledge of economics may come entirely from what the economics department tells them. How is the economics major described in the college catalogue or other online academic guide? Not only is this a key source of information for admitted students, but it is also often the primary source for college advisors. Be sure that your descriptions are up to date, reflective of the diversity of options within the economics major. Your overworked campus advisors will be grateful if you can give them a one-sentence summary of economics that they can use with students who are undeclared: "Economics is about using data to create solutions to society's problems."

For students in residence, again think through the content of any advertising that you are making available. Does your advertising assume that students know what an economist does? Be sure the catalog description for every course fully captures the questions addressed in that course. Some students will take the introductory course solely because it is a prerequisite to later courses that they are particularly interested in.

PROMOTING CONTINUING STUDY IN ECONOMICS

What happens in the Introductory Microeconomics course can influence who continues in the major. This section focuses on strategies to encourage women to continue studying economics.

Role Models

Seeing other women who are economists and who can serve as role models may encourage some students to continue with economics. Research on the role model effect is mixed. Carrell et al. (2010) find that having a women faculty member teach math and science has little impact on male students, but improves performance and the likelihood of continuing study for women students. Kato and Song (2022) find that matching female students with female advisers pays off in terms of retention and grades, particularly for women with weaker high school backgrounds. Fairlie et al. (2014) find that underrepresented minority (URM) students in community colleges are more likely to complete the course and earn higher grades if the instructor is also URM. Lusher et al. (2018) find that the role model effect extends to teaching assistants (TAs); having a TA of a similar race/ethnicity improves student grades and may impact the decision to pursue that major. Yet in a study of 159 institutions, Emerson et al. (2018) find no effect of having a woman faculty member on the share of economics majors who are female.

And in any case, we are who we are; we cannot individually change our identity in order to become a role model.[1] But we need not look only to ourselves when seeking out role models for students. Porter and Serra (2020) demonstrate that bringing women speakers into an introductory course can boost rates of continuing study for women students. Everyone's extensive experience with Zoom now makes this strategy even easier. A speaker can join an introductory class for 15 to 30 minutes via Zoom from anywhere. Consider inviting female faculty from your own or other schools, or recent alumnae.

Active Learning

Instruction that invokes active learning practices provides a more positive and successful learning experience (Freeman et al. 2011). Eddy and Hogan (2014) found that implementing active learning in the biology classroom boosted average exam scores for everyone, and particularly benefitted black and first-generation students, but they did not isolate the effects on women. *Div.E.Q.*, *Starting Point*, and Chapter 14 in this book contain many suggestions for how to add active learning to any class.

Do not think that active learning is only the purview of those with small classes. In my own introductory class of 700 students, I relied heavily upon clickers, incorporating five to eight clicker questions in any 50-minute class (Olney 2016). Questions included quick recall, reading checks, problem-solving, polls, and simple experimental questions. In a 500-student class with nine TAs, we divided the room into ten physical zones, one for each of the TAs and myself. Students were given in-class exercises to complete and each of the TAs and I would circulate within our zone to answer questions and encourage students.

Examples

Think carefully about the examples you use to illustrate economic principles. Surely, we are light years away from the blatantly sexist examples that I and others heard as students in the 1970s. Yet still we need to consider what background knowledge is needed to understand an example. Is that knowledge equally accessible by all students? If not, either revamp the example or fill in the knowledge blanks for all.

Early impressions matter. On the first day, talk about the wide variety of questions addressed with economics. Include the big questions as well as the narrow ones: Why are some nations rich and others poor? What impact will rising commercial rents have on the ability of family-owned restaurants to survive in a rapidly gentrifying community? Perhaps use that week's news as a springboard. Cover a range of topics: transportation, health, energy, inequality, climate, urbanization, education, and perhaps even finance.

And then, over the semester, deliver. Incorporate examples that draw from these diverse topics. Even if your curriculum is entirely scripted, do your best to illustrate the principles with contemporary and varied social and economic issues.

Market imperfections resonate with many students. The more quickly the curriculum can move through perfect competition, the better. Illustrate monopolistic competition with family-owned restaurants. This can be an opportunity to discuss familial responsibilities and childcare. Consider together whether a family-owned restaurant which allows the parents flexibility for supervising homework or shepherding kids hither and yon will choose to operate with negative economic profit, even in the long run. Discuss externalities in depth. Consider delving into whether the implicit assumption of equal power across individuals in determining the socially optimal quantity of an activity is accurate, or fair. Should both men and women have an equal say in determining the socially optimal quantity of abortion? Prioritize discussion of inequality—wealth, income, unemployment—by class, by race, and by gender (see Chapters 10 and 11 in this book).

Small changes in examples can be effective. In a problem set question about comparative advantage and the gains from trade, I referenced Szuchman and Anderson's 2012 book *It's Not You, It's the Dishes* and set up an example about a married couple deciding who would take what responsibilities within the household. The example began, "Chris and Robin are a married couple. They both use they/them pronouns." The names were deliberately ambiguous as to gender. Students who use they/them pronouns saw themselves reflected in the example. Some even posted their appreciation on Twitter.

Math Skills and Confidence

Emerson et al. (2018) find that a college calculus requirement can increase the share of economics degrees awarded to women. While calculus is required for only a small handful of Introductory Microeconomics courses, comfort with and a basic ability in math is a necessity. Yet high school boys continue to be more confident in their math ability than girls (Travers 2020). Fennell and Foster (2019) describe formative assessments that can help students to build confidence in and hone the math skills needed to be successful in economics. In my own introductory course, I implemented Fennell and Foster's approach. In week one, students took a low-stakes math assessment. Students who earned fewer than three of the possible four points were offered the chance to raise their score to four points if they met with a free department tutor to review the incorrectly answered questions. While selection bias is clearly present, those who followed up performed better on the subsequent exams and were more likely to finish the course than other students with the same math score.

Grades and Nudges

Jansson and Tyrefors (2020) found same-sex bias in grading of exams, which was eliminated when anonymous grading was implemented. There are a number of platforms now available for grading anonymously, often financed through a contract between the college and the vendor, and then provided free of cost to the student and instructor. Even for grading essay questions, a platform such as Gradescope is valuable.

Women tend to be more sensitive to grades than men, particularly in male-dominated fields (Kugler et al. 2021). Avilova and Goldin (2018a) found that the decision to continue with economics was nearly impervious to grades in an introductory course for men, but strongly correlated with grades for women. An encouraging nudge can be effective. A letter of praise and encouragement received a few days to weeks before enrollment opens for next term's classes can boost enrollment rates in the next course in the sequence, especially for women and students of color (Dhar et al. 2018). Timing matters. Send a letter before, not after, students have enrolled in next term's classes.

BEYOND THE CLASSROOM

Students need friends and community. Encourage student organizations in your department for women and students of color. Starting a club may take some faculty time and investment. Sometimes a call for interested parties is sufficient to get a club started. At other times, students first need settings in which they can meet and get to know each other. Consider offering a one- or two-unit reading course for introductory students on a topic likely to draw a diverse audience. For instance, you could center a reading course around Claudia Goldin's book *Career and Family: Women's Century-Long Journey Toward Equity* (Princeton University Press, 2021), Mehrsa Baradaran's book *The Color of Money: Black Banks and the Racial Wealth Gap* (Belknap/ Harvard University Press, 2017), or William Darity and A. Kirsten Mullen's book *From Here to Equality: Reparations for Black Americans in the Twenty-First Century* (UNC Press, 2020). Each book is accessible by students with just Introductory Microeconomics. With your help, students can see how Introductory Microeconomics applies to diverse topics. They will make new friends. And perhaps out of the experience a student organization will emerge.

CONCLUSION

Doing the work of promoting gender diversity is often slow and without obvious or immediate payoff. Keep at it. Small and large efforts, occasional or continuous, can change lives.

NOTE

1. Those of us who identify as lesbian, gay, bisexual, transgender or queer (LGBTQ) are not consistently identified by students as LGBTQ. We can come out to our students. In my experience, coming out through off-handed in-class mentions of my

wife (much as many straight male colleagues do regularly) can have a powerful effect for LGBTQ students and for students with LGBTQ family members.

REFERENCES

Allgood, S., and Bayer, A. (2017). Learning outcomes for economists. *American Economic Review 107*(5), 660–664.

Auriol, E., Friebel, G., Weinberger, A., and Wilhem, S. (2021). Women in economics: Europe and the world. CEPR Discussion Paper No. 16686.

Avilova, T., and Goldin, C. (2018a). What can UWE do for economics? NBER Working Paper No. 24189. Accessed December 1, 2021 at http://www.nber.org/papers/w24189.

Avilova, T., and Goldin, C. (2018b). What can UWE do for economics? *AEA Papers and Proceedings 108*, 186–190.

Baradaran, M. (2017). *The Color of Money: Black Banks and the Racial Wealth Gap.* Belknap/Harvard University Press.

Bayer, A., and Rouse, C.E. (2016). Diversity in the economics profession: a new attack on an old problem. *Journal of Economic Perspectives 30*(4), 221–242.

Bayer, A., and Wilcox, D. (2019). The unequal distribution of economic education: a report on the race, ethnicity, and gender of economics majors at U.S. colleges and universities. *Journal of Economic Education 50*(3), 299–320.

Benjamin, D., Cohen, A.J., and Hamilton, G. (2020). A Pareto-improving way to teach principles of economics: evidence from the University of Toronto. *AEA Papers and Proceedings 110*, 299–303.

Buckles, K. (2019). Fixing the leaky pipeline: strategies for making economics work for women at every stage. *Journal of Economic Perspectives 33*(1), 43–60.

Carrell, S.E., Page, M.E., and West, J.E. (2010). Sex and science: how professor gender perpetuates the gender gap. *Quarterly Journal of Economics 125*(3), 1101–1144.

Chevalier, J. (2021). Report: Committee on the Status of Women in the Economics Profession (CSWEP). *AEA Papers and Proceedings 111*, 742–763.

Council for Economic Education (2020). Survey of the states: economic and personal finance education in our nation's schools. New York: Council for Economic Education. Accessed December 14, 2021 at https://www.councilforeconed.org/survey-of-the-states-2020/.

Crawford, C., Davies, N.M., and Smith, S. (2018). Women's Committee: why do so few women study economics? Evidence from England. *Royal Economic Society*, accessed December 1, 2021 at https://www.res.org.uk/resources-page/why-do-so-few-women-study-economics--2018-pdf.html.

Darity, W.A., Jr, and Mullen, A.K. (2020). *From Here to Equality: Reparations for Black Americans in the Twenty-First Century.* University of North Carolina Press.

Dhar, D., Gist, H.J., and Sadler, A. (2018). Race, gender, (and more!) and economics at Berkeley. Presentation for the April 2018 UWE Conference, Urbana-Champaign, IL.

Duoduo, X. (2018). Is gender equality at Chinese colleges a sham? *Sixth Tone.* Accessed December 1, 2021 at https://www.sixthtone.com/news/1002051/is-gender-equality-at-chinese-colleges-a-sham%3F.

Duval-Hernández, R., and Villagómez, F.A. (2011). Trends and characteristics of economics degrees in a developing country: the case of Mexico. *Journal of Economic Education 42*(1), 87–94.

Eddy, S.L., and Hogan, K. (2014). Getting under the hood: how and for whom does increasing course structure work? *CBE Life Sciences Education 13*(3), 453–468.

Emerson, T.L.N., McGoldrick, K., and, Siegfried, J.J. (2018). The gender gap in economics degrees: an investigation of the role model and quantitative requirements hypotheses. *Southern Economic Journal 84*(3), 898–911.

Fairlie, R.W., Hoffmann, F., and Oreopoulos, P. (2014). A community college instructor like me: race and ethnicity interactions in the classroom. *American Economic Review 104*(8), 2567–2591.

Fennell, M.A., and Foster, I.R. (2019). Revisiting the role of a basic math assessment in predicting student performance in Principles of Microeconomics. *Journal of Economics and Economic Education Research 20*(2), 1–13.

Freeman, S., Haak, D., and Wenderoth, M.P. (2011). Increased course structure improves performance in introductory biology. *CBE Life Sciences Education 10*(2), 175–186.

Goldin, C. (2021). *Career and Family: Women's Century-Long Journey Toward Equity*. Princeton University Press.

Hansen, W.L., Salemi, M.K., and Siegfried, J.J. (2002). Use it or lose it: teaching literacy in the economics principles course. *American Economic Review: Papers and Proceedings 92*(2), 463–472.

Jansson, J., and Tyrefors, B. (2020). The genius is a male: stereotypes and same-sex bias in exam grading in economics at Stockholm University. Working Paper No. 1362, Stockholm: Research Institute of Industrial Economics. Accessed December 14, 2021 at https://www.ifn.se/en/publications/working-papers/2020/1362/.

Kato, T., and Song, Y. (2022). Advising, gender, and performance: evidence from a university with exogenous adviser–student gender match. *Economic Inquiry 60*, 121–141.

Kugler, A.D., Tinsley, C.H., and Ukhaneva, O. (2021). Choice of majors: are women really different from men? *Economics of Education Review 81*, 1–19.

Lusher, L., Campbell, D., and Carrell, S. (2018). TAs like me: racial interactions between graduate teaching assistants and undergraduates. *Journal of Public Economics 159*, 203–224.

Müller, M. (2021). Intergenerational transmission of education: internalized aspirations versus parent pressure. Job Market Paper, U.C. Berkeley. Accessed December 14, 2021 at https://www.maximilianwmueller.com/#h.ss2y72nsz8gk.

Olney, M.L. (2016). Explaining "in the aggregate" concepts with clickers. *Journal of Economics Teaching 1*(2), 71–90.

Page, E. (2021). Economics 101: more college classrooms bring moral debates to the surface. *Christian Science Monitor* November 9. Accessed December 1, 2021 at https://www.csmonitor.com/Business/2021/1109/Economics-101-More-college -classes-bring-moral-debates-to-the-surface.

Porter, C., and Serra, D. (2020). Gender differences in the choice of major: the importance of female role models. *American Economic Journal: Applied Economics 12*(3), 226–54.

Project Implicit (n.d.). Project implicit: preliminary information. Accessed December 1, 2021 at https://implicit.harvard.edu/implicit/takeatest.html.

Quadlin, N. (2020). From major preferences to major choices: gender and logics of major choice. *Sociology of Education 93*(2), 91–109.

Stock, P.A., and Stock, E.M. (2018). Factors that influence a college student's choice of an academic major and minor. *Journal of Scholastic Inquiry: Business 9*(1), 56–78.

Szuchman, P., and Anderson, J. (2012). *It's Not You, It's the Dishes (Originally Published As Spousonomoics): How to Minimize Conflict and Maximize Happiness in Your Relationship*. Random House.

Travers, M. (2020). Even among elite students, boys are more confident in math than girls. *Forbes* April 9. Accessed December 14, 2021 at https://www.forbes.com/sites/traversmark/2020/04/09/even-among-elite-students-boys-are-more-confident-in-math-than-girls/.

PART IV

Pedagogy

13. Writing in the Introductory Microeconomics course

Nathan D. Grawe and George Cusack

Written communication is as foundational to microeconomics as the concept of elasticity. However, where the latter is included in every Principles of Microeconomics textbook (and so, we presume, in every course), the former is often excluded. Given economists' training, we assume that the decision to emphasize problem sets and exams over writing assignments follows from perceptions of two factors: benefits and costs. Regarding the former, we imagine some believe that the core content of the discipline lies outside writing; the perceived benefit of time spent helping students learn to communicate economic concepts is low. At the same time, effective writing assignments require substantial effort on the part of students and faculty alike. Taking these two factors together, to some it may seem that benefits and costs simply do not justify devoting time to writing that might instead, say, be put toward a more nuanced understanding of alternative solutions to externalities.

We begin by arguing for the essential nature of writing in economics. Our position is hardly novel. Even in 1906—long before the language of mathematics gained ascendency in our primary journals—Alfred Marshall articulated a preference for communication in English over mathematics wherever reasonably possible (Pigou 1925, p. 427). "[A] good mathematical theorem dealing with economic hypotheses [is] very unlikely to be good economics," he warned. As a result, as he matured he found it wise to follow several principles including "use mathematics as a shorthand language, rather than as an engine of enquiry." When the math had served that purpose, he counseled, "Translate into English … [and] burn the mathematics." If our argument for writing in economics lacks novelty, technological change has only increased the relative value of fluency in written communication. We will point to several spots in the traditional Principles of Microeconomics curriculum that seem particularly well suited to writing assignments.

As great as the value of writing instruction may be to an economics curriculum, we acknowledge the costs to the time of students and faculty. This chapter attempts to reduce these burdens by drawing on the deep scholarship surrounding writing across the curriculum (WAC) (or writing in the disciplines).

We offer numerous ideas for assigning and responding to Principles students' writing that are designed to fit the constraints of a typical introductory course.[1] In addition, we offer insights from the WAC literature on effective assignment design. Among these, three stand out. First, because writing is typically learned through the process of revision, effective writing assignments build in opportunities for students to re-write. Second, because effective rhetoric reflects the audience, professors should explicitly identify a reader for assigned student writing. Finally, as tempting as it may be to correct each grammatical mistake, pedagogical studies show this practice to be ineffective: students respond more to targeted comments, a result that dramatically reduces the necessary time spent in grading. We conclude with references to professional development resources for colleagues who would like to move forward with writing in their classrooms.

WHY WRITE IN PRINCIPLES OF MICROECONOMICS?

The most basic answer to this question is offered by McCloskey (1985, p. 188): "Writing is the economist's trade." McCloskey (1999, p. 5) elaborates a bit further by noting that "an economically trained person is likely to spend most of her working life writing papers, reports, memoranda, proposals, columns, and letters. Economics depends much more on writing (and on speaking, another neglected art) than on the statistics and mathematics usually touted as the tools of the trade." Allgood and Bayer (2016) concur, listing "communicat[ion of] economic ideas in diverse collaborations" among five "essential competencies of the discipline."[2] They explain:

> Economists do not answer multiple-choice questions. They formulate productive questions, and they convey their analyses in short and long form. They interpret data and construct and deconstruct arguments that explain observed phenomena. Communication is part of this process .... A person well trained in economics must be able to take information, whether statistical data or written material, and apply the appropriate economic methods to explain the context by which the information is created or the potential implications of this information. This will be difficult to do with any short form of response. (Allgood and Bayer 2016, p. 109)

Given the professions and lives that our students will lead, writing about economic ideas will be a skill so necessary that training should begin as early as possible.

As much as we agree with this argument, we also recognize that it is an argument for writing instruction in general rather than for writing instruction in economics courses. After all, arguments of comparative advantage lead toward a world of specialization in which economists focus on income and substitution effects, while writing instructors help students to develop clear arguments. This logic fails, however, because the process of writing about economics—and writing to a variety of audiences in particular—leads to new and deeper understanding of the material (Palmini 1996). Indeed, through writing for someone else's understanding, we often clarify our own: "what looked persuasive when floating vaguely in your mind looks exceptionally foolish when moored to the page. You'll discover, too, truths you didn't know you had .... [L]anguage is ... an instrument of thought" (McCloskey 2019, p. 8). More broadly, Bean (2001) argues that writing assignments improve content knowledge by deepening student engagement and critical thinking around the subject.

Scholars in the field of composition and rhetoric have advocated the concept of "writing to learn" (WTL) since the 1970s. Stated simply, WTL is the idea that practicing writing within disciplinary contexts does more than improve students' communication skills; it enhances their ability to process new information critically, learn and apply new concepts, and understand the guiding assumptions and methods of a discipline (Forsman 1985). Parker and Goodwin (1987) document the benefits of WTL projects in disciplines as diverse as psychology, nursing, and mathematics, all of which seemed to enhance students' understanding of the material as well as teaching them the basic genres and techniques of the discipline. In the late 1990s and early 2000s, numerous science, technology, engineering, and mathematics (STEM) programs adopted WTL approaches at all levels of education, with consistently positive results (Poirrier 1997; Brewster and Klump 2004; Galer-Unti 2002; Thaiss and Zawacki 2006; Graham and Perin 2007). Taken as a whole, the literature of the past five decades clearly indicates that when disciplinary courses incorporate writing alongside content instruction, students tend to achieve a better understanding of the material (Carter et al. 2007; Anderson et al. 2015), retain this understanding better in future courses (Yancey et al. 2014), and develop a stronger interest in and enthusiasm for the study of that discipline (Thaiss and Zawacki 2006; Anderson et al. 2015).

The low frequency of writing assignments on Principles of Economics syllabi suggests that many in the field question these arguments. Revealed preference suggests that the majority view writing assignments—especially quantitative writing assignments—as an opportunity to contribute to general education rather than as central components of economics instruction. Evidence, however, falls on the side of Marshall and McCloskey. For example, Greenlaw (2003) reports on an experiment in which students experienced two essentially identical classes of Principles of Macroeconomics, except that one section completed a series of short papers while the other did not. While differences in affective measures of student engagement with and appreciation for the course were not clearly correlated with engagement with writing, students in the writing-rich course outperformed their non-writing peers on exams. Specifically, while the two sections earned very similar grades on the first midterm exam (as one would expect from random assignment to the two sections), in the second midterm and the final exam students whose introduction to macroeconomics was writing-rich earned (statistically and practically) significantly higher scores.

If empirical studies are not persuasive, we end this portion of our argument with an appeal to introspection, extending our own experiences to those of our students. In an argument for greater use of quantitative writing assignments, Burke (2007) observes: "We [the professoriate] write, after all, to figure out what we think. And we ask our students to write so that they will learn how to think." If we expand and shape our own economic thinking through the process of putting words down on paper, surely we should teach our students to do the same; this is literally to say: we should teach them to learn to think like economists.

If economists' traditional tendency to shift writing instruction outside the discipline hampers students' economic understanding, it also dooms students to be poor economic writers. Many studies show that because students struggle to transfer skills learned in one domain to another, they are unlikely to learn to write effectively about economics without practice within the discipline. For example, based on a survey of faculty from a variety of disciplines (including economics), Thaiss and Zawacki observe that while faculty tend to use the same basic vocabulary to describe the standards of "good writing" within their disciplines, this similarity of terms hides a variety of discipline-specific expectations that students are generally expected to master with little explicit instruction (Thaiss and Zawacki 2006, pp. 88–90). The authors ultimately conclude that students' mastery of these discipline-specific conventions depends on their "sense of place within the disciplinary enterprise," a sense of themselves as practitioners of a discipline that students develop through the experience of writing to a variety of assignments within major courses (ibid., p. 139). Ultimately, if writing is fundamental to the working lives of economists, economics faculty must take on the responsibility to teach it. Writing courses may provide basic instruction, but only economists can teach students how to apply those skills effectively within the discipline.

EXAMPLES OF WRITING IN PRINCIPLES OF ECONOMICS

Before looking at how workload can be managed, consider several representative writing assignments that exemplify the intersection between writing and common Principles of Microeconomics learning outcomes. Indeed, effective writing-to-learn moments run throughout the Principles of Microeconomics course. We focus on three example assignment types to demonstrate potential variety with connections to major elements of a typical section.

Because students often enroll in introductory courses with a crude, topic-bound notion of economics, most textbooks and instructors begin the course by showing students the broad range of questions addressed within the field. While a short reading or lecture often serves as the vehicle for this content, an annotated bibliography paper would arguably accomplish similar goals more effectively. The assignment is simple: using EconLit, students identify between three and five papers published in the *American Economic Review: Papers and Proceedings* in the past five years. For each paper, they are to compose a short bibliographic entry that identifies the question studied and the results found. Because the purpose is to explain to a peer audience the range of topics studied by economists, in addition to rewarding clear writing, points are given for the subject variety represented in the annotated bibliography. Note that the assignment does not require that students read the full articles; that would surely be more than can be expected of Principles students in the first week of their economics education. Thoughtful skimming will suffice.

Despite the brevity of the writing product required, the assignment achieves three important learning goals. First, short writing assignments like this are wonderful opportunities to focus on concision, sentence construction, and word choice. Freed from larger questions of organization and argument, the student can pay close attention to these narrower writing concerns. Second, the assignment broadens students' perceptions of the field, and does so in a more personal and memorable way than the standard textbook treatment. By leading a brief class discussion on the day the bibliographies are due, a broader view of the discipline emerges—and one that inherently speaks better to students' interests—than any textbook treatment. Moreover, the definition of the field comes from students' own observations rather than assertions from authority (the instructor or textbook author). Finally, the assignment introduces students to EconLit, an invaluable tool for more advanced undergraduate study in economics.

Of course, models form the core of Principles of Microeconomics. We hope that students will begin to "think like economists," using models of perfect competition, oligopoly, or monopoly to understand current events and policy debates. Written assignments are well suited to cementing content lessons through active application. One such assignment asks students to take on the role of an aide to a United States (US) Senator considering legislation that would relax immigration law to allow larger numbers of workers to enter the country. (The purpose of giving students an explicit role and audience is discussed in detail later in this chapter.) They are asked to write a three-page memo explaining the labor market consequences following from the model of supply and demand.

Take a moment to consider likely responses. The weakest papers might model the entire US labor force as a single market: 160 million homogenous laborers. With an increase in supply, wages fall and domestic workers are hurt. While consistent with many textbook applications, writing such words should give students pause. And so the learning begins. Weak papers may uncover the direction of effects, but what would determine whether those effects are large or small? (Elasticity of demand makes a return visit to the stage.) Is it reasonable to treat all workers as substitutes for immigrant labor? Given educational attainment in the most common immigrant countries of origin, a better version might focus the essay's analysis around the market for low-skill labor. Having recognized that workers are not homogeneous, the best essays might take a final step to acknowledge that there are actually at least two labor markets: low- and high-skill. In the former, immigrant labor is a substitute with supply-side effects; but in the latter, immigrants' labor hours are complements such that we might anticipate demand-side effects.

While it is possible that strong students would make these connections when completing a typical in-class exam, these discoveries seem far more likely in the context of a written assignment. First, a paper provides more time and so signals to students that the question might be more complex than first realized. Second, the process of writing forces students to sit with their ideas, prompting reflection and the questioning of assumptions. Of course, recognition of complexity and the questioning of assumptions mark the economist's way of thinking.

Both Palmini (1996) and Thaiss and Zawacki (2006) argue that learning opportunities expand when students are asked to write to different audiences. Modest tweaking of the supply and demand assignment described above demonstrates the potential. The product might become a letter written to a grandfather who is passionate about immigration. Or the analysis can be directed to a classmate who is apathetic about immigration reform. Or perhaps the student takes on the role of a columnist working for a newspaper. Maybe the journalist produces a blogpost rather than a printed column. Change the audience, the writer's relationship to the audience, or the genre, and writing choices will necessarily change. It is relatively easy to imagine a series of short writing assignments—one for supply and demand, one for externalities, one for monopoly, one for public goods, one for trade, and so on—all based on this template but never repeating the same audience or genre. Of course, the same principles apply to the stylistic choices that professional economists make as they shift from writing an academic paper, to writing a report for a private-sector client, to writing a policy-relevant op-ed; once again we see that teaching students to use effective economic rhetoric is teaching "how to think like an economist."

Finally, we offer example assignments that engage students with data. Quantitative literacy (QL) might be viewed as a general education goal. For example, the Association of American Colleges and Universities (2011) includes it among a short list of "essential learning outcomes" for undergraduates. However, Allgood and Bayer (2016), Hansen (1986, 2001), and Wolfe (2020) argue that QL is central to our discipline, and among the basic competencies aspired to among economics majors. Specifically, Hansen (2001, p. 232) argues that our majors should be able to "track down economic data and data sources [and] [f]ind information about the generation, construction, and meaning of economic data." Meyers et al. (2011) report widespread agreement within the field: a large majority of department chairs strongly agree that "ability to find economic data and use it in appropriate ways" is very important as a learning outcome for our discipline.

Writing assignments in Principles of Economics can support these goals by introducing students to commonly used data sources in stand-alone assignments, or by incorporating data in an "explicate the model" paper like the one described above. For example, in teaching a module on input markets, some introductory texts introduce students to the Hotelling conjecture. Students can be asked to go to the Federal Reserve Bank of St Louis's FRED database to find the Spot Crude Oil Price since 1946. In a one-page paper they might present a graph of the data and answer whether the time series is consistent with the conjecture. Alternatively, in a unit on demand, annual percentage change in oil prices might be compared with percentage change in vehicle miles traveled (also available in FRED) to find evidence of own-price effects in the gasoline market. (Or students might compare growth in vehicle miles to that of real gross domestic product to explore the income effect.)

The Statistical Abstract of the United States is another go-to data source that students can be exposed to with short data description assignments. For example, many textbook treatments of Smith's diamond–water paradox replace the former good with K-12 (kindergarten to twelfth grade) teachers. Students can be asked to estimate the number of K-12 teachers in the United States based only on the fact that the total population is around 330 million. Then they can find the actual number of teachers reported in the Statistical Abstract and, in one page, reflect on the difference between their estimate and the truth. (In my experience, students vastly underestimate the number of teachers, because lacking first-hand experience in low-attendance, special education classrooms, they dramatically overestimate the pupil-to-teacher ratio.) This one short writing assignment reinforces the diamond–water paradox, introduces students to a common data source, provides practice in estimation, highlights the problem of experience-based biases, and engages students with technical writing tasks common to our field.

Writing with numbers can also be incorporated into a writing-about-models assignment. Consider again the application of supply and demand to immigration expansion. If we were to expand immigration levels by 10 percent, should we expect the effects on low-skill wages to be pronounced or negligible? Obviously, the elasticity of demand is important to this question, as is the degree of substitutability between immigrant and domestic labor. But even setting these theoretical issues aside, the impact of such immigration reform clearly depends on whether the proposed policy adds relatively many or few workers to the labor force. How many new immigrants would we add if immigration rose by 10 percent? And how does that compare with the size of the current low-skill labor market? Using data from the Statistical Abstract, students can put some empirical flesh on the concept of elasticity to get a sense of whether the qualitative predictions of the model are likely to be quantitatively important.

A QUESTION OF EXPERTISE

Because most economists lack graduate school training in the art of writing instruction, it is natural that many avoid giving writing assignments due to fears of limited expertise.[3] For at least three reasons, students benefit when we set these anxieties aside and ask them to write in the economics classroom. First, our fears overlook two other critical forms of expertise: subject area and reader expertise. Bean (2001, p. 11) notes that:

> Teachers simply need to be honest readers, making comments like these:
> "I got lost in this part."
> "You need more evidence here."
> "You seem to be overlooking Baker's research on this problem. Can you summarize and respond to Baker's views?"
> "Excellent point!"

He argues that engaging in honest dialogue gives students sufficient focus for the work of revision and re-writing. This is not to say that there is no expertise relevant to writing instruction: indeed, George has benefitted from years of powerful formal training in this area, while Nathan has not. Rather, despite lack of training, Nathan is still capable of pushing students forward through use of his training as an economist and many years of reading others' writing. Focusing on what he lacks distracts from the numerous things he can do to move student writing to the next (if not final) level.

Second, while George may be a more specialized and experienced writer/ writing instructor, students are incapable of learning everything at once. And, for better and worse, they come to college with many opportunities for development as writers. Even though Nathan might not recognize everything that is going wrong with a piece of a student's writing, and even though he may not know how to address every problem he identifies, he still finds plenty to comment on when responding to papers. In fact, a key to effective commenting is limiting comments to only the most important issues. As Bean (2001, pp. 83–84) notes, this strategy of "minimal marking" both encourages students to "develop their own mental procedures for finding and correcting errors" and "avoid[s] sending the message that a poorly written essay simply needs editing rather than revision."[4] Perhaps concision is your strength. Then, help students to exclude extraneous verbiage. Perhaps you are expert in crafting topic sentences: then work with students on organization. Perhaps you have a deep vocabulary: then help students in the art of word choice. No matter the case, students will never learn to write in a single term. Embracing that truth allows us to focus on the most productive feedback for the present moment. What is more, if an entire economics department commits to writing instruction—even if each person brings a limited scope to the endeavor—students have more opportunities to write, which research suggests is more effective than when writing is limited to a single course (see Quesenberry et al. 2000; Thaiss and Zawacki 2006, pp. 139–141).[5]

Third, economists have important knowledge that some writing instructors lack: specifically, training and experience with technical writing. It is an unusual piece of economics writing that is entirely free of tables, graphs, or quantitative data. These staples of business writing involve their own set of writing questions. Where do I place a graph or table? How should the written text interact with these visual elements of the piece? Are there tips for creating captions or labeling axes and table columns? How should color choices be made when graphing? How might I contextualize a large number (in sentences such as "The federal government's debt totals $27 trillion," for example) so that readers better understand its meaning? Even economists who have never enrolled in a technical writing course will likely have received extensive instruction from editors and co-authors on these kinds of questions. Students who only receive writing assignments in English literature or religion courses will likely enter the workforce without even knowing that these questions might be asked.

So, we honor the importance of formal training in writing instruction. And yet we argue that economists have much to teach their students about writing in economics.

HOW TO REDUCE THE COST OF WRITING ASSIGNMENTS WHILE IMPROVING THE WRITING PRODUCT

Time represents one of the largest impediments to assigning writing in Principles of Microeconomics. Sections are often heavily enrolled, so that the grading load is substantial. Insofar as studies show that the process of revision is critical to gaining writing skills, the grading costs seem only to multiply when students are given the opportunity to revise and resubmit assignments. Meaningful and recurring invitations for student writing (including meaningful opportunity for revision) can easily overwhelm available time for both faculty and students.

Recognizing this problem, WAC professionals have developed a wide range of practices to craft better assignments with extensive feedback and learning through revision, while killing neither doctor nor patient. We provide a few of these ideas here, including further assignment examples with connections to specific teaching goals in Principles of Microeconomics.

Remember that Small Can Be Powerful

We often assume that the most powerful writing assignments are long essays or reports, where students practice multiple writing skills at once. However, students often learn as much, if not more, from smaller assignments that target one or two key operations, because shorter length reduces the cost of revision, and simpler tasks enable students to practice core skills in isolation. This is good news for those teaching large sections for which grading loads preclude longer written assignments. For example, consider the annotated bibliography prompt described above. The final product is three to five short paragraphs. Despite the modest length, students learn about the breadth of the field and a key tool for accessing the economics literature (the primary content goals), while simultaneously honing the skill of writing strong sentences and paragraphs.

Another short writing assignment might focus on data literacy. In a unit on externalities, students could be asked to write a paragraph to their peers on the topic "one number we all should know."[6] They would find one piece of data in the Statistical Abstract that is pertinent to the production of energy or resulting externalities. Then, in a substantial paragraph, students present their number and make an argument as to why everyone in the class should have this particular figure at their fingertips as we analyze externalities. Such one-page papers allow students to engage repeatedly with written economics without creating an impossible grading task.

Constrain Topics, Particularly When Incorporating Data

Grading flows more quickly when mistakes are predictable. The instructor can plan in advance how various content errors will affect papers' scores. By contrast, when novel mistakes show up deep into the stack, fairness often requires combing through previously graded work, followed by awkward comparisons of "Is this error of the same magnitude as that?" Moreover, when data are involved, the explanation for why a cited figure is misused often requires detailed knowledge. And when students are writing on a wide range of topics, obtaining that information may involve a time-consuming investigation of the numbers. For example, when Nathan first assigned the paper applying supply and demand to immigration reform, the prompt allowed students to write on a legislative debate of their own choice. The resulting stack covered dozens of disparate topics and much time was spent looking up facts and figures to make sure they were being used appropriately. The revision described above largely avoids these costs by making all students write on the same topic. As a side benefit, students are better able to serve as peer reviewers when they are all studying the same proposal.

Scaffold Assignments

Scaffolded assignments break up a larger paper into a series of writing opportunities that are combined in the final product. For example, in the version of the supply and demand analysis that incorporates data on immigration and the labor market, Nathan has found it useful to assign a mini-writing assignment in which students describe the data they will use and how. Then students submit another mini-assignment showing their analysis of the economic model. Finally, they submit the full paper combining the two parts. The mini-assignments allow Nathan to identify fundamental problems of data interpretation or economic analysis before they become the basis of an entire paper. What grade does a student earn for a competent manipulation of supply and demand, that is made ridiculous by a fundamental misinterpretation of data? Scaffolding avoids the cost of answering such questions.

From the learner's perspective, scaffolding works by requiring revision. It is literally impossible to begin the ultimate assignment the night before it is due. Some sections of the mini-assignments can find their way into the final product, but the focus of each preliminary assignment is sufficiently different from that of the final paper that rewriting is inevitable.

Scaffolding also reduces cognitive load. (See, for example, Wood et al. 1976; Bamberg 2000.) Papers in Principles of Microeconomics often represent the first time that students will be asked to include graphs, figures/models, or tables in their writing. With considerable mental energy spent on so many new tasks, basic writing skills such as sentence or paragraph construction can falter. Scaffolding allows students to focus on new elements in isolation before incorporating them into the larger whole. By dividing up the content this way, cognitive load is reduced to a manageable level which can improve ultimate writing quality. Of course, the challenges of cognitive load never go away, which is one of the reasons that revision is critical. Galbraith (1978) notes: "Thinking ... is also a very tedious thing which men—or women—will do anything to avoid. So all first drafts are deeply flawed by the need to combine composition with thought. Each later draft is less demanding in this regard. Hence the writing can be better."

Engage Peer Review

Even though revision is critical to the writing process, instructors need not read all papers twice. Judicious use of peer review can provide feedback that informs revision without instructor input. In a workshop, John Bean shared that he required his students to have an acknowledgment on the cover page identifying at least two peer readers who had given feedback before he saw that paper. He explained that this requirement modeled professional practice: who among us submits writing to journals without first getting feedback from others? The peer readers can be student employees in the writing center or friends. Or the instructor can organize reading groups within the class. One advantage of using classmate peers is that students benefit doubly: first as readers when they encounter alternative models of the paper they are writing, and again as writers when they respond to comments from peers.

Assign Iterative Writing Portfolios[7]

This assignment combines scaffolding and peer review. Early in the course, when first encountering market effects of taxation, students are asked to write a two-page paper explaining the efficiency consequences of unit taxes. A first draft is submitted to an assigned reading group. Based on feedback from peer readers, students then revise the two-page paper. A short class discussion further assures that students are identifying crucial concepts such as price wedges.

After learning about externalities, students are asked to write a four-page paper with the same prompt. Informed by greater theoretical understanding, they should now be capable of writing a more nuanced argument (which explains the longer assignment length). Clearly, content from the two-page version will contribute to the four-page assignment (scaffolding), but the extended length coupled with new ideas encountered in lectures prompt mean-ingfully new papers. Again, peers give feedback on first drafts, which guide revision. Students ultimately turn in a portfolio with four papers, two versions each of the two- and four-page essays. Grades are assigned for the final product and revision across the portfolio.[8] The ultimate grading load is only slightly greater than grading a single paper, yet students experience two opportunities to compose, along with two revisions.

Give Students a TIP and a RAFT

Students struggle to engage material when assignment prompts lack clarity about students' role and purpose. Resulting papers generate less student learning and can be a chore to grade. To draw students into the material, Bean (2011) recommends that each assignment should offer students a TIP and a RAFT. The TIP is a "task as intriguing problem." That is, the prompt should invite students into a dialog or argument rather than ask for a rote solution. For example, consider an assignment exploring the market for Christmas trees, designed as an application of the monopoly model. An overly narrow prompt might ask students to write a two-page paper explaining the effects of monopolization on the price and quantity of Christmas trees, along with resulting changes in consumer and producer surplus. This is a dead-end problem: students immediately sense that there is a single correct answer and focus on reproducing it, rather than contemplating alternative choices for articulating their thoughts. A variation on the same prompt might ask students to consider the pros and cons of a government proposal to relax anti-trust regulations, such that Christmas tree producers might act as a cartel. It is the same economics at the core, but the revised prompt has no right answer; it exposes trade-offs that students can explore in a variety of ways resulting in diverse conclusions.

Bean's RAFT is a "role, audience, format, and task." The prompts in the previous paragraph so far identify only the task. By augmenting the assignment to include a role, audience, and format (or genre), we invite students to think more critically about situational aspects of writing, such as, "What is my relationship to my audience and how does that constrain my writing choices?" Recall the assignment applying a model of supply and demand to immigration expansion. The original prompt gave students the role of an aide writing a policy brief to a US Senator. A twist of the same assignment became the student writing a letter to her grandfather. While the economics content is unchanged, alterations to the audience create distinct learning opportunities. For lengthier discussion of the importance of a clear sense of audience or creative examples, see Bean (2011, pp. 40–46) and Greenlaw (n.d.-a).

With clear direction on all four elements of the RAFT, students are better prepared to engage the subject matter and produce a richer (and more varied) reading experience when it is time to grade the stack. Perhaps most relevant to the purpose of the present discussion, better writing prompts lead to better writing which is much easier to grade. Clarity in the assignment decreases the probability that students fundamentally miss the mark. While such papers are always a minority, instances of fundamental misunderstanding of the assignment consume a disproportionate amount of grading time.[9]

Develop Metacognitive Assignments

Metacognitive writing assignments require students to articulate their methods, assumptions, or thought processes, either in a general context (for example, what they understand about Economics as a discipline) or in the context of a specific assignment (for example, what led them to select a particular model). This genre of assignment is also referred to as reflective writing, but that phrase is often associated with informal, introspective activities such as journaling. In contrast, metacognitive writing assignments can be tightly structured exercises that serve as a valuable extension of the learning process in any course.

Metacognitive assignments can be prospective, asking students to plan or predict their work on a future assignment; or retrospective, asking students to document their work on an assignment they have already completed. Common prospective assignments include:

- Knowledge statements. Students identify what they already know or believe about a given topic and what they hope to learn by studying it in the class.
- Writing proposals. Students identify the topic they have chosen for an upcoming report, why they chose it, and how they intend to approach it (where they will obtain their data, how they will use it, and so on).
- Literature reviews or annotated bibliographies (also discussed above). Students specifically identify their sources for an upcoming report and explain how each source will fit into their argument.
- Writing plans. Students lay out in detail the steps they will undertake for a major assignment, how long they expect to spend on each step, and when they expect to complete each step before the deadline.

Common retrospective assignments include:

- Author's notes. Students write a brief note to accompany either a working draft or the final draft of a major assignment. In their note, students might identify what they see as the major strengths or weakness of their draft, identify areas they plan to improve in revision (or in future assignments), or ask for feedback on specific areas.
- Process analyses. After submitting a major assignment, students critically examine their writing processes: what they believe they did well, what they

might have done better, and how they might adapt their process for future assignments.

- Knowledge statements. Used retrospectively, students articulate what they learned from a given topic, unit, or assignment, and what questions, if any, they still have going forward.

Metacognitive assignments serve two major purposes. First, they allow students to crystalize and document aspects of their learning and writing processes that would otherwise happen entirely in their heads. This allows the students themselves to externalize, examine, and even discuss these processes, with the goal of improving them over time.

Second, metacognitive assignments allow instructors to see and respond to aspects of the students' writing and learning processes that would otherwise be invisible to them. Prospective assignments such as writing proposals allow instructors to identify false assumptions or faulty understandings before they pose significant problems for the student. They also allow the instructor to present alternative suggestions—sources students might consult, methods they might employ, and so on—that could significantly improve a student's final product. Retrospective assignments can provide instructors with deep insight into how students are learning from and engaging with the course material. They create opportunities to help students learn from their mistakes, capitalize on their successes, apply what they have learned to future assignments, and cement learning gains.

Crucially, metacognitive assignments generally take minimal time for students to complete and for instructors to read and return. Short assignments such as author's notes can involve a page or less of writing on the student's part, and can sometimes be completed in class on the day an assignment is due. Longer assignments such as annotated bibliographies, when completed in conjunction with a formal research report, simply document work that students are already doing (or should be doing). In all cases, since metacognitive assignments by definition represent a student's work in progress, there is little need or advantage to writing detailed marginalia or critiquing the formal aspects of student's writing. Thus, instructors can respond to most metacognitive assignments with just a few holistic comments, affirming things that the student is doing well, identifying mistakes or areas for improvement, and providing key suggestions for moving forward.

Use Reader Response Rubrics

Well-constructed rubrics allow instructors to provide detailed feedback at a fast pace. Before giving the assignment, identify the dimensions relevant to feedback.[10] For example, in the data-supported supply and demand analysis of immigration reform, dimensions might include: analysis of the policy using the economic model, quality of data used to support the analysis, quality of the required data figure, and attention to task and audience. Then, for each dimension, provide short descriptions of student work at levels of performance ranging from ineffective to exemplary. Table 13.1 provides an example of descriptors for each dimension. Note that descriptors can be narrowly tailored to one specific assignment, or crafted in more general language such that a single rubric can be reapplied to multiple assignments (Bean 2011, pp. 270–275). The example in Table 13.1 is of the latter variety.

With rubric in hand, the time-consuming process of writing notes is replaced by a few check boxes or underlinings. With the addition of one or two sentences of holistic feedback (see the Comments section at the bottom of the rubric in Table 13.1), students receive a large quantity of input for improvement at a low cost to the grader. Moreover, effective rubrics discipline instructors to focus attention on critical skills, keeping them from spending inordinate time and effort on issues of second-order importance (for example, overfixating on grammar). Some instructors further use the rubric to assign points that can be quickly tallied to arrive at a final grade. Others question whether the dimensions are summable and prefer the freedom to assign holistic grades. In this case, the rubric provides a concise visual summary of the paper that can considerably reduce grading time.

RESOURCES FOR THOSE WHO WANT TO LEARN MORE

In an ultimate appeal to incentives, McCloskey (2019, p. 4) argues for the importance of writing instruction in economics, because it is well rewarded: "The big secret is that good writing pays well and bad writing pays badly." We hope that by providing a modest number of tips and examples we have convinced readers that the cost of writing instruction can be reduced sufficiently so that its benefits exceed the costs. However, as with any teaching innovation, addition of student writing to the syllabus requires a modest, up-front investment in professional development. We conclude with reference to several resources to reduce these fixed costs.

Starting Point: Teaching and Learning Economics Website

Greenlaw (n.d.-b) provides a useful introduction to many teaching methods including quantitative writing.[11] Brief essays offer tips and examples for designing writing assignments, developing criteria and rubrics for assessment (complete with example rubrics for adaptation to new assignments), and framing the writing assignment as a process. In addition, the site includes

Table 13.1   Example reader response rubric

	Ineffective	Weak	Clear	Exemplary
Analysis of the policy using the supply-and-demand model Was reasonable market selected? Was the model effectively employed? Was the model clearly explained? Was the graphical presentation effective?	Supply-and-demand model incorrectly implemented; Unclear explanation; Ineffective graph associated with model	Explanation is weak so that reader must work hard to understand; Model graphic may be muddled or hard to understand	Clear explication and explanation of correct model; Graph is easy to read and properly demonstrates theory; May not be most important labor market	Graceful, nuanced explication and explanation of correct model; Graph easy to read, properly demonstrates theory, and is aesthetically pleasing
Quantity and quality of data used to support your analysis Have you missed opportunities to support your claims and/or argument with numerical evidence? Have you overused data so that the numbers detract from your brief? How well have you selected your data? Are these powerful pieces of information or are they less useful? Are the data well connected to the policy under consideration?	Essentially no data used; Data used are incorrectly interpreted; Connection of data to policy unclear	Insufficient or distracting amount of data used; Data choices may not be particularly potent, though interpretation is correct; Weak connection between data and policy	Appropriate quantity of data used; Data chosen are powerful, though perhaps not uniformly so; Correct interpretation of data; Solid connection between data and policy	Appropriate quantity of data used; Data chosen are consistently powerful; Interpretations are nuanced and insightful; Nuanced connection between data and policy

	Ineffective	Weak	Clear	Exemplary
Quality of the data presentation in text, table, and chart (if applicable) Is the table/chart clear? Does the table/chart reflect the lazy reader principle? Are sources and definitions appropriately defined and explained? Are limitations of the data appropriately considered?	Missing labels or titles; Missing notes; Unclear use of jargon/ column labels; No reference to tables/charts in the text	Clear labels or titles; Unclear or incomplete notes; Reference in the text may not clearly explain what reader should; Limited understanding of limitations of the data presented	Clear labels or titles; Clear and complete notes; Reference in the text clearly explains what I should be seeing; Reasonable understanding of limitations of the data presented	Particularly insightful labels or titles; Clear and complete notes; Text clearly explains the important content of the chart/ table; Nuanced consideration of limitations of the data presented
Attention to task and audience Does the paper provide useful information for making a policy decision? Do rhetorical choices reflect role and audience?	After reading brief, it is not clear how information would inform decision; no reflection of the status of the audience relative to writer	After reading brief, the relevance of some information is unclear but most is obvious; Limited reflection of the status of the audience relative to writer	After reading brief, the relevance of information is clear; Status of the audience relative to writer is clear from rhetorical choices, but may be inconsistent	The brief provides insightful information for a decision-maker; Rhetorical choices consistently show a graceful recognition of the relationship between author and audience

Comments:

Note: Well-constructed rubrics make expectations clear to students and allow instructors to provide detailed feedback at a fast pace.

a collection of 11 examples of economics paper assignments. Each example is presented with a detailed description and the teaching tips that one might expect when sharing an assignment with a colleague. Some example assignments might be borrowed "as is"; most likely, modest revision will adapt an assignment idea to the particular context of your course. The example assignments in Greenlaw (n.d.-b) are part of a larger collection of quantitative writing assignments in Bean (n.d.). While the larger collection includes examples from multiple disciplines, assignments in other disciplines have often been the germ of a new assignment in our own courses.

Economical Writing by McCloskey (2019)

McCloskey's book provides economics-specific writing instruction. At 140
pages, the book is likely too long to be assigned in Principles courses (though
we recommend it for advanced courses). As a whole, it may better serve as
inspiration for instructors looking for a few points which they wish to emphasize in writing instruction. (Remember, none of us needs to teach everything.)
A choice or two from the 35 short chapters, however, might serve as a reasonable reading assignment for students, particularly when those choices line
up with the instructor's points of emphasis. As an added bonus, McCloskey
engages with wit, while offering challenging insights that inspire even seasoned professionals to improve their writing.

Writing Economics by Neugeboren and Jacobson (2001)

Developed as a guide for Harvard students, Neugeboren and Jacobson's
focus is on upper-level course work rather than Principles sections. Still, like
McCloskey (2019), the guide can be excerpted for use with students. While
less witty than McCloskey, Neugeboren and Jacobson shine when providing
samples of initial and revised student work that exemplify their lessons. In
addition, appendices list data sources and indices to the periodical literature
that are commonly used by economists. The lists are useful to instructors
designing annotated bibliography or data-driven assignments like those we
describe above.

Engaging Ideas: The Professor's Guide to Integrating Writing, Critical Thinking, and Active Learning in the Classroom, 2nd edition, by John C. Bean (2011)

While not specific to writing in economics, this short but powerful book
provides practical advice for enhanced writing instruction. Through specific
examples, Bean gives concrete guidance on the creation and revision of assignments, help in managing the grading load, and more.

NOTES

1. Those interested in a similar discussion applied to upper-level economics field
    courses should consult Schmeiser (2017).
2. In Table 3.1, Allgood and Bayer show the intersection between effective commu-
    nication and four essential concepts of economics: individual decision-making,
    markets and other interactions, the aggregate economy, and the role of government.
3. The expertise we speak of here is in teaching writing, and not, in particular,
    a detailed knowledge of the rules of grammar. Research shows that grammar is not

typically learned by memorizing rules or from copious copy-editing notes carved in red ink across a paper (Bean 2011, pp. 66–86). Some grammatical fluency might be taught by highlighting and correcting an example or two of a particular error, but more is less in this area of instruction. Embracing this research frees us from the unpleasant and time-consuming task of uselessly copy-editing our students' papers.

4. Both the phrase "minimal marking" and the overall technique advocated by Bean were first proposed by Richard Haswell (1983).
5. This departmental commitment to writing can, of course, manifest simply as individual instructors independently developing writing assignments within their courses. As Flash (2016) demonstrates, though, there is significant value, both for students and for faculty, in an explicit dialogue among departmental faculty about the roles and locations of writing within their curriculum.
6. This paper idea is adapted from Lutsky (n.d.). Nathan has used a version of this prompt in a first-year seminar, though not in Principles of Microeconomics.
7. This assignment is an adaptation of an assignment Nathan has given in an Economics of Inequality elective course, with the prompt adjusted to reflect the contents of Principles of Microeconomics.
8. To further speed grading in large sections, Nathan tells students that revision will be assessed by a comparison of the final paper with only one of the other papers. While the students do not know which prior paper will be used as the point of comparison, Nathan uses the second version of the two-page paper.
9. With the same goals in mind, just as we advise students to seek peer feedback before submitting an assignment, so we can also improve writing prompts by getting revision notes from directors of writing programs and reference librarians (who, whether we know it or not, often work with our students when assignments involve data).
10. Some instructors share their evaluation rubric with students as the assignment is given. Providing the rubric to students ahead of time gives a clear sense of expectations. Others only share the rubric when feedback is provided, contending that students learn by figuring out the important sub-parts of an assignment. We see value in both sides of this controversy, but believe that either way, teachers should articulate in advance (for themselves, if not for students) the dimensions most relevant to grading.
11. Greenlaw's economics-specific material is adapted from Bean (n.d.) which explores pedagogy surrounding quantitative writing more broadly.

REFERENCES

Allgood, S., and Bayer, A. (2016). Measuring college learning in economics. In R. Arum, J. Roksa and A. Cook (eds), *Improving Quality in American Higher Education* (pp. 87–134). John Wiley & Sons.

Anderson, P., Anson, C.M., Gonyea, R.M., and Paine, C. (2015). The contributions of writing to learning and development: Results from a large-scale multi-institutional study. *Research in the Teaching of English 50*, 199.

Association of American Colleges and Universities (2011). The LEAP vision for learning: Outcomes, practices, impact, and employers' views. Association of American Colleges and Universities.

Bamberg, B. (2000). WAC in the 90's: Changing contexts and challenges. *Language and Learning Across the Disciplines* 4.2 (2000), 5–19. The WAC Clearinghouse. Web. 1 June 2014.

Bean, J.C. (2001). *Engaging Ideas: The Professor's Guide to Integrating Writing, Critical Thinking, and Active Learning in the Classroom.* Jossey-Bass Publishers.

Bean, J.C. (2011). *Engaging Ideas: The Professor's Guide to Integrating Writing, Critical Thinking, and Active Learning in the Classroom* (2nd edition). Jossey-Bass Publishers.

Bean, J.C. (n.d.). Quantitative writing. Carleton College teaching activity collection. Accessed December 11, 2020 from http://serc.carleton.edu/13332.1093.

Brewster, C., and Klump, J. (2004). At the classroom level: Writing in the disciplines and writing to learn. In C. Brewster and J. Klump, *Writing to Learn, Learning to Write: Revisiting Writing across the Curriculum in Northwest Secondary Schools* (pp. 19–23). Northwest Regional Educational Laboratory.

Burke, M.C. (2007). A mathematician's proposal. *Carnegie Perspectives*, October.

Carter, M., Ferzli, M., and Wiebe, E.N. (2007). Writing to learn by learning to write in the disciplines. *Journal of Business and Technical Communication 21*(3), 278–302. https://doi.org/10.1177/1050651907300466.

Flash, P. (2016). From apprised to revised: Faculty in the disciplines change what they never knew they knew. In K. Yancey (ed.), *A Rhetoric of Reflection* (p. 227–249). Utah State University Press.

Forsman, S. (1985). Writing to learn means learning to think. In A.R. Gere (Ed.), *Roots in the Sawdust: Writing to Learn across the Disciplines* (pp. 162–174). National Council of Teachers of English.

Galbraith, J.K. (1978). Writing, typing, and economics. *The Atlantic Online*, March. https://www.theatlantic.com/magazine/archive/1978/03/writing-typing-and-economics/305165/.

Galer-Unti, R.A. (2002). Student perceptions of a writing-intensive course in health education. *Health Educator: Journal of Eta Sigma Gamma 34*(2), 35–40.

Graham, S., and Perin, D. (2007). *Writing Next: Effective Strategies to Improve Writing of Adolescents in Middle and High Schools.* Alliance for Excellent Education.

Greenlaw, S.A. (2003). Using writing to enhance student learning in undergraduate economics. *International Review of Economics Education 1*(1), 61–70.

Greenlaw, S.A. (n.d.-a). How to create context-rich problems. Teaching and learning economics. *Starting Point.* Accessed March 30, 2021 from https://serc.carleton.edu/econ/context_rich/how_create_cont.html.

Greenlaw, S.A. (n.d.-b). Teaching and learning economics. *Starting Point.* Accessed December 11, 2020 from http://serc.carleton.edu/30611.

Hansen, W.L. (1986). What knowledge is most worth knowing—For economics majors? *American Economic Review 76*(2), 149–152.

Hansen, W.L. (2001). Expected proficiencies for undergraduate economics majors. *Journal of Economic Education 32*(3), 231–242.

Haswell, R. (1983). Minimal marking. *College English 45*(6), 600–604. doi:10.2307/377147.

Lutsky, Neil. (n.d). Writing about numbers we should know. Carleton Quantitative Inquiry, Reasoning, and Knowledge Initiative. *Starting Point.* Accessed March 31, 2021 https://serc.carleton.edu/quirk/quantitative_writing/examples/numbers.html.

McCloskey, D. (1985). Economical writing. *Economic Inquiry 23*(2), 187–222.

McCloskey, D.N. (1999). *Economical Writing* (2nd edition). Waveland Press.

McCloskey, D.N. (2019). *Economical Writing* (3rd edition). University of Chicago Press.

Meyers, S.C., Nelson, M.A., and Stratton., R.W. (2011). Assessment of the undergraduate economics major: A national survey. *Journal of Economic Education 42*(2), 195–199.

Neugeboren, R., and Jacobson, M. (2001). *Writing Economics*. President and Fellows of Harvard University. https://writingproject.fas.harvard.edu/files/hwp/files/writing economics.pdf.

Palmini, D.J. (1996). Using rhetorical cases to teach writing skills and enhance economic learning. *Journal of Economic Education 27*(3), 205–216.

Parker, R.P., and Goodkin, V. (1987). *The Consequences of Writing: Enhancing Learning in the Disciplines.* Boynton/Cook.

Pigou, A.C. (1925). *Memorials of Alfred Marshall.* Macmillan & Co. http://pombo.free.fr/marshallmemorials.pdf.

Poirrier, G.P. (1997). *Writing-to-Learn: Curricular Strategies for Nursing and Other Disciplines.* National League of Nursing Press.

Quesenberry, L. et al. (2000). Assessment of the writing component within a university general education program. *Academic.Writing: Interdisciplinary Perspectives on Communication Across the Curriculum 1*(4). https://doi.org/10.37514/AWR-J.2000.1.4.07.

Schmeiser, K. (2017). Teaching writing in economics. *Journal of Economic Education 48*(4), 254–264.

Thaiss, C., and Zawacki, T. (2006). *Engaged Writers and Dynamic Disciplines: Research on the Academic Writing Life.* Boynton/Cook Heinemann Press.

Wolfe, M.H. (2020). Integrating data analysis into an Introductory Macroeconomics course. *International Review of Economics Education 33*, 100176.

Wood, D., Bruner, J.S., and Ross, G. (1976). The role of tutoring in problem solving. *Journal of Child Psychology and Psychiatry 17*(2), 89–100.

Yancey, K., Robertson, L., and Taczak, K. (2014). *Writing Across Contexts: Transfer, Composition, and Sites of Writing.* Utah State University Press.

14. Taking advantage of structured peer interaction: cooperative learning in the Principles of Microeconomics course

Scott P. Simkins, Mark Maier, and Phil Ruder

While many introductory economics courses continue to be dominated by "traditional lectures and chalkboard or whiteboard text and graphs," usually accompanied by a PowerPoint presentation (Asarta et al. 2021, p. 20), there is a rich body of research supporting the benefits of active, student-centered instructional techniques (Deslauriers et al. 2019; Freeman et al. 2014; Hake 1998). Many of these instructional techniques involve students interacting with each other in structured group work, ranging in complexity from simple think–pair–share activities to full-course implementations of team-based learning (TBL). There are many ways to incorporate structured group work in the Principles of Microeconomics course and in this chapter we provide a variety of examples to help you get started or expand your use of these active-learning strategies in this course.

THE CASE FOR COOPERATIVE LEARNING IN ECONOMICS

Our focus here is on the broad class of structured group work characterized as "cooperative learning," a pedagogical category that allows for a wide range of instructional activities grounded in a common set of foundational characteristics.[1] As noted by Barbara Millis (2010, p. 2), "Cooperative learning is founded on a deep historical research base, with new research on how people learn and on deep learning providing added insights into its efficacy." Emerson et al. (2018) and Yamarik (2007) provide additional research-based support for using cooperative learning instructional practices in economics.

Popular resources such as Barkley et al. (2014) provide pragmatic advice and an extensive set of classroom-based examples for implementing cooperative learning in undergraduate teaching. In economics, the *Starting Point: Teaching and Learning Economics* pedagogic portal (https://serc.carleton.edu/ econ/cooperative/index.html), McGoldrick (2011) and Maier et al. (2010)

provide a variety of discipline-specific examples for incorporating cooperative learning in introductory economics courses.

What Does Cooperative Learning Look Like?

Cooper (2009, p. 3) defines cooperative learning as "a structured, systematic instructional strategy in which small groups work together to produce a common product." As the definition suggests, cooperative learning can take many forms. Cooperative learning structures range from ad hoc pairs of students working together on short tasks, to four-student groups working on more complex and time-consuming tasks, to team-based learning, a whole-course pedagogy in which semester-long fixed teams of five to seven students work on challenging application of the material under study to real-world cases.

How Does Cooperative Learning Help Students to Learn Better?

An important purpose of cooperative learning structures is to permit all students in the class to engage with new ideas in simultaneous structured activities within a small group setting, achieving a level of student practice and feedback that is impossible in instructor-centered classes. These student–student conversations, when structured in intentional ways, promote a variety of powerful learning strategies supported by learning sciences research. These include prompt feedback that guides metacognition and improved understanding, retrieval practice that promotes durable and long-lasting learning, and elaboration of new ideas that encourages connections among ideas and concepts, along with transfer of learning to new situations (National Research Council 2000; Brown et al. 2014; Schwartz et al. 2016; Weinstein et al. 2019). These benefits provide a strong incentive for instructors to increase their use of cooperative learning in introductory courses, which enroll a disproportionate share of novice learners who may not yet have developed and internalized effective learning strategies.[2]

   While thinking through how to incorporate cooperative learning activities in your course will likely take more planning time than preparing a class lecture, the resulting increase in student engagement and learning offers considerable benefits.

KEY FEATURES OF COOPERATIVE LEARNING

Simply putting students into groups does not in and of itself lead to learning gains and, indeed, could be counterproductive in the absence of well-designed structures to foster student learning and engagement (Johnson et al. 1994,

p. 6). The wide range of effective cooperative learning structures share a small set of key characteristics that promote student learning gains.

All cooperative learning structures, from the simplest to the most complex, put into practice four important elements that research has shown are critical for improving student learning. Those characteristics are represented by the acronym "PIES" (Kagan and Kagan 2009): P, positive interdependence; I, individual accountability; E, equal participation; S, simultaneous work.

Positive Interdependence

Successful cooperative learning structures require participation by all group members. Cooperative learning activities must be designed to ensure that success by individuals is more likely when others are similarly successful, and contributions by all are necessary for the group's success (Kagan and Kagan 2009, pp. 5.9–5.10).

Individual Accountability

The cooperative learning literature advises strongly against "group grades" (Millis and Cottell 1997, pp. 12–13). The goal is learning—again promoted by positive interdependence—with the reward being individual success. Thus, most cooperative learning structures end with or lead to an individual product documenting each person's learning.

Equal Participation

Cooperative learning promotes—indeed, requires—participation by all group members through explicitly designed structures and activities, rather than simply listening to instructor-led lectures. The goal, of course, is not pre-cisely equal participation, but rather learning outcomes that require all group members to contribute to the discussion and final product of the activity. In economics, the cooperative learning literature addresses free-riding as a pos-sible drawback to cooperative learning (Maier et al., 2010, p. 160), and points to the importance of structures that encourage more equal participation (Kagan and Kagan 2009, pp. 12.14–12.22).

Simultaneous Work

Cooperative learning allows more students to actively engage in the learning process and receive more immediate feedback than whole-class discussion. The type of engagement and feedback experienced are dependent on both the composition and the size of cooperative learning groups. The cooperative learning literature recommends that the composition of groups be determined by the instructor (Millis and Cottell 1997, pp. 50–53). Allowing students to self-select teammates likely will create groups with a narrower range of viewpoints, greater likelihood of distracting conversation, and voting blocs among friends. With respect to group size, pair work can serve as an introduction to collaborative work, while larger groups create the possibility of more diverse perspectives, more available resources, and more demanding group tasks.

COOPERATIVE LEARNING IN THE PRINCIPLES OF MICROECONOMICS COURSE

The PIES characteristics, when intentionally embedded into the design and implementation of student group activities, make cooperative learning a powerful teaching and learning tool in the Principles of Microeconomics course. In particular, cooperative learning structures:

- Help each student to connect their experience to newly introduced concepts. That experience may be from outside the classroom or from the cooperative learning activity itself. In both cases, students have the opportunity to frame the microeconomic concept under study in the context of their own lives.
- Allow students to briefly engage in hands-on practice with real-world applications of newly learned concepts. Too often, microeconomics is experienced by students as a set of abstract rules rather than helpful concepts that can be applied to real-world behavior and decision-making. Cooperative learning structures in which students measure outcomes, analyze data, or evaluate policy decisions, allow students to see the real-world connections with economic concepts and how economists use economic analysis for decision-making.
- Encourage students to challenge preconceptions and consider other points of view. Cooperative learning activities that are designed to elicit and correct preconceptions, and that require input from all group members, provide a powerful opportunity to expand, revise, and deepen students' thinking.

Incorporating cooperative learning in classroom teaching can seem daunting to instructors unfamiliar with this instructional practice. The remainder of this chapter presents a variety of examples of cooperative learning structures and activities for the Principles of Microeconomics course, ordered from least-structured (think–pair–share) to most structured (team-based learning), that are intended to help economics instructors initiate or expand their use of cooperative learning in their courses.

Think–Pair–Share

In brief, "think–pair–share" involves the following steps. First, individual students are given "think" time on a problem or question (important to provide more reticent students with an opportunity to process their answer) posed to the entire class (for example, projected on a screen at the front of a classroom). The problem or question can be pre-scripted by the instructor or created on the fly based on perceived need in the class. Next, the instructor asks students to turn to a nearby student (advising students to turn to someone they do not know to promote greater on-topic discussion) and take turns in sharing brief responses and rationales. To conclude, the instructor calls on pairs to share their response (it is often best to ask students to share the response given by their partner) (Aronson 2021; Aronson and Patnoe 2011; Social Psychology Network n.d.).

Examples:

- After a lecture or reading on mergers and acquisitions, ask: What are two examples not already described of a recent merger or acquisition? Are these horizontal, vertical, or conglomerate mergers or acquisitions?
- After a lecture or reading on monopolistically competitive markets, ask: What is an example in your neighborhood of a firm in a monopolistically competitive market?
- After a lecture or reading on costs and benefits and/or marginal analysis, ask: You paid cash for a movie ticket but lost it. Should you buy another ticket?

Pairwise structures are particularly effective when combined with one of the active learning pedagogies for the Principles of Microeconomics course described elsewhere in this book (Chapters 15, 16, 18). For example:

How fast does a market reach equilibrium? The double auction classroom experiment (see Chapter 15) is the most commonly used experiment, and one with conceptual understanding that may be lost in student excitement to participate in the activity. To focus on understanding market equilibrium, how it occurs, and how quickly it occurs, the activity can follow three steps:

1. Think–pair–share. Use to generate a prediction about the timing of equilibrium.
2. Experience. Conduct the classroom experiment with a double auction.
3. Reflection (again in think–pair–share). Ask the following questions: Why did equilibrium occur? Why did it occur much more quickly than students

anticipated? What are the implications of this result for our understanding of markets?

In an online class, think–pair–share activities can be accomplished by putting randomized pairs into breakout rooms for the student-to-student discussions. For the subsequent whole-class discussion, a randomized member of each pair (for example, the one whose first name comes first in the alphabet) can be tasked with typing a sentence or two in the chat to state the pair's answer and/ or explain the pair's reasoning in a sentence. Students all hit Return to make their comment visible to the class simultaneously on the instructor's cue. The instructor can then facilitate a discussion about the answer, calling on selected students to elaborate on what they have typed in the chat.

Peer Instruction

Peer instruction, originally developed by Eric Mazur (1997), builds on think–pair–share with more carefully constructed questions addressing specific, previously identified student misconceptions. Such questions have been shown to improve student learning (Crouch 1998; Crouch and Mazur 2001; Boyle and Goffe 2018). Schell and Butler (2018) provide additional learning sciences-based support for peer instruction. Peer instruction questions require careful thought and must be prepared in advance.

Peer instruction typically uses multiple-choice responses submitted electronically via clickers or cellphones, initially by each student on their own, and then again after pairwise discussion. The responses quickly identify students' understanding and expose learning gaps. The instructor can immediately address student misunderstandings in class. Following the pairwise sharing, the instructor asks some students to explain how their pair arrived at their choice, and then presents the expert's view. Student discussions in pairs generate curiosity about the topic and greater readiness to learn from the instructor mini-lecture that follows (Schwartz and Bransford 1998).

Examples:

The following items are likely to be owned by a typical college student: pants, shirt, bookbag, water bottle, and shoes. Consider the markets in which these goods are sold. Which of the following assumptions of the competitive model is LEAST appropriate for these markets?

a.   Well-informed buyers and sellers.
b.   Standardized products.
c.   Many buyers and sellers.

d.   Freely mobile resources.

Which of the following is a characteristic of efficient regulation of pollution?

a.   The net benefit of each unit of pollution cleaned up is greater than or equal to zero.
b.   Large firms are required to clean up disproportionately more pollution than small firms.
c.   Pollutants that create irreversible harm to ecosystems are banned completely.
d.   Corporations pay for pollution clean-up without raising the price of their products.

More Structured Cooperative Learning

The cooperative learning literature provides extensive discussion of structures that support groups of more than two students—and typically four or more—using the PIES criteria (see Kagan and Kagan 2009; Millis and Cottell 1997; Barkley et al. 2014; K. Patricia Cross Academy n.d.). Below we describe structures especially applicable in the Principles of Microeconomics course. They require more instructor preparation than the pairwise group structures discussed previously, but have the advantage of greater student engagement, better replication of actual practice by economists, and higher potential to address specific student learning outcomes.

Survey

This cooperative learning activity uses students' individual experiences as a foundation, requires that each student contribute to the group's product, gives students practice with issues that arise in economic surveys, and provides practice that often exposes and corrects common calculation errors. In this activity, individual students survey other students in the class to obtain data that are then used by the group to create a real-world economic measurement.

Example:

A group is assigned a good or service and then identifies an appropriate range of prices to measure the effect of price changes on quantity demanded. (Possible examples include copies of previous tests used in the course; one hour of tutoring for the course; lunchtime sandwich.) Individuals survey other students in the class on how much of the good they would buy at different prices, bringing back data for the group to use to calculate price elasticity of demand and compare with price elasticities calculated by other groups in the class (or with published estimates).

Jigsaw

This multi-step activity requires more preparation by the instructor but has the benefit of strong positive interdependence, equal participation, and individual accountability. In a jigsaw, student "base teams" are temporarily broken up and each base team member is assigned a different topic that is usually accompanied by topic-specific reading or data. Each student joins others in the class who have been assigned the same reading or data. In this "expert" group, students work together to prepare a presentation that they each will bring back to their base group. In the next step, students return to their base group and contribute the presentation they have prepared. The base group then creates a final product that requires the expertise of each individual in the group.

Example:

Individual students receive Federal Reserve Bank of St Louis (FRED) database data on labor force participation rates over time for different subsets of the population (for example, by age, ethnicity or gender). Each expert group examines the data for one subset, identifying main trends and possible explanations for those trends. Back in the base group, teams use the different experts' information to explain overall changes in United States (US) labor force participation rates over time.

Pass a problem

This cooperative learning activity can take place within a group or among groups. In each case an individual (or group) creates a problem for another individual (or group) to solve. Instructions set parameters so that the problem is constrained to focus on the concepts under study. After the problem has been passed to the new individual (or group), it is either passed to yet another individual (or group) or returned to the problem preparer to check for accuracy and commentary.

Example:

Individuals (or groups) set preferred marginal tax rates and deductions for a simplified income tax structure. The responding group calculates tax due, tax rates, and the tax incidence. If desired, the group also can pass judgment on the tax structure in comparison with current US rates.

Cooperative controversy

Many issues in microeconomics are unsettled and provide opportunities for students to learn about conflicting points of view. The cooperative controversy activity forces students to appreciate the logic on each side of a controversial topic, rather than simply determine a winner. Students learn that disagreements often result from different value judgments or unresolved empirical questions. This activity occurs in three steps (outlined below), best accomplished if the group has exactly four members; before the activity, students will have studied an issue, perhaps reading opposing positions:

1. The activity poses a clear statement taking a position on the issue.
2. Each pair in the team is assigned randomly a "pro" or "con" position and works together to identify arguments in favor of their position (perhaps a list of three).
3. Pairs take turns describing their identified arguments and the opposing pair selects which argument is strongest and explains why.

There is no requirement that the group determine which side is "right." Instead, individual students can be asked to summarize the "pro" and "con" positions in the debate, along with the supporting arguments, perhaps in a follow-up short writing assignment.

Examples:

*   Should a merger be permitted between two firms?
*   Should the top marginal US personal income tax rate be increased?
*   Should the US minimum wage be increased to $15/hour?
*   Should large technology companies such as Google or Amazon be broken up?

Team-Based Learning[3]

Team-based learning (TBL) is a whole-course, highly structured cooperative learning pedagogy intended to develop student skills at making and evaluating economic arguments. In TBL courses, student groups work together during an entire semester, building advanced teamwork skills and knowledge. Team-based learning (Michaelsen et al. 2004) features large (5–7 student) fixed groups that take on challenging applications during most class periods. Haidet et al. (2014) summarize the evidence of learning gains in TBL courses reported in 130 articles in the educational literature; while Hettler (2015) provides evidence of TBL student learning success in economics courses.

Readiness assurance process
TBL courses typically are divided into six or seven modules per semester. Each module begins with a "readiness assurance process" in which students prepare by actively engaging with key readings, videos, and/or podcasts before the first class period of the module. Students next take an individual quiz on

the fundamental concepts of the module before taking the same (or a very similar) quiz as a team in the first class of the module, using immediate feedback assessment technique (IF-AT) cards (CognaLearn 2022). The instructor then presents mini-lectures on the most challenging concepts in the module to conclude the readiness assurance process.

Subsequent class periods in the module feature students working in groups on a series of increasingly challenging application exercises (AEs), each one followed by a class-wide discussion among team reporters. Regular formative assessments by teammates on contributions to the group help to develop teamwork skills, while the summative teammate assessment completed at the end of the course provides additional incentive for each student to regularly prepare for each class and engage productively in team-based activities.

Application exercises

Context-rich application exercises (AEs) form the heart of team-based learning and can also be used with other cooperative learning structures. Pre-class readings, podcasts, or videos are often assigned as homework to prepare students for in-class AE activities. Unlike typical numerical or analytical curve-shifting exercises often used in the Principles of Microeconomics course, AEs pose a choice among a limited number of defensible alternatives and require teams to select the "best" prediction, policy recommendation, or explanation of observed phenomena, supported by economic reasoning. After teams develop their responses, a reporter from each team presents and defends their team's choice to classmates in an instructor-facilitated discussion among the reporters. Good AEs lead to multiple feasible "best" answers, with reporters using economic reasoning and evidence developed by their team to convince each other of the merits of one choice relative to another.

The structure of AEs matters to maximize learning. TBL AEs follow a "4S" framework: the problems posed are significant to students, each team works on the same problem, teams must make a specific choice, and team choices must be revealed simultaneously. The significance of the problems promotes engagement by students. The fact that teams work on the same problem and make specific choices from a limited set of options makes possible a lively class-wide debriefing of the groups' work. The simultaneous reveal, along with AEs that pose numerous defensible answers, increases the probability that teams make diverse choices, which in turn makes the debriefing conversation interesting to all students.[4]

Examples:

Ranking explanatory factors. The group must rank explanations as most (or least) correct, or outcomes as most (or least) likely.

Consider the market for baseball caps. Rank the assumptions of the competitive model from least appropriate to most appropriate for analyzing the market for baseball caps in the United States.

a. All firms sell the same standardized product.
b. The market has many buyers and many sellers, each of which buys or sells only a small fraction of the total quantity exchanged in the market.
c. Productive resources are mobile; that is, firms face little difficulty in entering or exiting the market.
d. Buyers and sellers are well informed.

Choosing the best public policy. The group would be assigned a pre-class reading to prepare them for this exercise.

Consider the issue of nitrate pollution by farms in Iowa fouling the Raccoon and Des Moines Rivers, the sources of drinking water for the City of Des Moines. What policy measure should be enacted to remedy the problem?

a. Ban nitrate emissions from farms.
b. Tax each ton of nitrate applied to fields.
c. Assign property rights over the river water clearly to the City of Des Moines.
d. Assign property rights over the river water clearly to farmers.

Estimating a numerical result. Given a situation, students must estimate an economic result.

Anthony and Susie are roommates and they are discussing upgrading their internet service to provide a faster speed. Susie works from home and could really use the improved speed, so she is willing to pay up to $60 a month to pay for the improvement. Anthony is home less often, he would love faster speed for when he is home, but he would only pay $20 a month. Suppose the cost to upgrade the speed is $50. How do you suggest the roommates split the cost?

a. Anthony $25, Susie $25
b. Anthony $20, Susie $30
c. Anthony $12.50, Susie $37.50
d. Anthony $5, Susie $45
e. Anthony $0, Susie $50

Identifying the most important concept for policy-making. Groups select which economic concept that they have studied is most important for a policy decision.

To predict the impact of a minimum wage increase, the most important thing we need to know is the:

a.   Price elasticity of supply of labor.
b.   Price elasticity of demand for labor.
c.   Poverty rate.
d.   Inflation rate.

Using data to reach a conclusion. Students examine economic data to choose among various explanations.

Looking at data by gender, age, ethnicity, and race, which factor best explains the overall decline in US labor force participation?

a.   Women are no longer entering the labor force in large numbers.
b.   Men are leaving the labor force at a greater rate.
c.   Blacks and Hispanics are no longer entering the labor force in large numbers.
d.   Teenagers no longer work as frequently.

The examples above illustrate five different types of AEs that can be used to generate group-based activities that promote multiple defensible positions (depending on assumptions used, for example). This lack of a single "right" answer is what makes "good" AEs especially powerful for student learning. Like the more structured cooperative learning activities discussed in the previous section, note how TBL AEs promote the PIES criteria central to all cooperative learning structures.

SUMMARY

Evidence from the learning sciences and classroom-based instructional research provides strong support for cooperative learning in the Principles of Microeconomics course. The intentional, structured nature of cooperative learning activities, grounded in the PIES characteristics, promotes learning for all students in a class and provides hands-on practice in applying economic concepts and ideas.

As illustrated here, cooperative learning strategies vary from easy-to-use think–pair–share and peer instruction in pairs, to more structured activities such as jigsaw and pass a problem, which often use teams of four or more students. The most structured cooperative learning strategies employ whole-course cooperative learning structures and develop advanced teamwork skills in addition to a high level of economic understanding.

NOTES

1. Like Barkley et al. (2014), we sidestep the academic debate surrounding the distinctions between cooperative learning and collaborative learning (Bruffee 1995). The guiding view of cooperative learning which we focus on here shares many of the same key characteristics as collaborative learning, in particular the importance of purposeful student interaction and individual accountability in the learning process.
2. The *Learning Scientists* website (https://www.learningscientists.org/blog/2016/8/18-1), developed and maintained by a group of learning scientists, provides valuable two-page student-focused "how to" guides for carrying out six evidence-based strategies for effective learning, including retrieval practice and elaboration.
3. This section summarizes information presented in Ruder et al. (2021). For a more detailed introduction to the use of TBL in economics courses, see that article and the *Starting Point: Teaching and Learning Economics* website (https://serc.carleton.edu/econ/tbl-econ/index.html). In addition, Simkins et al. (2021) illustrate how TBL pedagogy aligns well with learning sciences research findings about how to enhance student learning.
4. Crafting good AEs is challenging. The TBL module at *Starting Point: Teaching and Learning Economics* (https://serc.carleton.edu/econ/tbl-econ/index.html) offers dozens of AEs—mostly for introductory economics classes—that can be used "off the shelf" or modified to suit an instructor's needs.

REFERENCES

Aronson, E. (2021). The jigsaw classroom: A personal odyssey into a systemic national problem. In N. Davidson (ed.), *Pioneering Perspectives in Cooperative Learning* (pp. 146–164). Taylor & Francis.

Aronson, E., and Patnoe, S. (2011). *Cooperation in the classroom: The jigsaw method* (3rd edition). Pinter & Martin.

Asarta, C.J., Chambers, R.G., and Harter, C. (2021). Teaching methods in undergraduate Introductory Economics courses: Results from a sixth national quinquennial survey. *American Economist 66*(1), 18–28. https://doi.org/10.1177/0569434520974658.

Barkley, E.F., Cross, P.K., and Major, C.H. (2014). *Collaborative learning techniques: A handbook for college faculty* (2nd edition). Jossey-Bass.

Boyle, A., and Goffe, W.L. (2018) Beyond the flipped class: The impact of research-based teaching methods in a macroeconomics principles class. *American Economic Association Papers and Proceedings 108*, 297–301.

Brown, P.C., Roediger, H.L., and McDaniel, M.A. (2014). *Make it stick: The science of successful learning*. Belknap Press of Harvard University Press.

Bruffee, K.A. (1995). Sharing our toys: Cooperative learning versus collaborative learning. *Change: The Magazine of Higher Learning 27*(1), 12–18. DOI: 10.1080/00091383.1995.9937722.

CognaLearn (2022). Immediate Feedback Assessment Technique (IF-AT) Forms. www.cognalearn.com. Accessed July 25, 2022 at https://www.cognalearn.com/ifat.

Cooper, J.L. (2009). What is cooperative learning? In J.L. Cooper, P. Robinson, and D. Ball (eds), *Small group instruction in higher education: Lessons from the past, visions of the future* (pp. 3–5). New Forums Press.

Crouch, C.H. (1998). Peer instruction: An interactive approach for large classes. *Optics and Photonics News 9*(9), 37–41.

Crouch, C.H., and Mazur, E. (2001). Peer instruction: Ten years of experience and results. *American Journal of Physics 69*, 970–977.

Deslauriers, L., McCarty, L.S., Miller, K., Callaghan, K., and Kestin, G. (2019). *Proceedings of the National Academy of Sciences 116*(39), 19251–19257. DOI: 10.1073/pnas.1821936116.

Emerson, T.L.N., English, L.K., and McGoldrick, K. (2018). The high costs of large enrollment classes: Can cooperative learning help? *Eastern Economic Journal 44*(3), 455–474.

Freeman, S., Eddy, S.L., McDonough, M., Smith, M.K., Okoroafor, N., Jordt, H., and Wenderoth, M.P. (2014). Active learning increases student performance in science, engineering, and mathematics. *Proceedings of the National Academy of Science 111*, 8410–8415.

Haidet, P., Kubitz, K., and McCormack, W.T. (2014) Analysis of the team-based learning literature: TBL comes of age. *Journal of Excellence in College Teaching 25*(3–4), 303–333.

Hake, R.R. (1998). Interactive-engagement vs. traditional methods: A six-thousand-student survey of mechanics test data for introductory physics courses. *American Journal of Physics 66*, 64–74.

Hettler, P.L. (2015). Student demographics and the impact of team-based learning. *International Advances in Economic Research 21*(4), 413–422. DOI: 10.1007/s11294-015-9539-7.

Johnson, D.W., Johnson, R.T., and Holubec, E. (1994). *Cooperative learning in the classroom*. Association for Supervision and Curriculum Development.

Kagan, S., and Kagan, M. (2009). *Kagan cooperative learning*. Kagan Publishing.

K. Patricia Cross Academy (n.d.). https://kpcrossacademy.org/.

Maier, M.H., McGoldrick, K., and Simkins, S.P. (2010). Implementing cooperative learning in introductory economics courses. In B. Millis (ed.), *Cooperative learning in higher education: Across the disciplines, across the academy* (New Pedagogies and Practices for Teaching in Higher Education) (pp. 157–180). Stylus Publishing.

Mazur, E. (1997). *Peer instruction: A user's manual*. Prentice Hall.

McGoldrick, K. (2011). Using cooperative learning exercises in economics. In G. Hoyt and K. McGoldrick (eds), *International Handbook on Teaching and Learning Economics* (pp. 57–67). Edward Elgar Publishing. DOI: 10.1080/00220485.2014. 978923.

Michaelsen, L.K., Knight, B.A., and Fink, D.L. (2004). *Team-based learning: A transformative use of small groups in college teaching*. Stylus Publishing.

Millis, B.J. (ed.). (2010). *Cooperative learning in higher education*. Sterling.

Millis, B.J., and Cottell, P.G., Jr (1997). *Cooperative learning for higher education faculty*. American Council on Education Oryx Press Series on Higher Education. Praeger.

National Research Council (NRC). (2000). *How people learn: Brain, mind, experience, and school* (expanded edition). National Academies Press.

Ruder, P., Maier, M., and Simkins, S.P. (2021). Getting started with team-based learning (TBL): An introduction. *Journal of Economic Education 52*(3), 220–230. DOI: 10.1080/00220485.2021.1925187.

Schell, J.A., and Butler, A.C. (2018). Insights from the science of learning can inform evidence-based implementation of Peer Instruction. *Frontiers in Education 3*. DOI: 10.3389/feduc.2018.00033.

Schwartz, D.L., and Bransford, J.D. (1998). A time for telling. *Cognition and Instruction 16*(4), 475–522.

Schwartz, D.L., Tsang, J.M., and Blair, K.P. (2016). *The ABCs of how we learn: 26 scientifically proven approaches, how they work, and when to use them* (illustrated edition). W.W. Norton & Company.

Simkins, S.P., Maier, M.H., and Ruder, P. (2021). Team-based learning (TBL): Putting learning sciences research to work in the economics classroom. *Journal of Economic Education 52*(3), 231–240. DOI: 10.1080/00220485.2021.1925188.

Social Psychology Network (n.d.). *The jigsaw classroom*. Jigsaw Classroom. Retrieved January 16, 2022, from https://www.jigsaw.org/#steps.

Weinstein, Y., Sumeracki, M., and Caviglioi, O. (2019). *Understanding how we learn: A visual guide*. Routledge.

Yamarik, S. (2007). Does cooperative learning improve student learning outcomes? *Journal of Economic Education 38*(3), 259–277.

15. Teaching with experiments in the Introductory Microeconomics course

Tisha L.N. Emerson

INTRODUCTION

Principles of Microeconomics is often perceived as a daunting and difficult course by undergraduates and one that is not particularly interesting or relevant to their lives. This perspective may be tied, at least in part, to the heavy reliance on lecture by most economics instructors. In comparison, active learning techniques produce better attendance, more engagement, and greater learning (see e.g., Deslauriers et al. 2011). Classroom experiments are one such active learning approach that has been demonstrated to be effective in promoting better outcomes in Microeconomic Principles courses (Emerson and Taylor 2004). A classroom experiment in economics is an activity that asks students to make economic decisions by putting them in the role of buyers, sellers, donors, depositors, and so on. In market and other economic situations, facing constraints, students make decisions which lead to a variety of economic outcomes. Student decisions create data that can then be used for analysis and further illustration of economic concepts. Through the use of experiments, economics comes alive in the classroom.

EXPERIMENT EXAMPLE: COMPETITIVE MARKET

For those unfamiliar with classroom experiments, an example will illustrate the pedagogical technique. A foundational experiment for Microeconomic Principles courses is the competitive market experiment, also known as double oral auction, pit market, and demand and supply. This experiment introduces students to the demand and supply model that is generally presented early on in the Microeconomic Principles curriculum. At the start of the experiment, each student is assigned a role of either buyer or seller and provided with personal information about their role; that is, buyer value(s) and seller cost(s). The goal for participants is to maximize their earnings where earnings are calculated as the difference between: (1) their buyer value and negotiated price for buyers;

or (2) the negotiated price and seller cost for sellers. During trading, participants make offers/asks and negotiate with other participants. The instructor keeps track of the price of trades, the buyer value and seller cost to each trade, and the total number of trades. After trading finishes, these data are used to debrief the experiment, including predicting the outcomes (that is, equilibrium price and quantity, consumer and producer surplus, and market efficiency) based on the distribution of buyer values and seller costs, and comparing those predicted outcomes to the experiment's outcome data.

In addition to introducing students to the concepts of demand, supply, and equilibrium, adding relatively simple treatments to the competitive market experiment's basic structure can illustrate shifts in demand or supply (where buyer values or seller costs are changed relative to the initial distribution), the effects of price ceilings and/or floors, and taxes. The competitive market experiment can also be modified to illustrate externalities by adding an external cost or benefit that accrues to the entire population of participants for each trade. Alternatively, the competitive market experiment can demonstrate implications of prohibition by classifying the hypothetically traded good as "illegal" and imposing a random chance of seizure by enforcement authorities (that is, the instructor). To illustrate the implications of information asymmetries, the competitive market experiment can be altered so that buyers and sellers have different information about the quality of a good. Thus, through straightforward modifications, the competitive market experiment may serve as a workhorse by illustrating many important concepts that traditionally comprise the Microeconomic Principles curriculum.

Beyond the competitive market experiment and its derivatives, other experiments demonstrate key Microeconomic Principles concepts. Table 15.1 provides a summary of topics traditionally covered in Microeconomic Principles courses and some corresponding experiments.

PEDAGOGICAL EFFICACY

Early on, much of the evidence supporting the use of classroom experiments was anecdotal, but compelling nonetheless. My experiences using classroom experiments were positive from the start. Students enjoyed participating in the experiments, seemed to develop a deeper understanding of the concepts than they had with lectures alone, and I had never before witnessed such an active and involved economics classroom. Now, more than 20 years later, my store of positive experiences with experiments has only grown. For example, my students frequently come to class particularly excited on experiments days. They have also reported to me that they have shared both the experience of the experiments and their newfound knowledge with their roommates, friends, and parents. This is a far cry from the many people I have met over the years

Table 15.1   *Classroom experiments for Microeconomic Principles topics*

Topic	Experiment
Demand and supply, market equilibrium, consumer and producer surplus	Apple market,[a] Competitive market (continuous double auction),[b] Supply and demand[c]
Price controls	Competitive market experiment with price controls,[a,b,c] Minimum wage experiment,[a] Simple labor market[b]
Taxes	Competitive market experiment with taxes[a,c]
Production	Measuring productivity (airplane experiment),[a,d] Production entry and exit,[b] Cost curves[c]
Perfect competition	Entry and exit[a]
Monopoly	Monopolies and cartels,[a] Price discrimination,[b] Local monopoly and trade[c]
Oligopoly and game theory	Prisoner's dilemma,[b,c] Cournot,[b,c] Stackelberg,[b] Bertrand,[b,c] Ultimatum game,[b,c] Battle of the sexes[b,c]
Externalities and public goods	Externalities,[a,b,c] Public goods (contribution),[b,c,d] Tragedy of the commons,[b,c] Energy and the environment[d]
Information imperfections	Adverse selection (lemons market),[a,c] Insurance market[b]
Comparative advantage and trade	Comparative advantage,[a,b] Specialization and gains from trade,[c] Value of exchange[d]

Sources: Experiment sources: a. Instructor's Manual to Bergstrom and Miller (2000); b. *MobLab* (https://moblab.com/); c. *VeconLab* (http://veconlab.econ.virginia.edu/admin.htm); d. *Starting Point: Teaching and Learning Economics* (https://serc.carleton.edu/econ/experiments/index.html).

who have told me how awful their undergraduate economics course experience was, when I revealed my profession to them. Instructors, however, need not rely on the veracity of anecdotal evidence, as formal research has supported these informal experiences and observations.

Student Achievement and Engagement

The continued reliance on lectures by economics instructors is disheartening given the extensive evidence that active learning strategies, in general, improve student performance in an array of disciplines (Wieman 2014; Freeman et al. 2014). Further, research in economics specifically demonstrates that classroom experiments promote student achievement (see e.g., Emerson and Taylor 2004). Over the last two decades, considerable evidence of the value of classroom experiments has been amassed. Importantly, multiple studies demonstrate that students exposed to a pedagogy using classroom experiments outperform their counterparts whose Principles courses adopt a lecture-based format (Emerson and Taylor 2004; Dickie 2006; Durham et al. 2007; Ball et al. 2006; Frank 1997). And, while we certainly care about what our students learn, classroom experiments provide more benefits than just higher achievement. For example, Ball et al. (2006) found that student evaluations of teaching were higher in the experiment sections. Specifically, students exposed to the experiment pedagogy rated more highly the instructor's communication of the subject matter, and found the class more stimulating than did their counterparts in the lecture-oriented control group. Students in the experiment group also rated their instructor more highly overall. In terms of longer-run measures, though, Emerson and Taylor (2010) report no change in economics majors associated with exposure to the pedagogy in Microeconomics Principles; however, they do find limited evidence that some students took more upper-level economics courses than did their counterparts in lecture-oriented Microeconomic Principles courses.

Experiments and Promoting Diversity in the Economics Classroom

There are even more benefits from using experiments. We have reason to believe that adopting a pedagogy of classroom experiments may also help to promote diversity in the economics discipline. The lack of gender and racial diversity in economics is well documented (Bayer and Rouse 2016). Only about a third of all students majoring in economics are female. This has been consistently the case for decades, even as the proportion of female bachelor's degree graduates overall has increased. Underrepresented minorities (URM) are similarly observed in low numbers, with just over 10 percent of all economics majors identifying as Black, Hispanic, or Native American. Speaking to diversity specifically, both Emerson and Taylor (2004) and Ball et al. (2006) find that females exposed to a pedagogy of experiments experience greater achievement gains than do their male counterparts, closing the gender gap in performance. Since females are more sensitive to grade signals than are males (Rask and Tiefenthaler 2008), by closing the gender performance gap, experiments may increase female persistence in studying economics. Additionally, Bayer et al. (2020) suggest that certain aspects of an introductory student's experience are key in promoting student success and persistence. The elements are relevance, belonging, and a growth mindset. Classroom experiments place students in the economic environments being studied and make them decision-makers. Through their experiences in experiments, students more readily see the relevance of the topics studied and apply them to their own lives. Experiments also build community in the classroom which contributes to students' sense of belonging. Finally, through participation in the experiments and the subsequent debrief, students discover economic concepts for themselves. Through this process of discovery, students realize that their economic knowledge is malleable and developing rather than fixed; this supports a growth mindset with regard to economics.

LOGISTICAL CONSIDERATIONS

How Much Time Does It Take to Run an Experiment?

When considering adopting the classroom experiment pedagogy, instructors usually have many questions. The first often involves how much time the experiments will take and, relatedly, how they can possibly fit all of their content in once they have added experiments to their course schedule. These questions are based on the assumption that experiments are strictly a complement to rather than a (partial) substitute for lectures. Since experiments illustrate concepts, they can be used in place of part of the lecture time allocated to topics without reducing content.

Consider the competitive market experiment's role in my demand and supply unit. I usually allocate four 75-minute class sessions to demand and supply, which include presentation of the concepts (including equilibrium and consumer and producer surplus), examples and practice problems. When I adopted the competitive market experiment to illustrate demand and supply concepts, I simply replaced the first 75-minute class lecture/discussion with the experiment. During the 75-minute period, I review the experiment instructions, run the experiment (where students make decisions as buyers and sellers), collect data, and perform a debrief reviewing both what happened during the experiment and how we can use economic theory to predict the outcomes. Students draw demand and supply curves during the debrief, identify the predicted equilibrium, and are introduced to calculation of consumer and producer surplus. Students are exposed to as much or more information as during a 75-minute lecture. Instructors with 50-minute class sessions can complete all but the debrief during a single class meeting. The debrief should take place during the subsequent 50-minute class, and discussion of the theoretical concepts flows directly from the debrief.

Many experiments are designed to be completed during a 50-minute class. Some take even less time. For example, prisoner's dilemma and public goods experiments can generally be completed—including the debrief—in a 50-minute class or less. These short experiments provide an easy introduction to the pedagogy for an instructor new to classroom experiments. Finally, experiments often have different treatments (for example, shifting demand or supply, adding a price control or tax to the competitive market experiment). To run more treatments will take longer, as will running more rounds of trading within a single treatment. If an instructor is short on time or simply wants to reduce the time allocated to an experiment, they can always limit the number of treatments and/or limit the number of rounds of trading.

During Class or Outside of Class Time?

To this point, the discussion has assumed that experiments will be run during class time. That need not be the case if an instructor opts to use computerized experiments, as these may be run outside of class, either synchronously or asynchronously. Conducting experiments outside of class time offers the possibility that class time can be devoted to other activities. When run outside of class time, experiments may substitute for other student homework assignments. One important cost of conducting experiments outside of class comes in the form of losing the possibility to support community-building in the classroom. Carter and Emerson (2012) found that students exposed to manually run experiments reported more favorable views of the experiment pedagogy and higher levels of interaction with their classmates than students exposed to computerized experiments. An additional cost of moving synchronous experiments out of class time arises from the difficulty of scheduling a time when most students can be available to participate.

Computerized or Manually Run Experiments?

Instructors of face-to-face classes must decide whether to run experiments manually or on computers. As mentioned in the previous section, running experiments manually in class offers the possibility of supporting community-building in the classroom. However, manually run experiments require preparation of materials (for example, photocopying) prior to the experiment and can be difficult to manage in large (100+) classes. Computerized experiments require that students have access to computers (or tablets/smartphones) to participate. None of these requirements is terribly onerous, but one or the other may prove a more significant constraint for some instructors. These factors should all be considered when an instructor selects the form of experiment administration for their course. Instructors need not be concerned that one mode of administering experiments leads to greater student achievement than the other; Carter and Emerson (2012) found no significant difference in student performance in Microeconomic Principles classes in which some students participated in computerized experiments and others participated in manually run experiments.

Within each administration mode, instructors have an array of options from which to draw experiments. With respect to manually run experiments for Principles of Microeconomics, many published experiments are available. These include the Instructor's Manual to *Experiments with Economic Principles: Microeconomics* (Bergstrom and Miller 2000) which contains 14 experiments including an overview of each experiment, detailed instructions for the instructor, possible outcomes, and materials to photocopy for class use.[1] There are also many published journal articles detailing experiments on a wide array of microeconomic topics.[2]

Similarly, there are several options for adopters of computerized experiments. In particular, I recommend the following platforms: *MobLab*, *VeconLab*, and *classEx*.[3] *MobLab* is a fee service, though adopters of Cengage textbooks and the online supplement *MindTap* have access to *MobLab* experiments at no additional fee. *VeconLab* and *classEx* are completely free services. Each platform has a selection of experiments for use in a Microeconomics course. All three require the instructor to set up an account, but it is simple and quick to do so. Instructors and students only need a computer and internet connection to run and participate in an experiment (no software download is required). *MobLab* and *classEx* even allow students to participate using a tablet or smartphone. The various platforms also allow the instructor to modify experiment parameters (for example, adjust the level of a price control or tax) and, post-experiment, provide summary reports of experiment data and predicted outcomes based on economic theory.[4]

MobLab and *VeconLab* allow for asynchronous as well as synchronous play. Asynchronous play is made possible through the use of automated players based either on specific assumptions about decisions (*MobLab*) or on decisions from players in previously played games (*VeconLab*). The asynchronous option not only facilitates play outside of class time, but can also be used for synchronous play to add players to the market if an instructor has very few students and is concerned that the market may be too thin to produce results consistent with theory.

BEST PRACTICES

Where to Start?

For instructors new to classroom experiments, I recommend starting with one or two experiments in your first semester. Switching completely from a lecture-based approach (or some other pedagogy) to a full semester of experiments may be too overwhelming initially. By slowly adding a couple of experiments, the instructor will be better able to manage their pedagogical transition and to assess whether classroom experiments truly are right for them and their teaching style. While I am an ardent advocate of the classroom experiment pedagogy, I recognize that this pedagogy (or any other one) is not for everyone. Experiencing a couple of experiments, instructors will gather necessary information as to whether the pedagogy suits their personal pedagogical style and how it fits in their institutional environment. My first experience included using two experiments (competitive markets and prisoner's dilemma) in my Microeconomic Principles course. For me, the match was fast and clear, and from there I expanded my use to implement a pedagogy that makes heavy use of classroom experiments.

How Many Experiments Should I Use? Which Ones?

I recommend a pedagogy of classroom experiments using multiple experiments throughout the semester. With such an approach, students not only benefit from increased understanding of the material addressed by the experiments in which they participate, but they also experience positive spillovers to material not directly covered by an experiment. Additionally, students benefit from a more engaging classroom environment overall. To maximize student benefits, research suggests that the optimal number of experiments in a semester falls within the 5–7 experiment range. Fewer than five experiments are unlikely to maximize positive spillovers, while experiments beyond the seventh one yield diminishing marginal value (Emerson and English 2016a). Research further indicates that some experiments may be better than others. For example, there is some evidence that certain experiments produce more positive learning (for example, productivity) while others are associated with less negative learning (for example, minimum wage).[5] Additionally, some experiments appear to promote learning of the topic they illustrate, while others are associated with positive spillovers to other topics. For a full discussion of individual experiments, see Emerson and English (2016b).

What Preparation Do Students Need?

Once the instructor has selected the experiments they will use in their course for the semester, there are additional considerations in terms of administration. I recommend listing all of the experiments in the course syllabus and schedule. Doing so will allow students to plan and anticipate class activities. Prior to the class meeting in which an experiment will run, the instructor should provide students with experiment instructions so that they will be prepared to participate. Manually run experiments frequently come with written instructions that the instructor can share with their students. Computerized experiments may have written instructions or instructional videos. Even though instructions are provided to students beforehand, the instructor should review all of the instructions and rules associated with the experiment at the start of the class meeting during which the experiment will take place. Students will also benefit from the instructor working through possible decision-making scenarios that the students may encounter during the experiment, and answering any remaining questions.

While presenting and reviewing the experiment instructions is vital to the success of the experiment, equally important is that the instructor does not present any relevant theory prior to the administration of an experiment. From the learning science literature, we know that students better understand their text and classroom presentations when readings and lectures activate the students' prior knowledge. If the students are unfamiliar with the topic, there may be no prior knowledge to activate. Experiments address this issue as they provide students with an opportunity to participate in and experience markets and environments relevant to the course's economic theories. Participating in the experiment provides students with knowledge that can then create "a time for telling" where instructors then present economic concepts during the debrief and subsequent lecture (Schwartz and Bransford 1998). Further, through participating in the experiment and the following discussion, students will be able to discover some of the theory for themselves. This process supports a growth mindset amongst students, and they will take greater ownership of the material. Presenting the underlying economic theories prior to experiment administration would not only short-circuit this process, but it would also undermine students' confidence in the experiments and the predictive power of the economic theory being presented.

Incentives?

As economists, we know that incentives are important. Both intrinsic and extrinsic motivation play a role in experiments. Students quickly learn that experiments are fun and will eagerly anticipate them for this reason alone. I also make a point of telling students why I use the experiment pedagogy, emphasizing its efficacy in promoting student learning and engagement. This information, too, should promote intrinsic motivation to participate. However, I do not rely solely on students' intrinsic motivation because experiments function best and most consistently, as theory would predict, when students take the experiments seriously. Also, students learn more when they carefully make their decisions in response to the experiment's environment and constraints. So, I provide extrinsic motivation as well. How best to incentivize active participation and performance is still under some debate. Commonly used incentives include extra credit, grades, "treats" (for example, candy), and monetary rewards. I usually use extra credit, as I am uncomfortable with assigning a grade tied specifically to a student's experiment performance, and monetary rewards are not feasible in my context. For some experiments, I supplement extra credit incentives with candy.[6] Others, however, are uncomfortable even with extra credit, and suggest hypothetical earnings or small monetary rewards (Holt 1999). Speaking of monetary rewards, on common exam questions, Rousu et al. (2015) found that students who played a prisoner's dilemma game for monetary rewards outperformed their counterparts who either played for hypothetical earnings or did not participate in the experiment. In contrast, Dickinson (2009) found evidence supporting the use of hypothetical rewards. Finally, Dickie (2006) reported that grade incentives did not affect learning associated with experiments. Given the mixed findings and the variation in constraints different instructors face, I recommend using an incentive that you feel fits your situation the best; but do use some sort of incentive. For additional discussion of incentive use in the classroom experiment context, refer to "Should I provide incentives?" at the *Pedagogy in Action* portal (https://serc. carleton.edu/sp/library/experiments/incentivesecon.html).

Does Everyone Participate?

I highly recommend that all students participate in each experiment. They will gain far more from actively participating in making decisions than they will from passively watching others do so (Crouch et al. 2004). Before computerized experiments were available, instructors with large enrollments may have opted for having a subset of their class participate while everyone else observed, due to logistical issues. With computerized experiments, enrollment size is less of a constraint on full class participation.

What Is the Instructor's Role During the Experiment?

During the experiment, the instructor should answer any clarifying questions, but provide no direction regarding student decisions. Simply make sure that the students understand the decision-making circumstances of the experiment. If the instructor directs students on what decisions they should make during the experiment, this will undermine the learning process and students' belief in the economic concepts underlying the experiment. Instructors should ask students to predict the experiment's outcomes before running different treatments. For example, in the competitive market experiment, the baseline condition of the experiment establishes the equilibrium in the market. Subsequently, price controls or taxes may be added. After announcing the policy intervention, instructors should ask students to predict how the market outcomes will change as a result of the change in the environment. Doing so promotes learning (Crouch et al. 2004). Finally, the instructor should also collect data on the outcomes of the experiment. Examples include trade prices, which students are trading, quantity of trades, and so on. These data will be used during the debrief following the conclusion of the experiment. Computerized experiments generally capture all the necessary information for the instructor as the experiment is run. Those using manually run experiments will need to collect the data themselves. Preparing an Excel spreadsheet beforehand is quite helpful for data collection, analysis, and presentation when using manually run experiments.

Debriefing the Experiment

At the conclusion of an experiment, the instructor should always hold a debrief of the exercise with the class. A debrief should include a review of the data generated through the experiment, and an introduction to the economic theories motivating the experiment. For example, in the competitive market experiment, the instructor should present the list of actual trades, the trade prices, and the buyer and seller values for each trade. This allows for the calculation of the average trade price, the total quantity of trades, and the consumer and producer surplus realized. During the debrief, the instructor should also provide students with the distribution of buyer values and seller costs for the experiment. These values can be used to draw the demand and supply curves for the market, predict equilibrium price and quantity, and calculate expected surplus. Ultimately, expected outcomes should be compared to actual outcomes from the experiment. Through the discussion, students are introduced to the concepts of demand and supply, market equilibrium, consumer and producer surplus, and market efficiency. They also realize the predictive power of the simple demand and supply model. And, importantly, students will participate in uncovering this knowledge for themselves, which promotes a growth mindset. An important final step to support student learning involves a follow-on exercise (Cartwright and Stepanova 2012). Through a follow-on exercise, each student reflects on their experience in the experiment and how that relates to economic theory, and this constitutes a vital component in the learning process. The exercise could take the form of a homework assignment that mirrors the analysis performed in the debrief. Alternatively (or in addition), instructors could assign reading that illustrates the concepts in current events, and/or assign an essay where students reflect on the experiment.

CONCLUSION

A pedagogy of classroom experiments increases student achievement and engagement in Microeconomic Principles courses. Evidence also suggests that it closes the gender gap in performance. Through the experience of making decisions in response to economic stimuli, students are actively involved in the learning process and discover economic concepts for themselves. This process demonstrates the relevance to students of economic theory, builds a sense of community and belonging in the classroom, and promotes a growth mindset toward economics. By employing an experiment pedagogy, instructors create a more conducive environment for learning Principles of Microeconomics as well as promoting diversity in their classroom and the larger discipline.

NOTES

1. A pdf of the Instructor's Manual can be found at https://www.econ.ucsb.edu/ ~tedb/eep/instman2.html. The textbook includes student instructions and home-work exercises to accompany each experiment.
2. In particular, I recommend the vast array of experiments Charles Holt has pub-lished in a variety of journals. Other good sources for published classroom exper-iments include the *Journal of Economic Education* and the *Southern Economic Journal*.
3. https://classex.de/.
4. Notice that with manually run experiments, instructors will have to collect and analyze experiment data themselves and create their own diagrams. While not terribly onerous, these tasks may be challenging to complete for classes with larger enrollments and/or instructors without a teaching assistant.
5. In a pre-post test environment, students who answer a question incorrectly on the pre-test but answer the same question correctly on the post-test are said to have experienced positive learning. Students who initially answer correctly but later answer incorrectly exhibit negative learning.
6. I usually run 5–8 experiments per semester. For each experiment during the semester, I record the student's "earnings." At the end of the semester, I calculate the fraction of total earnings for the class that each student earned. They are then awarded the same fraction of a pool of extra credit points. Thus, if the pool consists of 400 extra credit points and Student A earns 3 percent of the class's total exper-imental earnings, then Student A would receive 12 extra credit points.

REFERENCES

Ball, S., Eckel, C., and Roja, C. (2006). Technology improves learning in large Principles of Economics classes: Using our WITS. *American Economic Review* 96(2), 442–446.

Bayer, A., Bhanot, S.P., Bronchetti, E.T., and O'Connell, S.A. (2020). Diagnosing the learning environment for diverse students in Introductory Economics: An analysis of relevance, belonging, and growth mindsets. *American Economic Review Papers and Proceedings 110*, 294–298.

Bayer, A., and Rouse, C.E. (2016). Diversity in the economics profession: A new attack on an old problem. *Journal of Economic Perspectives 30*(4), 221–242.

Bergstrom, T., and Miller, J. (2000). *Experiments with economic principles: Microeconomics* (2nd edition). McGraw-Hill Higher Education.

Carter, L., and Emerson, T. (2012). In-class vs. online experiments: Is there a differ-ence? *Journal of Economic Education 43*(1), 4–18.

Cartwright, E., and Stepanova, A. (2012). What do students learn from a classroom experiment: Not much, unless they write a report on it. *Journal of Economic Education 43*(1), 48–57.

Crouch, C., Fagen, A., Callan, J., and Mazur, E. (2004). Classroom demonstrations: Learning tools or entertainment? *American Journal of Physics 72*(6), 835–838.

Deslauriers, L., Schelew, E., and Wieman, C. (2011). Improved learning in a large-enrollment physics class. *Science 332*, 862–864.

Dickie, M. (2006). Experimenting on classroom experiments: Do they increase learning in Introductory Microeconomics? *Journal of Economic Education 37*(3), 267–288.

Dickinson, D. (2009). Experiment timing and preferences for fairness. *Journal of Socio-Economics 38*, 89–95.

Durham, Y., McKinnon, T., and Schulman, C. (2007). Classroom experiments: Not just fun and games. *Economic Inquiry 45*(1), 162–178.

Emerson, T., and English, L. (2016a). Classroom experiments: Is more more? *American Economic Review 106*(5), 363–367.

Emerson, T., and English, L. (2016b). Classroom experiments: Teaching specific topics or promoting the economic way of thinking? *Journal of Economic Education 47*(4), 288–299.

Emerson, T., and Taylor, B. (2004). Comparing student achievement across experimental and lecture-oriented sections of a Principles of Microeconomics course. *Southern Economic Journal 70*(3), 672–693.

Emerson, T., and Taylor, B. (2010). Do classroom experiments affect the number of economics enrollments and majors? A study of students in the United States. *International Review of Economics Education 9*(2), 42–58.

Frank, B. (1997). The impact of classroom experiments on the learning of economics: An empirical investigation. *Economic Inquiry 35*(4), 763–769.

Freeman, S., Eddy, S., McDonougha, M., Smith, M., Okoroafor, N., et al. (2014). Active learning increases student performance in science, engineering, and mathematics. *Proceedings of the National Academy of Sciences 111*(23), 8410–8415.

Holt, C. (1999). Teaching economics with classroom experiments: A symposium. *Southern Economic Journal 65*(3), 603–610.

Rask, K., and Tiefenthaler, J. (2008). The role of grade sensitivity in explaining the gender imbalance in undergraduate economics. *Economics of Education Review 27*(6), 676–687.

Rousu, M., Corrigan, J., Harris, D., Hayter, J., Houser, S., et al. (2015). Do monetary incentives matter in classroom experiments? Effects on course performance. *Journal of Economic Education 46*(4), 341–349.

Schwartz, D., and Bransford, J. (1998). A time for telling. *Cognition and Instruction 16*(4), 475–522.

Wieman, C. (2014). Large-scale comparison of science teaching methods sends clear message. *Proceedings of the National Academy of Sciences 111*(23), 8319–8320.

16. Teaching the Introductory Microeconomics course with social media

Abdullah Al-Bahrani, Darshak Patel, and Brandon Sheridan

INTRODUCTION

Social media is so deeply ingrained in our current society that it would be difficult to teach an economics course—or, indeed, any course—without at least an occasional reference to it. To use the language of economists, social media is becoming a complement to instruction, and its presence in a course is at least a necessary, if insufficient, condition for learning to occur. The goal of including social media in a course is to increase engagement, help students see that economics is relevant in their everyday lives, and hopefully deepen learning by reinforcing key economic concepts (Al-Bahrani and Patel 2015). The most important measure of a teacher's successs is their students' learning, which in turn requires engaging students and building a positive rapport (Pike et al. 2012). For the Introductory Microeconomics or Microeconomic Principles class, in particular, this means meeting students where they are and gradually introducing how to think more like an economist. What does this mean for the instructor? The current variety of social media platforms provides ample choice for an instructor to identify the best option for their particular context. However, social media platforms have proliferated at such a rapid rate that the choice of which platform to use to engage students may seem complicated. Indeed, the landscape has changed significantly in just the short time since Al-Bahrani et al. (2015, 2017a) surveyed students and faculty about their usage of social media platforms.

In this chapter, we focus on the use of social media, broadly defined, including current popular platforms such as Instagram, Twitter, and YouTube; we also include podcasts under our social media definition. We discuss the motivation for using such tools as well as their efficacy, we provide specific examples of how to incorporate social media into your teaching, we explain potential roadblocks and concerns you may encounter, and we conclude with a discussion of the future of social media in the classroom. While you may not choose to incorporate all of the strategies and tools we present, we are confident that you will find at least one that appeals to you and that will improve your teaching.

WHY USE SOCIAL MEDIA?

The ubiquity of social media begs the question of whether we should use it in our teaching. There are valid concerns (Manca and Ranieri 2016) which we will address, but we first want to discuss why you should consider using social media as part of your pedagogical strategy. It helps to think of social media as a toolbox, in which platforms such as Instagram, Facebook, Twitter, and so on, are the individual tools. Different tasks require different tools, but there can be a time and place for everything. As instructors, we also must realize that the majority of our students are now constantly connected to each other and the world around them via some type of social media, including while they are in our classroom. Kim et al. (2019) found that first-year college students were on their phones for up to 25 percent of class time and experienced a phone distraction in every four-minute time period measured. Therefore, we must leverage the tools we have to reach our students where they are and try to convert that distraction into engagement. Done well, social media can serve as a bridge into the social world of our students, with the intent of increasing competency and familiarity with course-related content, and without being overly invasive of their personal space.

There are multiple potential benefits from incorporating social media into your pedagogy toolkit. First, a primary feature of most social media platforms is communication, so it stands to reason that using social media in your courses can improve communication along the instructor–student dimension as well as the student–student dimension. There is evidence that students prefer social media to learning management systems, and that communication improves when using social media (Rahman et al. 2020; Schroeder and Greenbowe 2009; Al-Bahrani et al. 2017b). Second, the core focus of most social media platforms is engagement, and keeping students engaged is key to improving learning (Carini et al. 2006). There is mounting evidence that social media use within a course improves students' engagement with the content, each other, and the instructor (Hamadi et al. 2021; Henderson et al. 2017; Junco 2012), for both in-person and online courses (Martin and Bolliger 2018). Studies also find that more engagement is positively related to improved learning outcomes, especially for the lowest-achieving students (Carini et al. 2006). A related benefit, perhaps arising from better communication and more engagement, is higher reported satisfaction at the instructor, class, and university levels (Rahman et al. 2020). An implicit, related benefit is the potential for social media to increase access for all students to their instructors and peers because of the removal of the traditional classroom boundaries and structure. Finally, while perhaps not an explicit benefit, social media allows instructors an option to diversify their assessment methods.

WHAT SOCIAL MEDIA TO USE?

Over the past decade, the time people spend using social media has increased significantly (Levitz 2019). Many of us are familiar with the various social media platforms—Twitter, Facebook, Pinterest, Instagram, and so on—and use them for various personal interests. A 2015 study by Al-Bahrani et al. indicated heavy student presence on Facebook, YouTube, Instagram, and Twitter. Since then, students have continued to evolve their use based on availability of new platforms, features, and trends. According to the "Social Media Use in 2021" report by Pew Research Center (2021), the top three social media sites among United States adults are YouTube, Facebook, and Instagram, with those between ages 18 and 24 being more likely to use Instagram, Snapchat, and TikTok. Two of these social networking sites did not exist when we conducted our survey in 2015 (Al-Bahrani et al. 2015).

As new platforms proliferate, we highly recommend that instructors stay flexible and open-minded in engaging students in various ways. One possible approach is for instructors to survey students to stay up to date on current social media trends, but instructors should ultimately use a platform with which they are comfortable. Table 16.1 outlines various popular social media sites and provides different ways in which these tools can be used in Principles of Microeconomics courses. Although all social media platforms are unique in their functionality, a common denominator across all is the encouragement to engage with others. This opens the possibility for increased communication along the student–student, student–instructor, and instructor–instructor dimensions.

Instructors should select the social media platform with which they are comfortable and whose features support the learning goals of the assignment. We recommend instructors use a platform that is familiar to both them and their students to reduce their learning curve, and one that allows for one-way connection. Students report privacy concerns in connecting with instructors, but are more willing to connect and engage with classroom material as long as the connection is "one-way" (Al-Bahrani et al. 2015). To maintain privacy, many social media platforms provide these one-way connections. This means that students can connect with the instructor account and see material which the instructor posts, but the instructor does not need to connect back with a student account. This helps to maintain student personal account and content privacy.

Table 16.1   Summary of social media features

	Main method of communication			Type of connection		Micro-blogging
	Video/media sharing	Visual image/ document sharing	Text	One-to-one	One-to-many	
Facebook	•	•	•	•	•	•
Twitter	•	•	•	•	•	•
Instagram	•	•		•	•	
YouTube	•				•	
Pinterest		•			•	
Snapchat	•	•		•	•	
LinkedIn	•	•	•	•	•	
TikTok	•	•			•	

In this case, more students will feel comfortable in engaging with instructors. It is important for instructors to carefully evaluate their choice of a social networking site that aligns with their learning goals. Finally, we recommend that participation not be required, but rather be a complementary resource to the teaching approach (Al-Bahrani et al. 2017b).

Table 16.1 provides a summary of the features that various currently popular social media sites contain that could be helpful for an educational setting. Each platform provides users with a way to communicate and connect with others. Users can communicate using video/media, documents, images, or plain text. From Table 16.1, Pinterest does not allow for video messages and YouTube does not allow for communication via images. Facebook, Twitter, and LinkedIn have plain-text functionality. The platforms also allow for variability in type of connections. Users can connect with another user privately, or share their thoughts with all their connections. While all platforms allow for the latter, YouTube, Pinterest, and Tiktok do not have one-to-one functionality. Lastly, instructors interested in microblogging via social media should focus on using Facebook or Twitter.

HOW TO USE SOCIAL MEDIA?

Social media provides a platform for participants to share user-generated content, ideas, and information. These interactions help to build stronger virtual communities, relationships, and networks. Each social media platform comes with unique interaction functionality, and deciding which social media platform to use should also be a function of the pedagogical role an educator wants social media to fulfill. Platforms vary in popularity with students, and allow educators to create different types of learning opportunities. Al-Bahrani and Patel (2015) introduce several ways in which Facebook, Twitter, and Instagram can be used to engage students, and many other examples are continually added to the growing literature on this topic. Kassens (2014) used Twitter to help students improve the precision of their writing. Social media has been shown to increase student satisfaction through activities that lead to better communication, increased engagement, and unique assessment techniques (Rahman et al. 2020). This section highlights the main roles that social media can play in your classroom.

Social Media as a Communication Tool

The initial attraction of using social media in education was its perceived benefit of being more effective in reaching students. In comparison to email and learning management systems, students visit social media more frequently (Al-Bahrani et al. 2015). Educators interested in reaching students "where they are" embraced social media as a method to communicate course information and announcements to students. Al-Bahrani and Patel (2015) warn against the use of social media as a replacement for official university communication methods. Al-Bahrani and Moryl (2020) advocated for the use of social media to maintain communication and enhance engagement; this was especially important during the Covid-19 pandemic and the shift to virtual education. This communication aspect could become increasingly important as more education moves online.

Examples for instructors

Example 1: Announcements. Instructors can replicate announcements made in the institution's learning management system (LMS). The social media announcement can be short and direct, asking students to refer to the school platform for further details. Announcements may include but are not limited to tweeting/posting due dates, readings, class cancellations, reminders of exam dates, and so on. Various forms of reminders have been shown to increase classroom performance (Humphrey et al. 2021).

Example 2: Sharing an article. One of the most important tools of Twitter is the hashtag (#); this denotes the topic of discussion or conversation. Any topic associated with the # allows users to find or search content related to that topic in real time. For example, #TeachEcon is popular among economic educators when looking for examples of economic concepts with real-life connections. Instructors can share a link to an article, summarize it with an interesting question, and then use # to link to classroom topics. This helps students to relate the content of the article to classroom concepts. The # in this case will be any topics covered in the course; for example, #Incentives or #ChangeInDemand.[1] Students are encouraged to share their thoughts by engaging with the article on social media and/or sharing articles that either agree or disagree with the shared content. It is important for instructors to share the same article within the LMS or in the classroom to maintain the inclusive nature of the classroom.

Social Media as an Engagement Tool

A major benefit of using social media to communicate with students, and for students to share their work, is that it allows students to connect with a broader audience. These connections can serve as a way to expand the diverse voices to which students are exposed. The economics profession has increased its efforts towards diversity and inclusion in recent years. Special attention has been given to the importance of having diverse role models and, relatedly, the role of educators in recruiting new students to economics (Al-Bahrani 2022; Bayer et al. 2020; Porter and Serra 2020).

Social media allows educators to connect students to economists from other institutions. Consider providing students with a list of recommended economists to follow on social media. Carefully curate a list of diverse economists and researchers that will allow students to connect with social media. Instructors teaching at the Principles level can leverage social media connections to invite researchers from the field to talk to the students. The use of social media makes more researchers accessible compared to relying on traditional networks. Students can see that economists study a diverse range of topics, and that economics can be applied to almost anything. Many academics have shifted to using social media as a way of increasing awareness of their research (Gruzd et al. 2012).

Examples for instructors

Example 1: On Twitter, students can access the "hidden curriculum" using #EconTwitter. "Hidden curriculum" refers to knowledge that is unconsciously gained by consuming content from outside the classroom. Think about the unwritten rules and norms that are not taught in class. Economists on Twitter openly discuss their research, tips on applying to graduate school (answers differ based on whether you went to an Ivy League, regional college, and so on), among many other things, that students may not necessarily learn about during a typical course or semester.

Ask students to find an economist specializing in a topic of their interest on Twitter. Students can do that by searching hashtags such as #EconTwitter, #topic. The topic can be provided by the instructor or picked from class concepts. Ask students to follow the economist and engage with their research. Students can either ask a follow-up question to the economist or summarize the research and submit within the LMS.

Example 2: Once students have completed a classroom research project, ask them to share a summary of their research on their LinkedIn profile. This summary can be a short post on what the student research topic is about, with the presentation uploaded within their post. The presentation can be either through a series of photos or a PowerPoint presentation. To engage the community, students should tag their summary with several hashtags that relate to the class and the topic of their work. Students can also tag the educators or industries closest to their research, asking for feedback on their work.

Social Media as an Assessment Tool

Although we recommend the use of social media as a complementary resource, researchers have provided several ways to incorporate social media to assess students' understanding of classroom material. Instructors can create graded homework assignments or projects that are evaluated through submissions on a social media platform.

#EconSelfies

Social media provides an opportunity for students to communicate knowledge concisely. One form of such communication is through visual economics narratives. Al-Bahrani et al. (2016) introduce the "EconSelfie" assignment. The assignment uses images as a tool to assess students' ability to connect economic concepts to the world around them, which is particularly useful in a Microeconomics Principles class because students are at the early stages of thinking like an economist. While many social media platforms allow for the sharing of images and captions, Instagram provides a particularly useful platform for the image and caption combination. However, the researchers recognize that not all educators are comfortable with the use of social media (Al-Bahrani et al. 2015). For educators reluctant to incorporate social media in the classroom or for assessment, this assignment can be modified and incorporated as an assignment on any learning management system that accommodates discussion boards.

> *Example: Students are asked to take a photo of themselves (a selfie) that illustrates an economic concept covered in a classroom, and share a short caption of how the selfie relates to the economic concept. Submissions can be made on social networking sites such as Twitter, Instagram, Pinterest, Tumblr, or a closed Facebook group for privacy purposes. It is important for students to see their peers' submissions to create a learning community. This assignment is suitable for all modes of instruction (face-to-face, online, hybrid) and learning goals of a course. Instructions, rubrics, and recommendations can be found in Al-Bahrani et al. (2016).*

Podcasts

Social media provides educators with a platform where students can be active learners and create content. Project-based learning allows students to develop workforce readiness skills through inquiry (Bell 2010). Some great resources for Microeconomic Principles include Planet Money, Freakonomics,

EconTalk, This American Life, among others. A one-stop shop for instructors to incorporate podcasts that are geared towards Microeconomics Principles into their classroom is through audioecon.com summarized in Moryl (2014). The site provides a searchable library with many resources that make it easy for classroom implementation.

Example: One form of assessment via social media is to ask students to produce podcasts. Students are asked to apply economic concepts to the real world through the creation of a podcast. Moryl (2016) used student-generated podcasts and project-based learning to reinforce economic concepts. Podcasts can be shared internally or externally, through hosting platforms, or through YouTube as an audio file. While it requires more student time and effort, instructors can assign a video interview instead of an audio podcast. Instructions, rubrics, and recommendations can be found in Moryl (2016).

Twitter

Social media also provides a platform to generate discussion outside the four walls of classroom, on topics ranging from textbook readings, to news articles, or educational videos. Kassens (2014), designed a course in which students were required to microblog using Twitter and finds that students improved their writing and communication skills. That finding is consistent with Lowe and Laffey (2011) in a similarly designed study with a sample of marketing students. Malik et al. (2019) review 103 studies on the use of Twitter that were published between 2007 and 2017 and find that Twitter allows for increased communication and accessibility due to the real-time format of communication. Jones and Baltzersen (2017), introduce the use of Twitter in large principles courses. The authors leverage Twitter as a communication and assessment tool to create case study discussions in large lectures.

Example: Students are asked to complete a reading on a certain topic. Instructor should create two discussion questions for students to address on Twitter. The instructor should also provide a # so that they are able to easily search student responses (beneficial when the connection is one-way) and grade them. To enhance the engagement, students can also be required to respond to the responses of two classmates. Instructions, rubrics, and recommendations can be found in Kassens (2014).

ADDITIONAL CONSIDERATIONS

Privacy and Impact

Given the pervasiveness of social media, the professional and social boundaries are sometimes blurred. This raises privacy concerns and increases the possibility of misuses of the communication tools. Economics instructors have been slow in adopting social media as a teaching tool, citing concerns of privacy and of it being more of a distraction than a useful resource (Al-Bahrani et al. 2017a; Lau 2017). There have also been few attempts to quantify the impact of social media on student learning outcomes in economics courses, which further hinders adoption. Al-Bahrani et al. (2017b) study the impact of disseminating course material using Twitter versus an institution's LMS on learning outcomes and find no significant impact. It is important to note that the instructors' part of the study limited their use of Twitter in engaging students. The study only focused on using Twitter as a substitute for the LMS as a communication tool, and other forms of engagement were restricted to maintain the conciseness of the research hypothesis. Hence, we should not conclude that Twitter is ineffective as a pedagogical tool.

Using Social Media for Professional Development

Social media can be a positive and impactful tool when used appropriately, and instructors can help students to identify how to leverage it professionally. Using social media professionally may require some planning on the instructor's part to help students clean up their social media footprint, but this is important for students who are going on the job market. One way to implement this is to flex your own social media muscles, showing students how to professionally maintain an account that is inclusive and engaging. Other suggestions include using your institution's development/career centers that help with each student's brand creation. It is also vital to motivate students to share their presentations, research, and other accomplishments on social media to maintain their brand value.

EDUCATORS' APPREHENSION TOWARD SOCIAL MEDIA

Instructors and students might shy away from embracing social media because these platforms can be abused and exploited, with harassment and bullying not uncommon, especially for students from historically marginalized communities. This potentially harmful behavior should be taken into consideration when considering the type and purpose of use. Instructors should strive to create an inclusive classroom environment, and this extends to the online realm as well.

Another reason why economic educators are reluctant to incorporate social media in the classroom is to protect intellectual property and the privacy of classroom discussion (Al-Bahrani et al. 2017a), which has been a concern as far back as the introduction of email (Manning 1996). The boundaries of what discussions or content remain accessible to only enrolled students are being blurred. We expect at least some of these privacy concerns will decrease as online education and virtual teaching become more widespread, and instructors and students each become more adept at using social media.

The apprehension about incorporating technology in the economics classroom is not novel to social media. Goffe and Parks (1997) were the first to introduce economists to web-based resources and the tools available to them to reduce the cost of storing and sharing information. A reluctance to embrace technology in economics education was also evident with email and the internet (Manning 1996; Agarwal and Day 1998; Goffe and Sosin 2005). During the transition from "chalk and talk" to "PowerPoint and talk" some researchers found a negative effect on student outcomes in classes using PowerPoint relative to classes using traditional chalkboards, which suggested that PowerPoint should be used with caution (Sosin et al. 2004). It is difficult to imagine a classroom today that does not incorporate PowerPoint as part of the traditional teaching method.

Technology adoption and innovation in economic education may lag due to economists needing to be convinced of the causal improvements to student outcomes associated with innovations. Given how long it may take to design, implement, and conduct research, this need for evidence implies that the field will incorporate new technologies only long after they are introduced. There is also an implementation and learning lag of technology as educators work to find the most effective ways to use new tools in the classroom.

From a student's point of view, there are concerns that students might be inhibited about posting class-related material on social media, specifically Instagram or Twitter, where posts are sometimes public, due to the fear and stigma of publicly showing enthusiasm for a subject, class, or instructor. A solution is to have students create class-specific accounts. However, the concern then is that students do not encounter the class material during their regular engagement of social media through various interactions across social media users. While each choice does have tradeoffs, it is important to note that the same scenario is equally likely in an in-person setting. Many students do not volunteer to answer questions or engage in discussions out of shyness or fear of being stigmatized. Social media helps to mitigate this "stigma" risk, especially when students can engage by making themselves anonymous to other students while remaining known to the instructor (for graded work). In this case, one could argue that social media may be more inclusive relative to an in-person setting.

THE FUTURE OF SOCIAL MEDIA IN EDUCATION

The 2020–2022 coronavirus pandemic highlighted the importance of virtual connections in education. Perets et al. (2020) found that student engagement decreased due to the emergency transition to online teaching. However, classes that required student blogging were more effective in retaining student engagement. As schools develop online education strategies, it is imperative that these strategies also include student engagement plans.

Social media, due to open student access and high use, presents an opportunity to engage students and maintain a connection between student and university, or between student and a specific class. Al-Bahrani and Moryl (2020) present tips on using social media to maintain and develop connections based on their transition to online education. The authors present opportunities to target the whole student (investing in the student's overall well-being beyond just success in the course) and encourage faculty to use social media to communicate with students about university-level opportunities. By complementing traditional communication, faculty can amplify and promote university-led support systems with which students might not be familiar. The authors suggest that this form of communication can deepen ties between student and institution, particularly during difficult times such as those presented during the remote-learning transition of the pandemic. Stronger connections between students and higher education institutions will be even more important moving forward, especially in an educational landscape where online content is readily available.

The role of educators in the economics classroom is to help students learn the content, connect it to the world around them, and provide an opportunity to engage with the lessons. As more content becomes available online, higher education will have to define the value it provides. Connecting students with subject matter experts, and providing educational content created by reliable academics, is an important part of signaling the content's value. Social media allows educators to expand their communication reach beyond the traditional reach of classroom discussions and lessons. We recommend that educators embrace these new tools and learn how to use social media in an effective manner to engage and educate more people.

NOTE

1. When using hashtags, be sure to capitalize all individual words so that screen readers will properly read the hashtags for students using such devices (that is, #ChangeInDemand, not #changeindemand).

REFERENCES

Agarwal, R., and Day, A.E. (1998). The impact of the Internet on economic education. *Journal of Economic Education* 29(2), 99–110.

Al-Bahrani, A. (2022). Classroom management and student interaction interventions: Fostering diversity, inclusion, and belonging in the undergraduate economics classroom. *Journal of Economic Education* 3(53), 259–272.

Al-Bahrani, A., Holder, K., Moryl, R.L., Murphy, P.R., and Patel, D. (2016). Putting yourself in the picture with an 'ECONSelfie': Using student-generated photos to enhance introductory economics courses. *International Review of Economics Education 22*, 16–22.

Al-Bahrani, A., and Moryl, R. (2020, June 24). Using social media to retain and connect with students in the shift to online education. Faculty Focus. https://www.facultyfocus.com/articles/online-education/online-student-engagement/using-social-media-to-retain-and-connect-with-students-in-the-shift-to-online-education/.

Al-Bahrani, A., and Patel, D. (2015). Incorporating Twitter, Instagram and Facebook in the economics classroom. *Journal of Economic Education 46*(1), 56–67.

Al-Bahrani, A., Patel, D., and Sheridan, B. (2015). Engaging students using social media: The students' perspective. *International Review of Economic Education 19*, 36–50.

Al-Bahrani, A., Patel, D., and Sheridan, B. (2017a). Have economic educators embraced social media as a teaching tool? *Journal of Economic Education 48*(1), 45–50.

Al-Bahrani, A., Patel, D., and Sheridan, B. (2017b). Evaluating Twitter and its impact on student learning in Principles of Economics courses. *Journal of Economic Education 48*(4), 243–253.

Bayer, A., Bhanot, S.P., Bronchetti, E.T., and O'Connell, S.A. (2020, May). Diagnosing the learning environment for diverse students in introductory economics: An analysis of relevance, belonging, and growth mindsets. *AEA Papers and Proceedings 110*, 294–298.

Bell, S. (2010). Project-based learning for the 21st century: Skills for the future. *Clearing House: A Journal of Educational Strategies, Issues and Ideas 83*(2), 39–43.

Carini, R.M., Kuh, G.D., and Klein, S.P. (2006). Student engagement and student learning: Testing the linkages. *Research in Higher Education 47*(1), 1–32.

Goffe, William L., and Parks, Robert P. (1997). The future information infrastructure in economics. *Journal of Economic Perspectives 11*(3), 75–94.

Goffe, W.L., and Sosin, K. (2005). Teaching with technology: May you live in interesting times. *Journal of Economic Education 36*(3), 278–291.

Gruzd, A., Staves, K., and Wilk, A. (2012). Connected scholars: Examining the role of social media in research practices of faculty using the UTAUT model. *Computers in Human Behavior 28*(6), 2340–2350.

Hamadi, M., El-Den, J., Narumon Sriratanaviriyakul, C., and Azam, S. (2021). A social media adoption framework as pedagogical instruments in higher education classrooms. *E-Learning and Digital Media 18*(1), 55–85.

Henderson, M., Selwyn, N., and Aston, R. (2017). What works and why? Student perceptions of "useful" digital technology in university teaching and learning. *Studies in Higher Education 42*(8), 1567–1579.

Humphrey, W., Laverie, D., and Shields, A. (2021). Exploring the effects of encouraging student performance with text assignment reminders. *Journal of Marketing Education 43*(1), 91–102.

Jones, M.D., and Baltzersen, M. (2017). Using Twitter for economics business case discussions in large lectures. *International Review of Economics Education 26*, 14–18.

Junco, R. (2012). The relationship between frequency of Facebook use, participation in Facebook activities, and student engagement. *Computers and Education 58*(1), 162–171.

Kassens, A.L. (2014). Tweeting your way to improved #writing, #reflection, and #community. *Journal of Economic Education 45*(2), 101–109.

Kim, I., Kim, R., Kim, H., Kim, D., Han, K., et al. (2019). Understanding smartphone usage in college classrooms: A long-term measurement study. *Computers and Education 141*, 103611.

Lau, W.W. (2017). Effects of social media usage and social media multitasking on the academic performance of university students. *Computers in Human Behavior 68*, 286–291.

Levitz, R.N. (2019). 2019 E-expectations trend report. Ruffalo Noel Levitz. Available at www.RuffaloNL.com/Expectations.

Lowe, B., and Laffey, D. (2011). Is Twitter for the birds? Using Twitter to enhance student learning in a marketing course. *Journal of Marketing Education 33*(2), 183–192.

Malik, A., Heyman-Schrum, C., and Johri, A. (2019). Use of Twitter across educational settings: a review of the literature. *International Journal of Educational Technology in Higher Education 16*(1), 1–22.

Manca, S., and Ranieri, M. (2016). Facebook and the others. Potentials and obstacles of social media for teaching in higher education. *Computers and Education 95*, 216–230.

Manning, L.M. (1996). Economics on the Internet: Electronic mail in the classroom. *Journal of Economic Education 27*(3), 201–204.

Martin, F., and Bolliger, D.U. (2018). Engagement matters: Student perceptions on the importance of engagement strategies in the online learning environment. *Online Learning 22*(1), 205–222.

Moryl, R.L. (2014). Podcasts as a tool for teaching economics. *Journal of Economic Education 45*(3), 284–285.

Moryl, R.L. (2016). Pod learning: Student groups create podcasts to achieve economics learning goals. *Journal of Economic Education 47*(1), 64–70.

Perets, E.A., Chabeda, D., Gong, A.Z., Huang, X., Fung, T.S., et al. (2020). Impact of the emergency transition to remote teaching on student engagement in a non-STEM undergraduate chemistry course in the time of COVID-19. *Journal of Chemical Education 97*(9), 2439–2447.

Pew Research Center (2021). Social media use in 2021. https://www.pewresearch.org/internet/2021/04/07/social-media-use-in-2021/.

Pike, G.R., Smart, J.C., and Ethington, C.A. (2012). The mediating effects of student engagement on the relationships between academic disciplines and learning outcomes: An extension of Holland's theory. *Research in Higher Education 53*(5), 550–575.

Porter, C., and Serra, D. (2020). Gender differences in the choice of major: The importance of female role models. *American Economic Journal: Applied Economics 12*(3), 226–254.

Rahman, S., Ramakrishnan, T., and Ngamassi, L. (2020). Impact of social media use on student satisfaction in higher education. *Higher Education Quarterly 74*(3), 304–319.

Schroeder, J., and Greenbowe, T.J. (2009). The chemistry of Facebook: Using social networking to create an online community for the organic chemistry laboratory. *Innovate: Journal of Online Education 5*(4), 3.

Sosin, Kim, Lecha, Betty J., Agarwal, Rajshree, Bartlett, Robin L., and Daniel, Joseph I. (2004). Efficiency in the use of technology in economic education: Some preliminary results. *American Economic Review, 94*(2), 253–258.

17. Teaching Introductory Microeconomics online

Steven Greenlaw

Online courses have been offered for some three decades in the United States. They have been widely employed at for-profit institutions and community colleges. In both cases, they meet the needs of their students who often have jobs and families to work around. The Covid-19 pandemic brought online courses into the mainstream, especially at public four-year schools, and that is unlikely to change when the pandemic is over. Most students taking online courses at my institution take the bulk of their courses face-to-face. They also take online courses to speed up degree completion. Online courses may not work for all students or all courses, but there should be no doubt post-pandemic that they are useful for students.

Online courses have widely been considered second-rate, but is that necessarily accurate? Online courses replace face-to-face class time with a combination of synchronous and asynchronous learning activities. It is not the modality that makes an effective learning experience, but rather the pedagogy employed. This chapter explains how thoughtful course design, incorporating research-based pedagogies, can enable instructors to teach Principles of Microeconomics effectively in online or hybrid courses. The chapter provides specific examples from my experience; recent books, including Miller (2014), Major (2015), Darby and Lang (2019), and Boettcher and Conrad (2021), offer additional ways to develop excellent online or hybrid courses.

CHALLENGES OF ONLINE LEARNING

Online teaching is different from face-to-face. While the skills required overlap, they are not identical, and the two modalities have different strengths and weaknesses.

At present, the research on the efficacy of online courses is somewhat inconclusive. While the consensus seems to be that student learning suffers in online principles courses (in both microeconomics and macroeconomics) compared to traditional face-to-face courses (Goffe and Sosin 2005; Allgood et al. 2015), some studies show no significant difference (Vachris 1997; Coates et al. 2004; Gratton-Lavoie and Stanley 2009). Hybrid courses, which combine a limited amount of face-to-face class time (compared to on-site courses) with virtual learning activities, tend to combine the strengths of both online and face-to-face, so they generally do not suffer from an online penalty.

These results, though, are subject to at least two major shortcomings. First, course design matters for student learning, but in the efficacy research, course design tends to be subsumed under the categories of face-to-face and online. Just as on-site teaching varies from large lecture courses to laboratories, there are also a variety of formats for teaching online. Studies defining online courses merely as those which replace face-to-face class sessions with video-recorded lectures (e.g., Alpert et al. 2016; Schenck and Muriente 2020) use a narrow view of online modalities. As Bates (2021) notes, "if you just move traditional classroom teaching online, many students, especially the most disadvantaged, will do less well than if they were in class."

Second, most studies lack strong research designs. Few studies were based on random assignment to treatment and control groups. Large samples across courses, instructors, and institutions (e.g., Bettinger et al. 2017) leave too many confounding variables uncontrolled. Even with statistically significant results, it is not clear what may be causing the differences in learning outcomes.

We can draw two conclusions from the literature. Instructors can improve learning outcomes online by moving away from the lecture model. Gratton-Lavoie and Stanley (2009) note that online courses can employ personalized instruction and interactive hands-on learning materials. Second, student choice of modality and learning outcomes are endogenous. Online courses tend to attract older, female, and more able students (Gratton-Lavoie and Stanley 2009; Coates et al. 2004). For many students, who juggle jobs and families, online learning is the only modality that will work for them. Bates (2021) concludes: "[W]e need both online learning and face-to-face teaching. The issue is not which is better, but how do we make the teaching, in whatever form, effective for the students who are in those courses."

COURSE DESIGN

As faculty have begun teaching online, they have discovered the value of careful course design. Miller (2014, pp. 196–206) and Darby and Lang (2019, Chapter 1) provide thoughtful models.

Course design is the process of creating the learning environment for a course. Part of course design is conceptual: What are the course learning outcomes: that is, what should students know and be able to do by the end of the course? Principles of Microeconomics includes many concepts to learn, and a smaller number of analytical skills. What learning activities will help students achieve these learning outcomes? Concepts can be memorized, but deeper learning—especially of analytical skills—requires practice: problem sets, sample scenarios, and so on. How will student learning be assessed?

Part of course design involves the structure or scaffolding of the course. How much of the course will take place in the classroom? What will be the role for the learning management system (LMS) or other virtual spaces? What texts and course materials will be used? How much of the course will be synchronous? Will synchronous meetings be required or optional? Will they be recorded for later viewing? How much of the course will be asynchronous? Will students be expected to learn entirely on their own, or will there be group activities? Will students have regular opportunities to ask questions of the instructor in a way that all class members can benefit?

Traditional on-site courses have default learning designs, with which students and faculty are familiar. Students have internalized the learning environment, which revolves around attending class, generally multiple times each week. Class sessions embody more than just course content. Instructors tell students what they should be doing between class meetings, what readings to study, what exercises to complete, what upcoming deadlines they are facing, and so on. While these are likely explained in the course syllabus, good instructors remind students.

Online courses have no such defaults. They lack the predictable structure of class-time, and course structure in the online space is difficult for students to detect without significant scaffolding. Students do not have the long experience of transferring the consistent cadence of an on-site course when they take an online course. Consequently, instructors need to make an explicit effort to provide scaffolding in their online course designs. Miller (2014, p. 28) observes:

> In an online class … it may not be clear where to start, how to spend one's study time, or when the work is due. Good design, of course, offsets the problem of orienting students to the layout of the assignments—but even in a well-designed online course, students as well as teachers have to work harder to establish a basic understanding of how the course will work.

Students will need careful instruction on what they are expected to do and why they should do it. Darby and Lang (2019, p. 10) note:

> You can write all of those things to your online students, but when students are viewing everything through a screen, such text can become white noise that they filter out while they are getting to the requirements. So online teachers need to work a little harder to see that students see the purposes that underlie the activities they are undertaking.

What online course designs would promote student learning and possibly offset any online penalty? While not often taught in economics graduate programs, learning science has discovered a great deal about how to teach effectively (see Ambrose et al. 2010; Eyler 2018). Some of these findings have made their way into the literature on economic education. A consistent finding is that learning takes place when students interact with course content, with their classmates and with the instructor (see, e.g., Chizmar and Walbert 1999; Smith 2002). Courses should be designed to encourage such interaction.

Five elements can enhance course design: These are: (1) interaction with course materials (emphasizing active learning); (2) high expectations for students; (3) building intellectual community; (4) interaction between students and instructor; and (5) interaction between students and other students.

Active Learning

One way to offset the effect of any online penalty is by employing active learning pedagogies. Research shows that students learn more effectively from active learning than from passive learning. Koedinger et al. (2016) find that students learn six times as much from working with course materials than from watching a video or reading a text.

Economics instructors have long used active learning activities, such as problem sets, quizzes, and class discussions. This book includes chapters on several of these pedagogies. See, for example, Chapter 13 on teaching with writing, Chapter 14 on cooperative learning, Chapter 15 on teaching with classroom experiments, and Chapter 18 on teaching with Excel. However, the central focus of most Principles courses remains class lectures and readings. Active learning activities are used typically for assessment or ancillary opportunities for learning. Learning science research suggests that active learning should become the focus of the course design. Vachris (1999) describes an early approach.

The first step is to reconceptualize the role of assignments from serving primarily as assessments of learning to serving as integral to the learning process. Students should be assigned regular opportunities to work with the content, ideally using a variety of approaches. Selection of assignments should be based on achieving course learning outcomes. Second, regular feedback is necessary to allow students to make, but then learn from, their mistakes. Most learning activities should be low-stakes so that mistakes do not overly damage student grades. Feedback closes the loop on the learning process and catalyzes the next iteration of learning. To make this work, feedback must be timely and specific, identifying what the student needs to do to improve their performance, as well as explaining what has been done well.

Nearly all active learning pedagogies used in on-site courses can be modified for online courses. Students can be asked to create short videos explaining basic concepts in their own words. They can be assigned analytical problems or case study analyses to be done in groups. They can be asked to reflect on their own learning (Darby and Lang 2019, p. 17). After midterm exams, I ask: How much time do you study for this course during the average week? How much time did you study the week leading up the exam? Where did you make mistakes on the exam? What will you do differently to study for the next exam?

Synchronous sessions can play an effective role in online courses (Navarro 2015). Giving a 60-minute lecture is not generally a good use of scarce synchronous time. Count on the text to present the content; limit lectures to interpreting the content. Online lectures should be shorter than in-class ones: ten minutes or less. Students are unlikely to watch a 60-minute video lecture. Do not waste lecture on content that students can already learn for themselves. Focus on what you know students find challenging. Do not worry about production quality; simply using a webcam is fine (Darby and Lang 2019, p. 53). Synchronous sessions allow students to ask immediate questions. Recorded lectures can be viewed and re-viewed. There is a place for both in an online course.

Find and use pre-existing audio and video content. TED Talks, Freakonomics audios, and Planet Money (PBS) offer excellent examples. Scaffolding the note-taking process while watching a video lecture "encourages active listening and attentive processing of new information" (Darby and Lang 2019, p. 187). Alternatively, students can be given follow-up assignments based on each video/audio.

Chat functionality is common on video platforms. Students can use chat as a backchannel to ask questions, make comments, and so on. Alternatively, one can use polling to ask students questions in synchronous sessions.

Allgood et al. (2015, p. 304) note: "Past studies of achievement in introductory economics found that the choice of textbook does not appear to matter." If this is true, then instructors should consider open education resources (OER) since this saves the student significant expense. Instructors face costs when changing textbooks, but costs are no greater in adopting OER than another commercial text. Increasingly, OER publishers offer the same ancillary materials as those offered by traditional textbook publishers.

Digital courseware has the potential to promote greater student learning than traditional textbooks. Reading a text is usually a passive activity, even when homework follows. Digital courseware is more than an online text. Courseware described as adaptive and/or personalized embeds learning activities and short assessments through the content, which can be text, video, or simulation. The assessments are not meant primarily for grades, but to give the student and the instructor feedback about what the student is mastering and what they need more work with. Subsequent content is often based on the assessment results, meaning that different students take different paths through the content based on how well they are learning.

Digital courseware is offered by OER publishers, universities, and traditional commercial publishers. The price of the last of these, while lower than print textbooks, is generally significantly higher than that of the other two. Chapter 3 in this book provides an overview of the resources offered by a wide variety of texts and publishers, including two OERs.

For best results, one should adopt courseware that has been tested for efficacy at improving student learning. To date, there is not enough published research on the efficacy of digital courseware. Yarnall et al. (2016) examined seven controlled, side-by-side studies of efficacy, using scores on common exams, finding that the average impact of adaptive courseware was modest, but significantly positive. Dzuiban et al. (2017) found that adaptive courseware had significant positive impacts on student learning in psychology when differentiated by student ability. Gebhardt (2018) compared student completion of adaptive learning assignments with success on parallel questions on exams in Principles of Economics courses. She found that assignments lead to higher grades on the lower-level exam questions, though not on the more challenging questions.

If you accept that students learn more from working with the content, then it makes sense to adopt adaptive courseware. Courseware offers a nearly infinite number of problems, quizzes, and other exercises that can be assigned. Because they are machine-graded, students get immediate feedback. For best results, these activities should be assigned regularly with non-zero, but low stakes. While not limited to online courses, these learning activities can play a central role in online principles.

For adaptive courseware to work well, the course material, homework problems, quizzes, and exams must be aligned. This is not automatically the case. Terminology used in the course materials (including lectures) needs to match up with that of the various assessments. Material that is not taught will likely still show up in assessments, which undermines the alignment between assessment and exam performance. If the correspondence is weak, students wil not see much point in the learning activities, especially if they offer little credit. Instructors need to become familiar with the content being presented and the learning activities, to ensure a match with exam questions. At least in the past, test banks associated with textbooks have not been well done (Hammermesh 2019).

Setting High but Attainable Expectations for Students

Many Principles students have not taken an economics course before. They need to hear that economics is challenging, but that if they put in the effort, they will be successful. Ellenberg (2021) makes a similar point in the context of teaching mathematics: "When we say a lesson is 'easy' or 'simple,' and it manifestly isn't, we are telling students that the difficulty isn't with the mathematics, it's with them. And they will believe us. They won't think, 'I've been lied to,' they'll think, 'I'm dumb and I should quit.'"

For online courses, the problem is more acute. Miller (2014, p. 177) notes: "Motivational challenges are one of the main differences between online and face-to-face teaching." Online students need to take more responsibility for their learning than they do on an on-site course. They need to be told this explicitly.

Both Smith (2002) and Chizmar and Walbert (1999) support the use of high expectations to motivate students. Smith (2002) quotes Angelo (1993, p. 7):

> [W]e can increase a student's motivation to learn if we can positively influence that student's belief and expectations in four key areas. First, students need to see the value in what they are learning; second, they need to believe that learning will help them achieve other important goals; third, they need to believe they are capable of learning it; and fourth, they must believe they will succeed.

It is good practice to start the course with several early assignments that focus on effort: if students put the effort in, they will meet the standards. My first online Microeconomics assignment asks students to complete a ten-question syllabus scavenger hunt, that only requires them to read the syllabus carefully to find the answers. Nearly everyone scores 100 percent. My second assignment asks them to reflect on why they are taking Principles of Microeconomics. Is it a requirement for a desired major? If so, why is Microeconomics required? Is it to satisfy a general education requirement? If so, how does Microeconomics satisfy the requirement? Like the first assignment, if they take this assignment seriously, they are likely to get an A on it.

Subsequent assignments are more challenging. It is important for students to understand that working with the content and making errors is how learning happens (Mintz 2021). Key to this approach is the use of regular, low-stakes learning activities and feedback to students (Smith 2002). Chevalier et al. (2015) found that regular feedback on quizzes improves students' scores on exams. Even when students make mistakes, as long as the stakes are low and the feedback is helpful, they will persevere. Rubrics are also an excellent way of showing students that even challenging assignments are doable.

Mastery learning assumes that learning is iterative (Bloom 1984); students are given the opportunity to repeat their work until they attain some mastery level, 80 percent for example. It is easy to build elements of mastery learning into Microeconomics Principles. You can allow students to redo work that they scored poorly on. After mid-term exams, students can meet with me virtually to go over the questions that they got wrong. For each one they can correctly explain, I give them half a point back on their exam grade. The exam correction exercise works exceptionally well at teaching students why the right answers are right.

Building Intellectual Community

Online learning, by its very nature, is isolating (Navarro 2015). Isolation makes it easier for students to fall behind or drop out. Withdrawal and failure rates tend to be higher for online courses. A course design promoting intellectual community can reduce the isolation of online learning.

Walker et al. (2007) define intellectual community as a group with a shared purpose: "a commitment to help students develop into the best scholars possible." Members of an intellectual community feel a sense of belonging. Members need to feel comfortable in expressing themselves, taking risks, and even making mistakes without being judged. Intellectual communities do not just happen. They need to be intentionally designed and supported.

Intellectual community is more than just making students feel they belong: it can lead to greater learning. Smith (2020) observes: "Learning is a social as well as an intellectual and experiential activity. And learning environments that are short on community engagement and personal support will be, generally, less successful that those that are not." I emphasize that my Principles course is not a competition, but a collaborative effort to achieve the Microeconomics learning outcomes. By working together, students can all benefit.

Microeconomics should be a natural draw for students. Many are interested in the business world. All have personal experience with markets, budgets, and businesses. Darby and Lang (2019) affirm that asking students to draw connections between course content and their own lives can generate interest in the discipline. Why do markets, consumers, and businesses behave the way they do? Questions such as these can provide a structure for a community of inquiry in Microeconomics Principles.

At the beginning of each module, I provide a question that is designed to get students thinking about what they will learn in the module. These questions are designed to be engaging, relevant, and provocative, such as: What causes gasoline prices to go up and down? When a business runs a sale, how much more do they sell? How does a firm's market power affect how it operates? What specific strategies do firms use to increase sales? What determines a person's income? Do environmental problems represent a failure of the economic system or the legal system? Who is harmed when a nation imposes tariffs on imports? Questions such as these help the class to gel.

Interaction Between Students and the Instructor

Even in an online course, the role of the instructor is paramount (Darby 2019). Smith (2002, p. 541) points out that "interaction between teachers and learners is one of the most powerful factors in promoting student learning; interaction among learners is another." See also Chizmar and Walbert (1999).

Without instructor presence, there is much less intellectual community, much more of a feeling that one is taking a class alone. Many online courses are completely asynchronous with only machine-graded assessments. I once heard an economist describe this as "efficient" teaching, but it is not effective for student learning. Online instructors should allocate their time differently, with more time devoted to coaching, tutoring, and curating the course content. Darby (2019) describes this role as "explaining, guiding, asking, illustrating, answering questions."

In online courses, instructors must intentionally communicate with their students. While the default is text, Darby and Lang (2019) recommend using video messages to increase engagement. Many students have difficulty getting started in online courses, and it is easier to procrastinate (Miller 2014, p. 179). A first-year student once told me that they were so overwhelmed with college classes that while they went to their face-to-face ones, they simply forgot their online course.

Early in a course, it is a good idea to message students through the LMS several times a week, just to get them thinking about the course. The messages are simple, often just welcoming the students or reminding them what they should be working on. Once the course gets into a rhythm, it is important to communicate with the class at least weekly.

Online instructors need to be more explicit about messaging regarding deadlines, assignments, and exams. In a face-to-face class, when the instructor announces an exam, every student will take note; they often share that information with classmates who are not there. In an online course, it is not unusual for a student to miss an exam because they were unaware of it. Deadlines should be clearly announced, but it also helps to be flexible due to the complexities of many online students' lives. School is important, but so are families and employment.

I take every opportunity I can to talk to students individually, to build a relationship with them. This is not about sharing personal information, but it goes beyond my class to asking about majors, interests, and career plans. The goal is to help students feel respected as individuals. I also reach out to students who are struggling, offering appointments to get them back on track. This outreach should be framed as formative, so that students perceive this as a normal opportunity to improve, rather than punitive.

For my online courses, I offer online office hours. The first year when I scheduled fixed office hours, not a single student showed up. Instead, I offer virtual office hours as needed, at mutually agreeable days and times. I typically spend a few moments getting to know or checking in with the student. Video makes the conversation seem almost like face-to-face; you can read the student's body language. I have met far more students when I offer online appointments than I ever did with in-my-office hours.

I also offer a weekly virtual synchronous meeting. Many students appreciate the opportunity to interact with the teacher synchronously. The meetings last 10–60 minutes depending on how many questions are raised. I often give a mini-lecture on material I know will be challenging to students, such as deriving inferences from economic models. Each weekly meeting is recorded and archived on YouTube so that students who are unable to attend can still see what they missed. Not everyone comes to the weekly meetings, but nearly everyone watches the recordings.

Interaction Between Students and Other Students

Another way to build intellectual community is with student interaction. Chapter 14 in this book explains cooperative learning. While there are multiple reasons to promote student interaction (for example, student retention), the most important is that it enhances learning. As Eyler (2018, pp. 66–67) observes: "Sure, we can learn things on our own, but we rarely learn them as deeply because so much of our learning derives from our social nature and the visceral need to communicate with other people."

There are a variety of ways to encourage student interaction in online courses. To begin the course, I ask students to create a two- to three-minute video introducing themselves to the class. I provide a list of questions for students to answer, and I create my own introductory video to serve as a model. Students post their videos on the LMS discussion board. Personal videos make classmates (and the professor) visible and human. The videos need not be professional quality; in fact, they seem to be better received when they are not.

Study groups are another way to promote student interaction and intellectual community. Navarro (2015, p. 169) identifies study groups as being useful "to enhance student-to-student interactions and to help overcome some of the alienation and social isolation that can occur in an online learning format." Study groups are an integral part of my Principles course. I have found that groups of 3–4 students are the right size. Study groups can work in classes of any size. They may even be more important in larger sections.

I tell students that their study groups are important: many assignments will be completed as groups and the group is the initial place that students should go to get help. When I put the study groups together, I am careful to share the class talent. I place adult students with other adult students, and students from the same athletic team together. I take care not to create groups entirely of first-year students.

I often assign analytical problems that some students struggle with to groups (Vachris 1999). One is a supply and demand scenario where the groups must determine the effects of a demand and a supply shock on equilibrium price and quantity. Another analyzes the impact of a decrease in market demand on a perfectly competitive firm in the short and long runs. Both assignments are similar to what students will see in my exams.

Study groups can work together to prepare for exams. They can similarly work out correct answers after exams; I do not reveal these to students directly. Most study groups work well; a few work extraordinarily well. For the groups that do not, divorces can happen.

Another way to promote intellectual community is with online discussions (see, e.g., Vachris 1999; Chizmar and Walbert 1999; Darby and Lang 2019, pp. 82–85). As Navarro (2015, p. 168) observes: "The electronic discussion board has become a best practice and staple of online courses."

The best online discussions use open-ended questions with more than one reasonable answer. This reduces student anxiety about getting the answer "wrong." One good example is: "What is business?" The point of discussion is not to find "the answer" but to deepen students' understanding of the question and associated issues.

Outside readings from popular media also provide useful topics for online discussions. Articles such as Friedman's (1970) classic, "The Social Responsibility of Business is to Increase its Profits," are always excellent discussion prompts, as are articles on whether Microsoft or other large companies have too much monopoly power.

Asynchronous online discussions have certain advantages over synchronous face-to-face ones. They allow students to think before they respond. They also allow students who are reluctant to participate in person, to participate online. This includes women and minority students. Online takes longer, so a discussion that might last a class period face-to-face could play out over days asynchronously. This is both a bug and a feature. It requires more advance planning to fit into a course, but the time allows for more thoughtful discussion. Since many students are new to discussion and especially online discussion where the point is to generate knowledge, it is useful to make the topic of the initial online discussion, "How to have an online discussion." Miller (2014, pp. 144–145) finds having a series of online discussions leads to posts with higher-order thinking.

Finally, it is important that the instructor (or a trained teaching assistant) monitors the discussion, while not taking over. You would not have an in-class discussion without the instructor present. If you are not there, students will perceive that the discussion is not important. If you respond too frequently, the discussion will devolve into a dialog between the students and the instructor. Instructor presence need be no more than reviewing the posts daily, and occasionally responding in a way that keeps the discussion on track to its conclusion. A useful practice is to summarize the discussion to date, naming students' thoughtful contributions.

Note that online discussions in large classes can be overwhelming to participants, due to the number of posts. One solution is to divide the class into subgroups, each with its own discussion.

If you are skeptical about the value of online discussion, consider this: "[T]he single best predictor of final course grade was the number of discussion posts made over the course of the semester—even though these posts made up only a small proportion of the course points" (Miller 2014, p. 144).

CONCLUSIONS

Online courses have been offered for decades, but they entered the higher education mainstream during the Covid-19 pandemic. There is evidence that online courses, especially those that are designed to mimic traditional, lecture-oriented courses, lead to lower learning outcomes for students. To mitigate any online penalty, instructors should design online courses to focus on research-based pedagogies. These include a high degree of interaction between student and course materials (that is, active learning), high expectations for performance, intellectual community, interaction between student and instructor, and interaction between student and other students.

REFERENCES

Allgood, S., Walstad, W.B., and Siegfried, J.J. (2015). Research on teaching economics to undergraduates. *Journal of Economic Literature 53*(2), 285–325.

Alpert, W.T., Couch, K.A., and Harmon, O.R. (2016). A randomized assessment of online learning. *American Economic Review: Papers and Proceedings 106*(5), 378–382.

Ambrose, S.A., Bridges, M.W., DiPietro, M., Lovett, M.C., and Norman, M.K. (2010). *How learning works: 7 research-based principles for smart teaching.* Jossey-Bass.

Angelo, T.A. (1993). "Teachers dozen": Fourteen general, research-based principles for improving higher learning in our classrooms. *AAHE Bulletin* April, 3–13.

Bates, T. (2021, August 26). Research showing that online learning is less effective than classroom teaching—right? Online Learning and Distance Education Resources. https://www.tonybates.ca/2021/08/26/research-showing-that-virtual-learning-is-less-effective-than-classroom-teaching-right/.

Bettinger, E.P., Fox, F., Loeb, S., and Taylor, E.S. (2017), Virtual classrooms: How online college courses affect student success. *American Economic Review 107*(9), 2855–2875. https://doi.org/10.1257/aer.20151193.

Bloom, B.S. (1984). The 2 sigma problem: The search for methods of group instruction as effective as one-to-one tutoring. *Educational Researcher 13*(6), 4–16.

Boettcher, J.V., and Conrad, R. (2021). *The online teaching survival guide*. Jossey-Bass.

Chevalier, A., Dolton, P., and Lührmann, M. (2015). Making it count: Incentives, student effort and performance. *Journal of the Royal Statistical Association Statistics in Society Series A 181*(2), 323–349.

Chizmar, J.F., and Walbert, M.S. (1999). Web-based learning environments guided by principles of good teaching practice. *Journal of Economic Education 30*(3), 248–259.

Coates, D., Humphreys, B., Kane, J., and Vachris, M.A. (2004). No significant distance between face-to-face and online instruction: Evidence from Principles of Economics. *Economics of Education Review 23*(5), 533–546.

Darby, F. (2019). How to be a better online teacher. *Chronicle of Higher Education*, April 17. https://www.chronicle.com/article/how-to-be-a-better-online-teacher/.

Darby, F., and Lang, J.M. (2019). *Small teaching online: Applying learning science in online classes*. Jossey-Bass.

Dzuiban, C.D., Moskal, P.D., Cassisi, J., and Fawcett, A. (2017). Adaptive learning in psychology: Wayfinding in the digital age. *Online Learning 20*(3), 74–96.

Ellenburg, J. (2021). Want kids to learn math? Level with them that it's hard. *Washington Post*, June 25. https://www.washingtonpost.com/outlook/math-hard -easy-teaching-instruction/2021/06/25/4fbec7ac-d46b-11eb-ae54-515e2f63d37d _story.html.

Eyler, J. (2018). *How humans learn: The science and stories behind effective college teaching*. West Virginia University Press.

Friedman, M. (1970). The social responsibility of business is to increase its profits. *New York Times Magazine*, September 13.

Gebhardt, K. (2018). Adaptive learning courseware as a tool to build foundational content mastery: Evidence from Principles of Microeconomics, *Current Issues in Emerging eLearning* 5 (1), Special Issue on Leveraging Adaptive Courseware, October 22. https://scholarworks.umb.edu › cgi › viewcontent.cgi?article=1062&context=ciee.

Goffe, W.L., and Sosin, K. (2005). Teaching with technology: May you live in interesting times. *Journal of Economic Education 36*(3), 278–291.

Gratton-Lavoie, C., and Stanley, D. (2009). Teaching and learning principles of economics online: An empirical assessment. *Journal of Economic Education 40*(1), Winter, 3–25.

Hammermesh, D.S. (2019). 50 years of teaching introductory economics. *Journal of Economic Education 50*(3), 273–283.

Koedinger, K.R., McLaughlin, E.A., Jia, J.Z., and Bier, N.L. (2016). Is the doer effect a causal relationship? How can we tell and why it's important? In *Proceedings of the Sixth International Conference on Learning, Analytics and Knowledge* (pp. 388–397). ACM Digital Library.

Major, C.H. (2015). *Teaching online: A guide to theory, research and practice*. Johns Hopkins University Press.

Miller, M.D. (2014). *Minds online: Teaching effectively with technology*. Harvard University Press.

Mintz, S. (2021). Decolonizing the academy. *Inside Higher Education*, Higher Ed Gamma, June 22. https://www.insidehighered.com/blogs/higher-ed-gamma/decolonizing-academy.

Navarro, P. (2015). How economics faculty can survive (and perhaps thrive) in a brave new online world. *Journal of Economic Perspectives 24*(5), 155–175.

Schenck, S.M., and Muriente, C.L. (2020). Enhancing online learning through technology: Case study of Principles of Macroeconomics at Central Connecticut State University. *International Advances in Economic Research 26*(February), 131–133.

Smith, P. (2020). Maturing practice: Yellowdig. *Inside Higher Education*, May 13. https://www.insidehighered.com/digital-learning/blogs/rethinking-higher-education/maturing-practice-yellowdig.

Smith, W.D. (2002). Applying Angelo's teacher's dozen to undergraduate Introductory Economics: A call for greater interactive learning. *Eastern Economic Journal 26*(4), 539–549.

Vachris, M.A. (1997). Teaching Economics in a virtual classroom. *Virginia Economic Journal* 1997, 2 (September), 17–26.

Vachris, M.A. (1999). Teaching Principles of Economics without "chalk and talk": The experience of CNU online. *Journal of Economic Education 30*(3), 292–303.

Walker, G., Golde, C.M., Jones, L., Bueschel, A.C., and Hutchings, P. (2007). The importance of intellectual community. *Chronicle of Higher Education* (December 3). https://www.chronicle.com/article/the-importance-of-intellectual-community-123554/.

Yarnall, L., Means, B., Wetzel, T. (2016). *Lessons learned from early implementations of adaptive courseware*. SRI International.

18. Using Excel to teach Principles of Microeconomics

Humberto Barreto

INTRODUCTION

You might think that teaching Principles of Microeconomics is easy. After all, content is restricted to the basics, there is little mathematics involved, and the instructor can choose materials from a massive catalog of textbooks, videos, and other resources. However, the terminology and style of economics is so unfamiliar to the uninitiated that it presents a major hurdle for the instructor, an expert used to the jargon and formalism that permeates our discipline.

What should you do instead of endless performances of the "sage on the stage," plowing through a deck of prepared slides? Vary your delivery by mixing in active learning, visual stimulus, and numerical exposition that are the hallmarks of concrete pedagogy. A spreadsheet is ideal for this. Students have to click, see what happens, and respond. Abstraction is replaced by data on the screen, and clicking on cells reveals whether the display is based on a number or a formula.

A Principles instructor with a PhD in economics needs to worry less about content and, instead, focus intently on bridging the gap from expert to learner. Excellent teaching begins when the instructor is aware of the student's initial position. Absent context and a framework to organize new words and ideas, educational research confirms that concrete examples are absolutely essential. "Providing supporting information can improve the learning of key ideas and concepts. Specifically, using concrete examples to supplement content that is more conceptual in nature can make the ideas easier to understand and remember" (Weinstein et al. 2018, p. 11).

Of course, every teacher in every course is faced with the problem of communication: delivering content in a language and format accessible to the student. For Principles of Microeconomics, however, the communication problem is markedly more difficult. It is like teaching a foreign language; the first course is the hardest and has by far the highest failure rate. Students have no anchor, no framework with which to process information, and are over-whelmed by a flood of new words, symbols, and ideas.

One crucial strategy that improves learning outcomes is concreteness: be specific and vivid rather than general and vague, and never start a sentence with the word "imagine." As an expert, you implicitly call on a deep bank of knowledge to interpret the world around you. Students do not have this accumulated human capital, and therefore they have no way to process novel concepts and terminology. Abstract graphs are a jumble of lines and curves. Beginners require concrete examples, with numbers instead of letters, words instead of symbols, and phrases instead of abbreviations.

Traditionally, textbooks play the role of translator, recasting knowledge in a more digestible form. Even the best textbook is hampered by the fact that students read much less today than before the internet, and even when they do read, comprehension is a challenge (Johnson 2019). Repeated application of assigned textbook material combined with "chalk and talk" delivery—the usual approach—is undoubtedly low-cost for the professor, but student learning suffers under this pedagogical strategy (Miller and Rebelein 2012). Ironically, the most common way that we teach is one of the least effective ways to learn.

Spreadsheets offer a natural, relatively simple way to ease into concrete pedagogy. The typical economics professor is likely to be quite comfortable using a spreadsheet. Likewise, students have rudimentary knowledge of spreadsheets and can quickly acquire basic skills. Thus, it is relatively easy to include examples, homework, and computer lab exercises.

Another benefit of spreadsheets is that they enable us to develop compe-tency, not merely memorization of facts and definitions. Yes, you want your students to know that the price elasticity of demand requires computing the percentage change in quantity demanded divided by the percentage change in price. This is content mastery. But you want to move beyond this. You want your students to apply and transfer their knowledge of elasticity to new contexts and situations. You want them to be able to actually use the concept of responsiveness when interpreting a numerical elasticity estimate, or eval-uating a claim about how an exogenous shock affects other variables. This is competency.

Allgood and Bayer (2016) suggest that we measure college learning of economics via essential concepts and competencies. One of these is the use of quantitative methods: "We want students to be able to access, interpret, and manipulate economic data and to have knowledge of the primary methods of gathering and assessing evidence in economic investigations" (Allgood and Bayer 2016, p. 108). At the introductory level, spreadsheets provide a path to developing true competency because they are exceptionally good at displaying data, enable easy transformation through formulas that can be readily observed, and invite questions about connections between variables.

This chapter contains concrete examples of how Excel can be used to improve a Principles of Microeconomics course. Appendices include step-by-step instructions. It provides resources for infusing a Principles of Microeconomics course with concreteness via spreadsheets.

THE PRICE OF EGGS DURING THE PANDEMIC

Instead of the usual, boring example in your textbook, why not bring the world into your classroom and connect with your students? Covid-19 will leave a mark for years. Students will remember quarantine and lockdown. With this shared experience, you have a hook with which to attract and maintain their focus.

National Public Radio's (NPR) *Planet Money* produced a nine-minute podcast on rapidly rising egg prices in the summer of 2020 (http://tiny.cc/ eggprices). The audio is short enough to be played in class. You can download data from https://www.bls.gov/cpi/data.htm and prepare a spreadsheet, but there is a much better way: use the Federal Reserve Bank of St Louis (FRED) database Excel add-in to instantly download and graph the data, as shown in Figure 18.1. Step-by-step instructions are provided in Appendix A. The process is so easy and fast that it enables students to see the data downloaded live, making it part of the concrete pedagogical approach.

Armed with this eye-catching graph, you are ready to present supply (S) and demand (D). You have explained that price rises when demand increases, but with a concrete example, you can bring the shifting D chart to life. If students have access to the internet, it is easy to search and discover some basic facts about eggs: they cannot be easily stored, and that spike in 2015 was due to disease that resulted in a collapse in the number of hens. That is a very different story to the 2020 price spike from increasing demand (which, *Planet Money*'s podcast notwithstanding, has happened several times before). Now students have a way to deeply connect with two cases, increasing D and decreasing S. Both cause rising prices, but in different ways; and changes in equilibrium quantity are not the same.

Although not usually covered in discussions of supply and demand, since we have such a long series in Figure 18.1, you can point out that these are current, or nominal, prices. You could, of course, get the consumer price index (CPI), using the FRED add-in, and deflate the series to create real prices. You could provide hypothetical quantity data so students could compute change and percentage change in the price of a dozen large grade A eggs. Students could compute percentage change in quantity and then take the ratio of the quantity and price percentage changes to compute elasticity. Visual inspection

Eggs, Grade A, Large, Per Doz. in U.S. City Average

Note: Excel charts of FRED data provide a concrete sense of supply and demand events for students.
Source: Data from US Bureau of Labor Statistics (BLS) (n.d.).

Figure 18.1　　*FRED Excel add-in graph of egg prices over time (created July 22, 2021)*

can determine whether the elasticity estimates remain stable across the data. The elasticity estimates can then be discussed in the context of the determinants of inelastic and elastic demands, and perhaps compared with estimates of price elasticity of demand for a variety of goods. Finally, note that clicking on the series in the chart highlights the source cells in columns A and B and further reinforces the relationship between graphs and data.

In terms of delivery, there are several options, for example: conventional presentation of your computer screen as you download the data and make the chart; Socratic question-and-answer (Q&A) with the entire class where you solicit answers for what to do next; small groups working on questions together (ideal for a video breakout room); or a traditional assignment.

No matter the delivery method, you are grounding the supply and demand model in something that students readily understand. They know what an egg is and they have purchased eggs. This gives them the opportunity to connect concepts and terminology, such as increase in demand or decrease in supply, to the model. The concreteness in the pedagogy is what makes it work.

An extremely powerful feature of the FRED Excel add-in is that it provides a one-click update. The next time you teach the course, it is easy to get the latest data: clicking the *Get FRED Data* button will instantly download data from 1980 to the latest available prices. Another advantage is that you can give students different goods (or let them choose their own) to see how prices behaved during the pandemic. Now we have a discovery exercise; another mechanism well known to improve student learning outcomes. If conducive to your teaching style, you could set up a competition, individual or team, around a question such as: Which product had the highest percentage price increase during the pandemic?

EXCEL'S SOLVER

Although few Principles of Microeconomics courses use calculus, we still want students to understand the idea of optimization. Excel's Solver is a numerical optimization add-in that is easy to use and gives us the concreteness needed to teach the logic of optimizing agents that underlies the economic way of thinking.

A simple example is a competitive (price-taking) firm's profit maximization problem. Instead of U-shaped marginal and average costs curves, we can create a simple example with a squared functional form for costs, giving this profit function: $\pi = Pq - q^2$. With $P = 4$, we have the following concrete problem: max $\pi = 4q - q^2$.

Perhaps you are thinking that this is a waste of time since the answer is plainly $q^* = 2$, but the majority of students in your Principles of Microeconomics course do not have the tools to solve this problem. They stare at the equation and have no idea what to do with it or what it means. The ability to get out of your expert mindset and see the world through the eyes of a novice is critical to becoming a good teacher.

Appendix B offers step-by-step instructions for setting up and solving this optimization problem in Excel. It is simple enough to be done in a single class period, yet offers enough complexity to be interesting and challenging to an introductory economics student. Because they have to implement the problem in Excel, it requires the student to recast and organize the elements of the problem (objective function, endogenous, and exogenous variables). This is exactly what you want your students to do to learn about optimization and modeling.

Your economics course is not a computer science class, but basic understanding of an optimization algorithm and giving your students the opportunity to work with software is extremely valuable. By introducing them to Solver, you open the possibility of using this add-in for other models and problems. For example, a simple supply and demand model can be analyzed by using Solver to drive excess demand to zero.

Your textbook will undoubtedly have a series of profit maximization graphs, for perfect competition and monopoly in the short and long run. Using Solver gives your students a framework for understanding the optimization problems they see in the textbook. You can use the numerical examples in your textbook in your own Excel-based versions to give students a second bite at the apple. This kind of repetition, with variation in presentation, is an effective strategy and personalizes your teaching. Providing alternative ways of explaining the same thing will make you a better teacher, and your students will learn more.

MORE SPREADSHEET-BASED RESOURCES AND IDEAS

Another way to use spreadsheets in Principles of Microeconomics is by incorporating prepared materials. You need not radically and completely "Excelify" your course. Consider instead incremental change, with one or two class experiments. A change of pace in the routine of the regular schedule is a great way to break monotony and gives students a new opportunity to learn.

A Simple Presentation of Emergent Behavior

We try to explain the invisible hand and how interactions of buyers and sellers produce equilibrium that allocates scarce resources, but the idea that exchange in a market could somehow produce a pattern is a difficult concept. Conventional approaches, including readings (textbook and supplementary material), lectures, and videos may not be enough.

As an introduction to this concept, consider an Excel implementation of Langton's Ant. This two-dimensional cellular automaton was an early example of computer-based simulation and spawned many implementations and extensions, easily accessible by searching the web (https://www.google.com/search?q=langton%27s+ant). It provides a clear demonstration of the idea that following simple rules can produce complex behavior. A macro-enabled Excel workbook with explanation and instructions, *LangtonsAnt.xlsm*, is available from this book's website at https://www.e-elgar.com/textbooks/maier.

The *LangtonsAnt.xlsm* workbook is standalone and can be assigned as homework for subsequent class discussion, presented in class by the instructor, or used in a computer lab setting. It explains the two simple rules followed by Langton's Ant (change direction and move forward one step, flipping the color of the previous location) and produces its signature graph, with the highway (or tube), shown in Figure 18.2. Students can explore and discover the emergent pattern. They can also try a variety of different starting positions.

In addition to instructions and detailed explanation of how the ant moves, the spreadsheet contains a sheet with lessons that explicitly ties decentralized systems (such as supply and demand) to the work the student just finished. It

Note: The Langton's Ant computer simulation demonstrates how simple behavior can lead to complex equilibrium outcomes.

Figure 18.2   Emergent behavior from LangtonsAnt.xlsm available at https://www.e-elgar.com/textbooks/maier

concludes by pointing out that there is an open problem: the claim that the ant will always find a highway is unproven.

Using Langton's Ant will certainly surprise your students and maybe even captivate some of them. Its novelty and the mystery associated with an unsolved problem guarantees an engaged audience that is receptive to your explanation of how supply and demand is much more than two lines that intersect on a graph.

Doing Economics (https://www.core-econ.org/project/doing-economics/)

The webpage above says that, "*Doing Economics* is a unique, freely available, resource for learning a valuable array of data-handling, software and statistical skills that will be transferable to other courses and to the workplace. The 1.0 version is available in Excel, Google Sheets and R."

The lessons are grouped into specific areas such as measuring climate change or the effects of a sugar tax. Students work with data and complete tasks. In addition to Excel, materials are also available in Google sheets (and

R). New materials are being developed and added so it is worth checking back and seeing if there are any applications that you want to try.

Intro Econ Labs (https://www.depauw.edu/learn/introeconlab)

Published in the *Journal of Economic Education* in 2012, this website is for Introductory Microeconomics and Macroeconomics: "This website has a set of standalone computer labs for an Introductory Economics course. The student uses Microsoft Word and Excel to answer questions. Students fill in a lab journal containing their answers. Completed journals can be printed or electronically submitted. Answer keys are available to instructors who must first obtain a password."

One nice feature is that you can easily modify the labs. Delete questions which you do not like, or change them. Add better questions. The materials are open source and completely adaptable.

Search for the Latest Materials

Using spreadsheets to teach economics in general, and Principles of Microeconomics in particular, is no longer an original idea. There are many prepared spreadsheets (some macro-enhanced) and videos available on the internet, with a constant stream of new additions. It is worth searching for new materials as you prepare a Principles of Microeconomics course, because you might find a resource that fits neatly into your course. This, however, is unlikely.

The real payoff from a search of "principles economics Excel" is that you explore and entertain different ways to communicate beyond the textbook. Your search results, for example, may lead you to click on Mixon's website (at https://sites.berry.edu/wmixon/home/economics-in-excel/). As you navigate and evaluate materials, you are getting ideas for how to improve your teaching. You may even be stimulated enough to create your own spreadsheet to convey a lesson in your own words and style. This will make you a much more effective teacher.

CONCLUSION

Learning involves the joint inputs of teacher and student, but as professors we tend to focus on ourselves and the student fades into the background. As you prepare to teach any course, think carefully about what your students know and how to communicate with them. This student-centered framework will remind you that they do not know what you know.

A crucial concept, especially for teachers just starting out, is concreteness. The more detailed and grounded in reality your explanation, the better. Abstraction is not your friend when it comes to communicating with students.

A spreadsheet forces concreteness. It requires numbers and explicit functional forms. The output is dynamic (changing as inputs change) and visual. Furthermore, students are familiar with spreadsheets and they want to become more proficient in using them. Unlike reading or listening to a lecture, they are primed to learn via spreadsheets. This is why spreadsheets belong in our teaching toolkit.

In addition, spreadsheets naturally develop competency in quantitative analysis. Students work with data, including transformation and visualization. There is also obvious value in acquiring advanced spreadsheet skills.

The two Excel add-ins suggested above, FRED and Solver, are powerful tools for data gathering and optimization. They can be used to produce concrete examples that enhance the textbook and lecture presentation. Likewise, *LangtonsAnt.xlsm*, *Doing Economics*, *Intro Econ Labs*, and many spreadsheet-based materials on the internet provide an opportunity to inject variety into your course.

While there are clear benefits to using spreadsheets to teach Principles of Microeconomics, there are, of course, also costs. They require more time and effort than the traditional way economists teach: using the textbook's ancillary materials while droning on for an hour or so. Surely the low cost of "chalk and talk" explains its persistence, but I believe that the return on spreadsheet investment in terms of comprehending economics is quite high. You can decide the optimal rate of utilization in your course by starting slowly and experimenting with spreadsheets in a single class or two. You might be pleasantly surprised by what happens to your teaching and student learning outcomes.

REFERENCES

Allgood, S., and Bayer, A. (2016). Measuring college learning in economics. In R. Arum, J. Roksa, and A. Cook (eds), *Improving Quality in American Higher Education: Learning Outcomes and Assessments for the 21st Century* (pp. 87–134). Jossey-Bass.

Johnson, S. (2019). The fall, and rise, of reading. *The Chronicle of Higher Education*, April 21.

Miller, J., and Rebelein, R. (2012). Research on the effectiveness of non-traditional pedagogies. In G. Hoyt and K. McGoldrick (eds), *International Handbook on Teaching and Learning Economics* (pp. 323–333). Edward Elgar Publishing.

US Bureau of Labor Statistics (BLS) (n.d.), Average price: Eggs, Grade A, Large (cost per dozen) in U.S. city average [APU0000708111], retrieved from FRED, Federal Reserve Bank of St Louis. https://fred.stlouisfed.org/series/APU0000708111, accessed July 26, 2022.

Weinstein, Y., Madan, C. R., and Sumeracki, M. A. (2018). Teaching the science of learning. *Cognitive Research: Principles and Implications 3*(2), 1–17.

APPENDIX A: USING THE FRED EXCEL ADD-IN

Visit the Federal Reserve Bank of St Louis (FRED) database add-in page at https://fred.stlouisfed.org/fred-addin/ and follow the instructions to install the FRED Excel add-in. The add-in is free, but you must agree to the terms of service.

In Excel, click the *FRED* tab and click the *Data Search* button. Enter "egg prices" and select "Eggs, Grade A, Large, Per Doz. In U.S. City Average," as shown in Figure 18A.1. Click *Add Series ID*, then click *Close*.

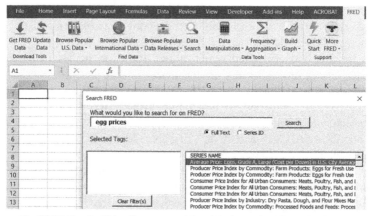

Note: The FRED Excel add-in offers a powerful tool for importing FRED data into spreadsheets.

Figure 18A.1   Getting egg prices from the BLS via the FRED Excel add-in

The FRED Excel add-in puts some information in the first four rows of columns A and B. Cell A1 has "APU0000708111" which is the series code used by the BLS for egg prices. In cell B1, "lin" means the data are in original form, without any transformation. Click *Data Manipulations* in the FRED menu to see ways the data can be transformed. Cell A3 shows "M" for monthly; changing this cell to A or Q would produce data in annual or quarterly time units. Finally, cell A4 shows the starting date for the series.

In the top-left of the FRED menu, click the *Get FRED Data* button. This downloads the series directly into the spreadsheet. Notice that cell A5 contains a hyperlink. Clicking it takes you to the FRED webpage for the series and provides full documentation.

You could graph the data with an Excel Scatter chart, but the add-in has its own charting tool that makes it easy to create a properly labeled graph. Click the *Build Graph* button and select *Create Graph(s)*. Select the series, check the *Include U.S. Recession Shading* option, and click *Build Graph(s)*. A chart with FRED's classic border, as shown in Figure 18.1, is placed on the spreadsheet. The chart you just created will look different since it will have data up to the latest month; the difference will be small if no large shocks have hit the egg market. In fact, since Figure 18.1 was produced, another large price spike hit the egg market in the summer of 2022. The FRED add-in makes it easy to always have up-to-the-minute news for your class.

As an additional exercise, if you wish to develop charting skills, you could ask students to create an Excel version of the chart. Using the dates as the x axis in a scatter chart, however, adds the complication that you need to change the minimum value of the chart.

APPENDIX B: USING THE SOLVER EXCEL ADD-IN

Excel's Solver can easily find the optimal solution to a simple problem such as max $\pi = 4q - q^2$. However, before we run Solver, we first have to implement the problem in Excel. Enter labels for profits and quantity in cells B1 and B2, respectively. Enter the formula "= 4*A2 - A2^2" in cell A1. (You could name cell A2 as "q" and the formula would be easier to read.) Excel displays a zero in cell A1 because it interprets the empty cell in A2 as zero. This, understandably, drives computer scientists crazy, leading to claims such as, "Friends don't let friends use Excel." While amusing, the message is misguided because spreadsheets are ubiquitous, so telling students not to use them because they can be dangerous seems like a poor policy prescription. We are much better served by showing students how Excel may do something unexpected that leads to mistaken conclusions.

Instead of diving in and using Solver, take a moment to show how Excel responds to changes in cell A2. Enter a 1 and explain why A1 displays a 3. Literally walk through the function: "Four times one is one, that means we have four dollars of revenues and one squared is one so that gives one dollar of costs. Four minus one is three dollars of profit and that is what Excel displays in cell A1 when 1 is in cell A2." Repeat with 3 (same profits as 1 so you are on the other side of the max), 5 (negative profits so you are in the fourth quadrant, below the x axis), and a non-integer, like 3.51 (harder to compute for a human, but trivial for a spreadsheet).

Ask students to draw the total revenue and total cost curves. Again, while trivial to you, some students may struggle with this. Rely on the concrete numbers in the example as you explain what is going on and why one relationship is linear and the other is not.

With the profit maximization problem implemented in Excel, we are ready to use Solver. Click the *Data* tab and click *Solver*. If it is not there, use the Add-ins Manager to install it. Walk your students through the Solver Parameters dialog box and enter A1 as the objective function and A2 as the changing cell, as shown in Figure 18B.1.

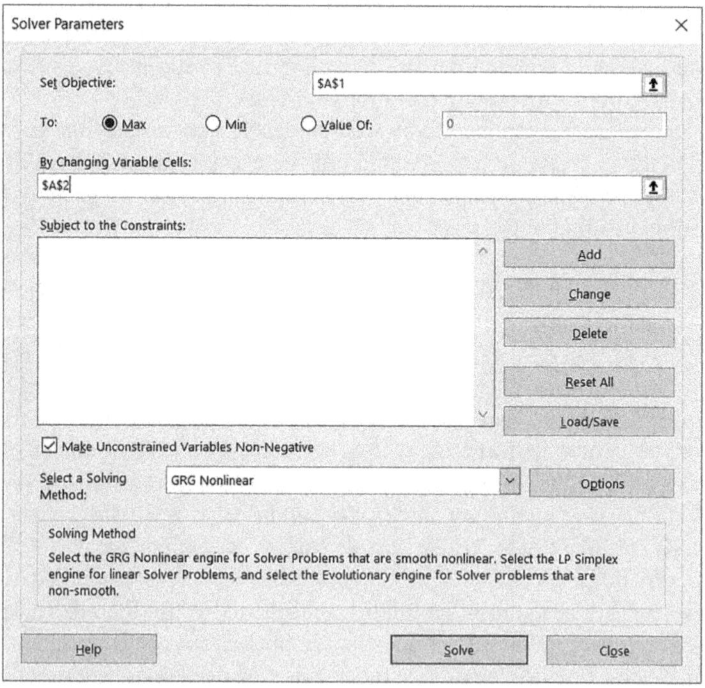

Note: Instructors will need to carefully explain the Excel Solver dialog box to students to enable them to use this powerful tool.

Figure 18B.1 The Solver Parameters dialog box

Click the *Solve* button at the bottom of the Solver Parameters dialog box. Excel displays the Solver Results dialog box, which announces that a solution has been found. Click the *OK* button and you can see that there is a 2 in cell A2 and a 4 in cell A1. This is the optimal solution.

Click on cell A2 to see that the actual number in Excel's memory is different from that displayed. Solver got extremely close to the exact answer, 2, but it is off by a little bit. Solver works by plugging in different values and seeing how much the solution improves. Once it improves by less than the convergence criterion, it stops and announces success. It may not get the exact answer, but practically speaking, Solver gives a substantially correct result.

Return to cell A1 and change the 4 to 5 in the formula. This represents an exogenous increase in P. How will the firm respond? Run Solver to find out. Repeat with $P = 6$. If you do this in front of your class, you are literally finding points on the firm's supply curve, and they are seeing a live demonstration of deriving supply. Concreteness in action.

Index